PRAISE FOR *AFTER THE RAIN*

"This exploration of trauma and family history through the body is perfectly adapted to the graphic medium."
 —Booklist

"*After the Rain* explores the boundaries we draw within ourselves, the way we seek to compartmentalize to fit in, and the remarkable people we find within ourselves when we break those barriers down."
 —Book Riot

"*After the Rain* is an intense realization of Okorafor's short story and uses the horror elements to thematic effect in a visceral and important way, and as a statement of intention for what will follow at Megascope, it hints at exciting work to come."
 —Comics Beat

"A phenomenal and haunting story . . . "
 —Comic Book Resources

"The story is best experienced rather than described, since its force is in its lush visuals and destabilizing twists. Okorafor's original language gets heavily employed in swathes of text boxes and Damian Duffy's kinetic lettering. That text from Okorafor's story conveys the fearsome uncertainty in being carried into this frightening sequence of otherworldly trials."
 —Multiversity Comics

"*After the Rain* is far more than a well-rendered tribute to a trailblazing black female writer. In this case, it's also a kind of visual incarnation of the story's theme . . . You don't simply observe Chioma's unwilling confrontation with the world her ancestors mythologized, you experience it."
 —NPR Books

"Brame's bold and arresting use of color and shading lends an unnerving atmosphere to the setting, while his attention to facial expressions injects the panels with emotion. This mostly faithful adaptation honors Okorafor's voice and paints a potent portrait of Nigeria and its folklore."
 —Publishers Weekly

AFTER THE RAIN

Adapted from the short story "On the Road" by

NNEDI OKORAFOR

Written by JOHN JENNINGS · Illustrated by DAVID BRAME
Lettering by DAMIAN DUFFY

ABRAMS COMICARTS · NEW YORK

MEGASCOPE Curator: John Jennings
Editor: Charlotte Greenbaum
Editorial Assistant: Jazmine Joyner
Designer: Charice Silverman
Managing Editor: Marie Oishi
Production Manager: Alison Gervais

Cataloging-in-Publication Data has been applied for and may be obtained from the Library of Congress.

Paperback ISBN 978-1-4197-4356-6
eISBN 978-1-68335-834-3

Adapted from the short story "On the Road" by Nnedi Okorafor, originally published in the anthology Kabu Kabu by Prime Books in 2013.

Published in paperback in 2022 by MEGASCOPE, an imprint of Abrams ComicArts®, an imprint of ABRAMS. Originally published in hardcover in 2021 by MEGASCOPE, an imprint of Abrams ComicArts®, an imprint of ABRAMS. All rights reserved. No portion of this book may be reproduced, stored in a retrieval system, or transmitted in any form or by any means, mechanical, electronic, photocopying, recording, or otherwise, without written permission from the publisher.

Printed and bound in China
10 9 8 7 6 5 4 3 2 1

Abrams ComicArts books are available at special discounts when purchased in quantity for premiums and promotions as well as fundraising or educational use. Special editions can also be created to specification. For details, contact specialsales@abramsbooks.com or the address below.

Abrams ComicArts® is a registered trademark of Harry N. Abrams, Inc. MEGASCOPE™ is a trademark of John Jennings and Harry N. Abrams, Inc.

ABRAMS The Art of Books
195 Broadway, New York, NY 10007
abramsbooks.com

MEGASCOPE is dedicated to showcasing speculative works by and about people of color, with a focus on science fiction, fantasy, horror, and stories of magical realism. The megascope is a fictional device imagined by W. E. B. Du Bois that can peer through time and space into other realities. This magical invention represents the idea that so much of our collective past has not seen the light of day, and that there is so much history that we have yet to discover. MEGASCOPE will serve as a lens through which we can broaden our view of history, the present, and the future, and as a method by which previously unheard voices can find their way to an ever-growing diverse audience.

MEGASCOPE ADVISORY BOARD

To Octavia E. Butler, Amos
Tutuola, and W. E. B. Du Bois for
introducing us to and showing us
how to embrace our most beautiful
of ghosts

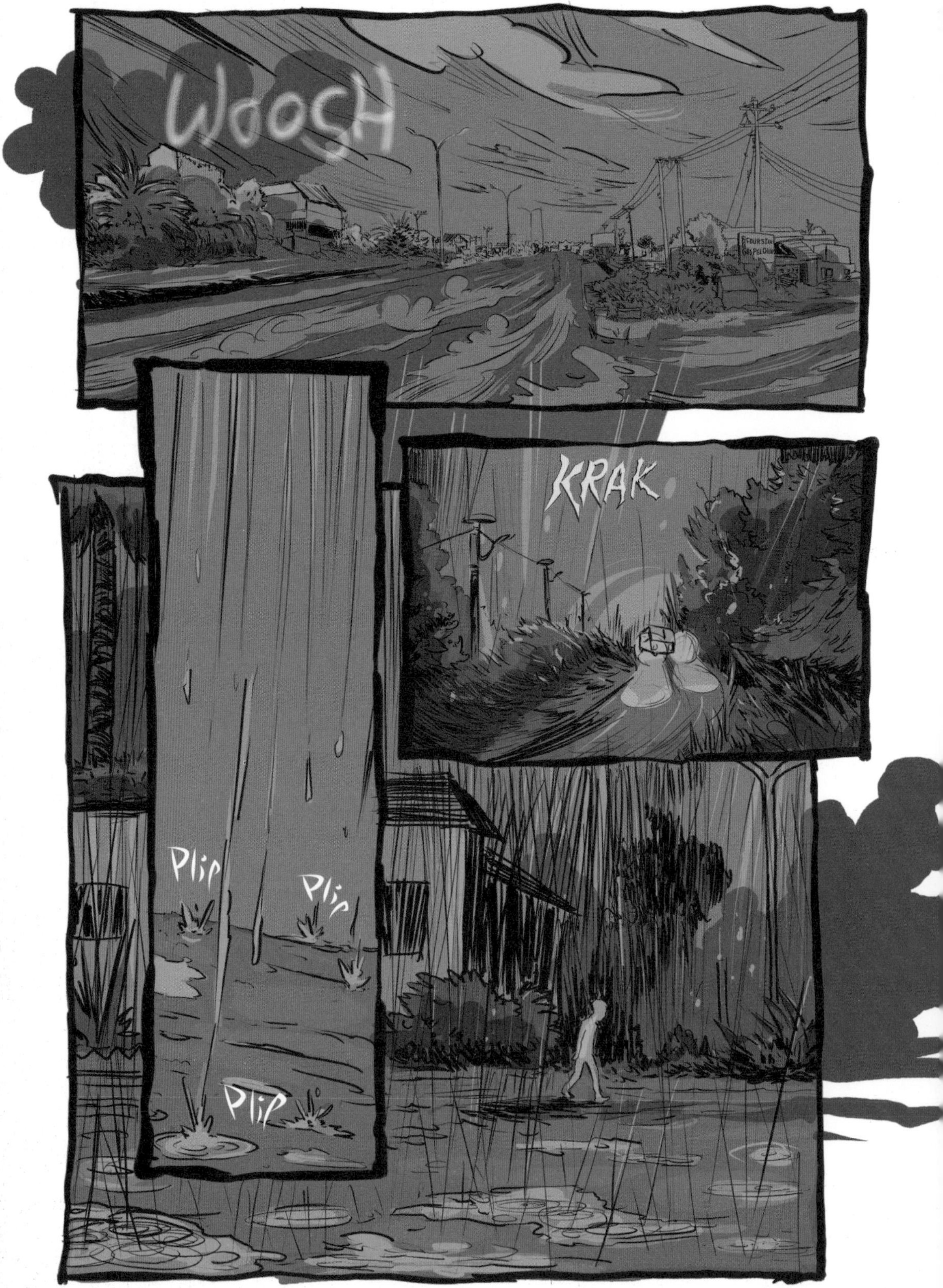
WOOSH
KRAK
Plip
Plip
Plip

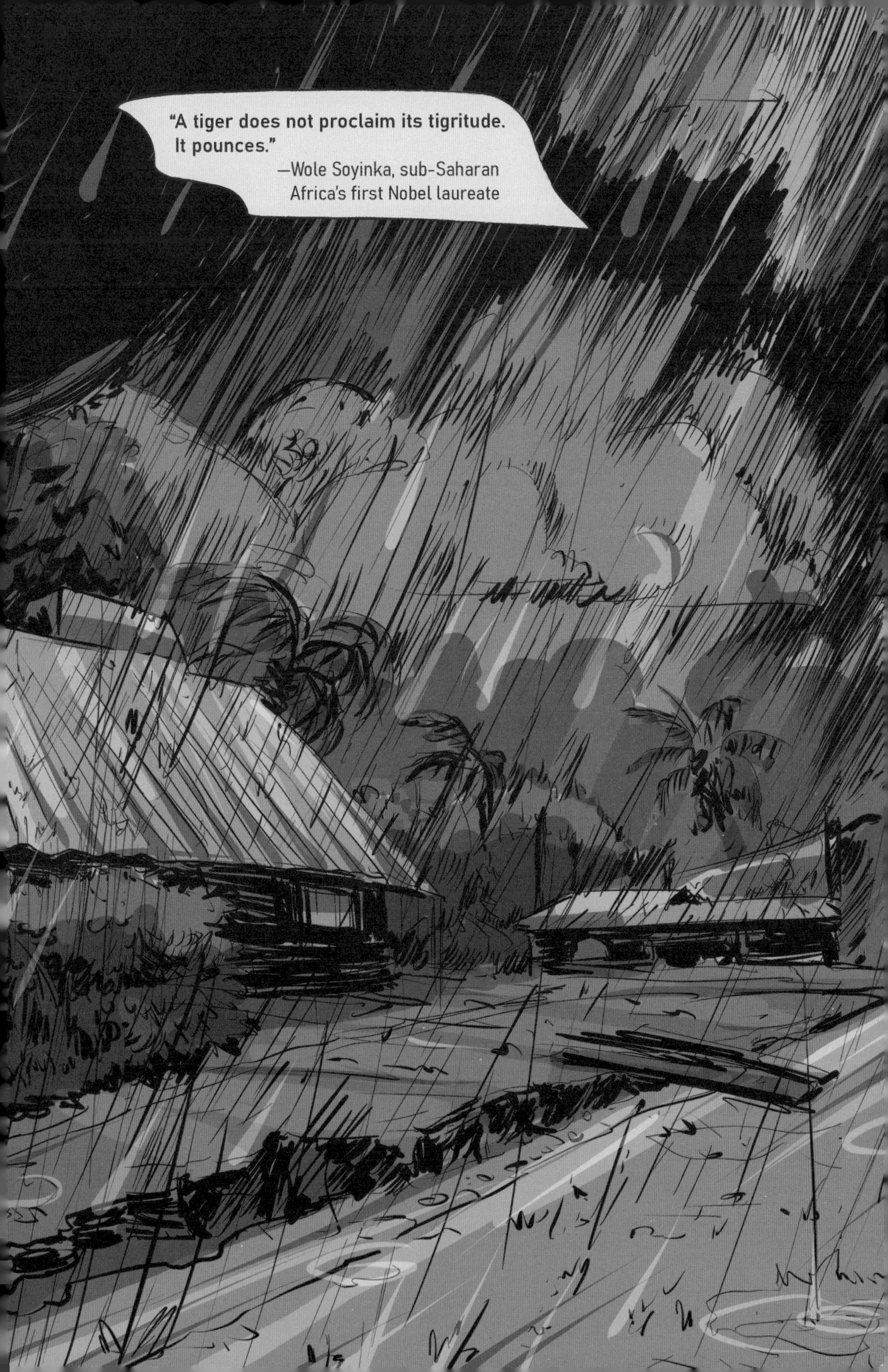
"A tiger does not proclaim its tigritude. It pounces."
—Wole Soyinka, sub-Saharan Africa's first Nobel laureate

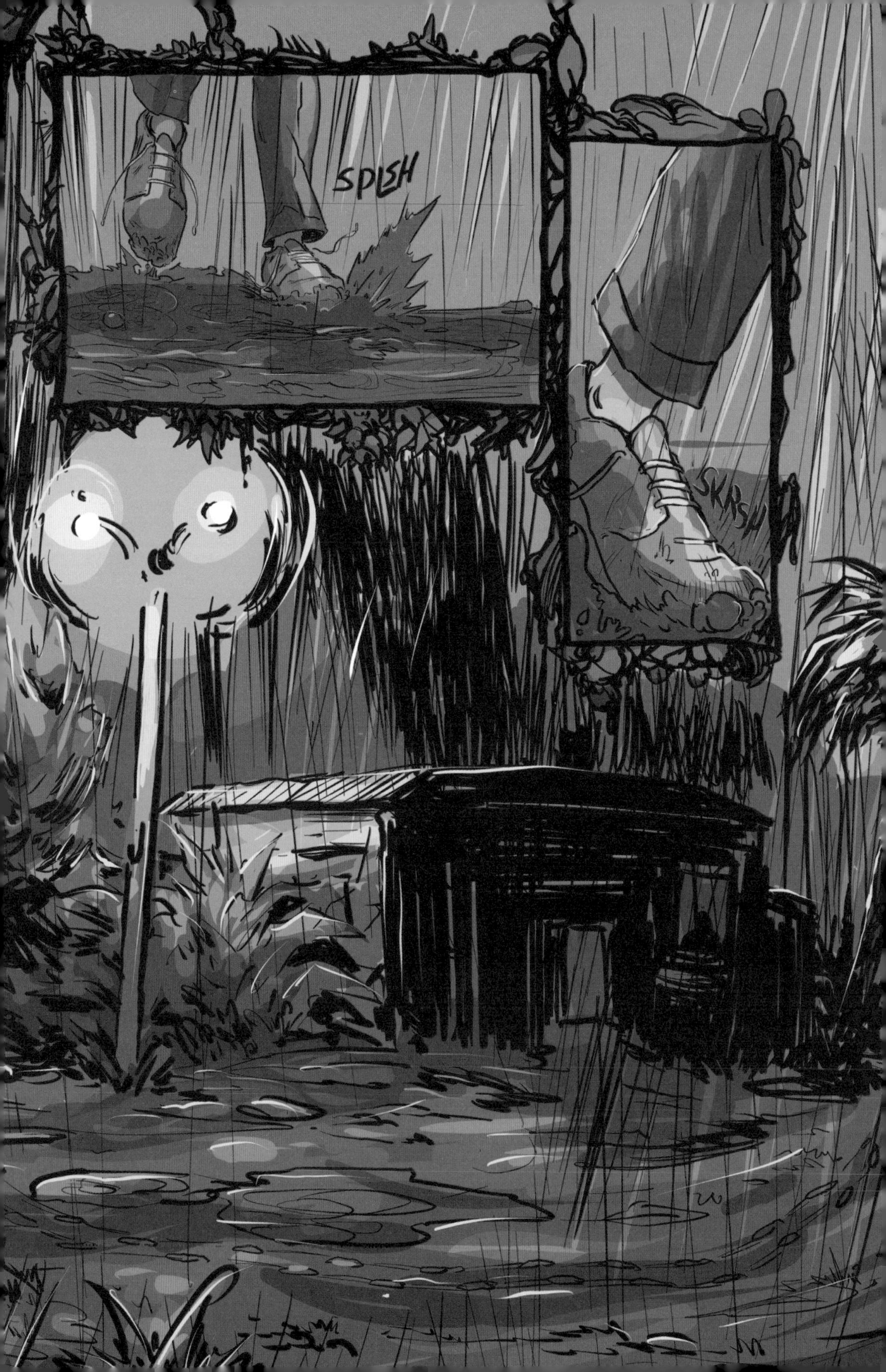
SPLSH
SKRSH

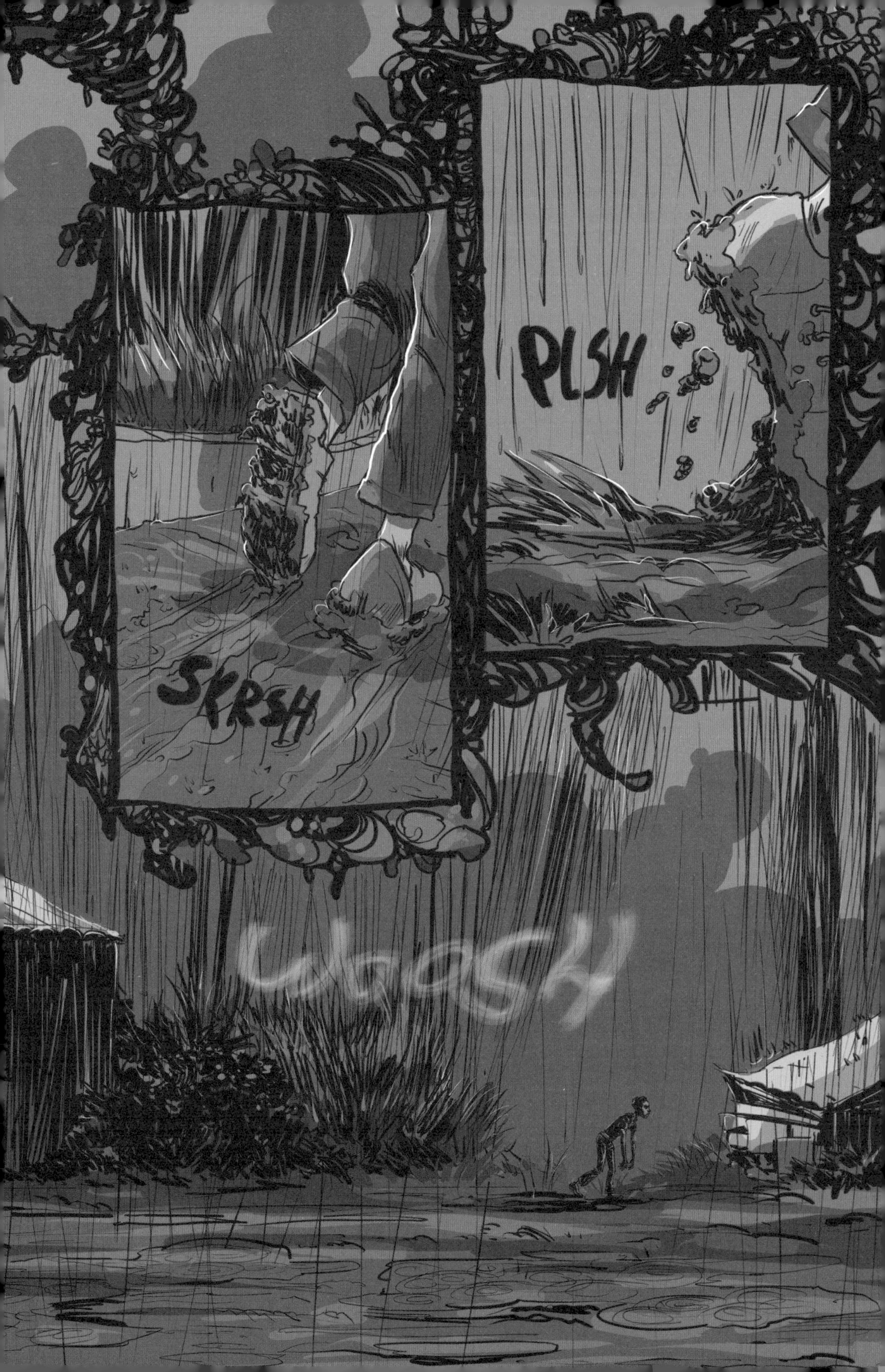
SKRSH
PLSH

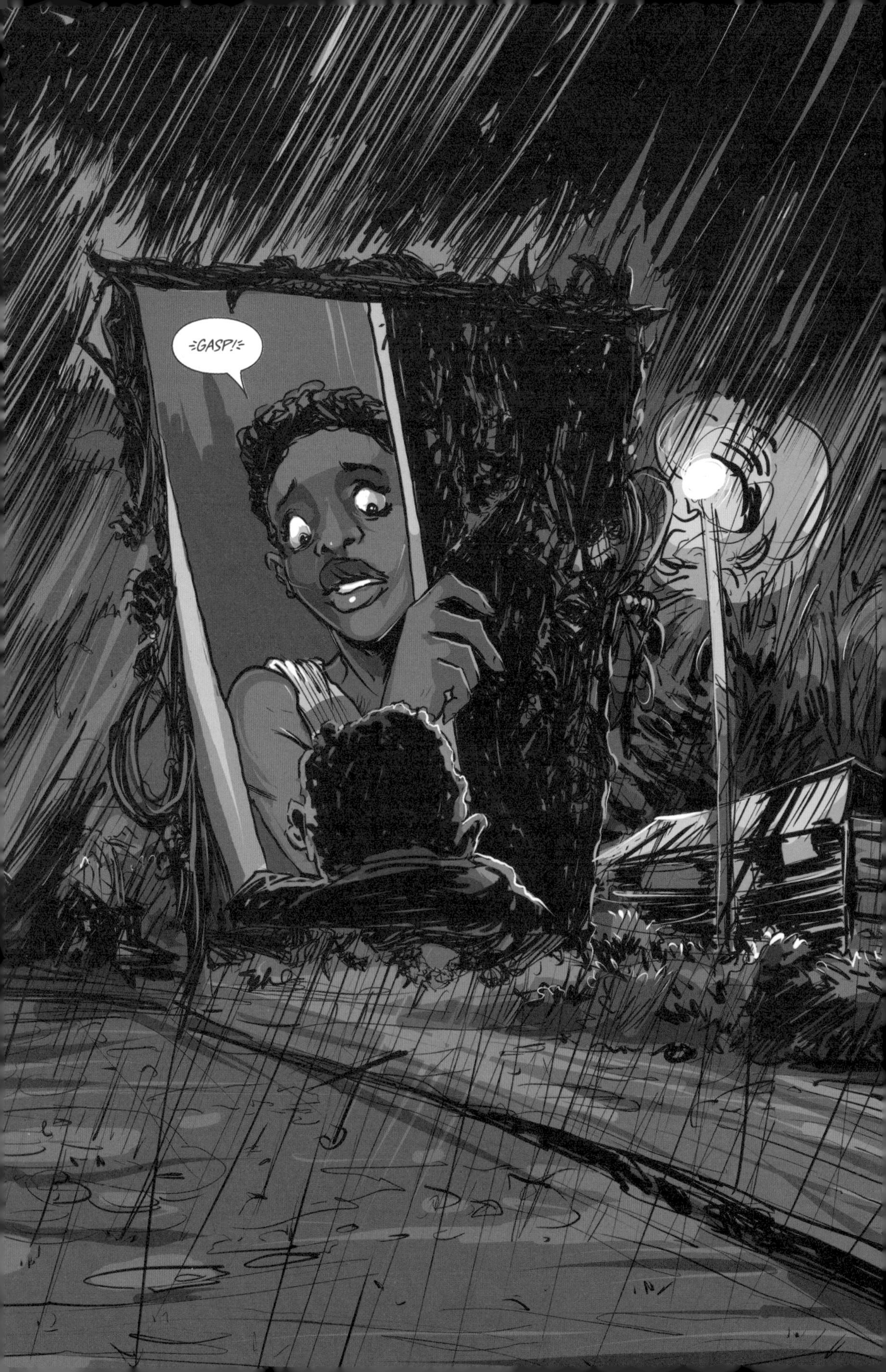
GASP!

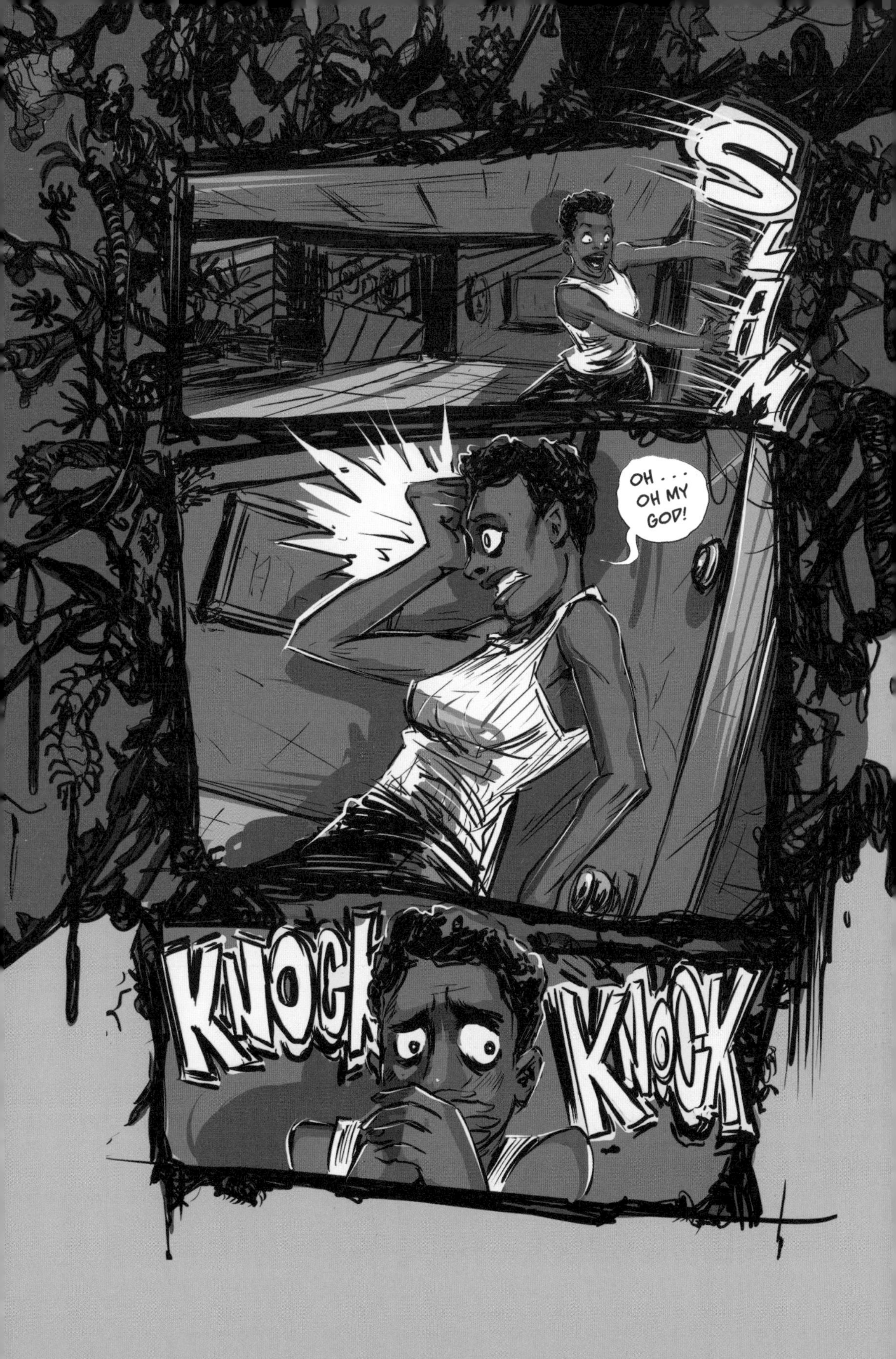
SLAM
OH . . . OH MY GOD!
KNOCK
KNOCK

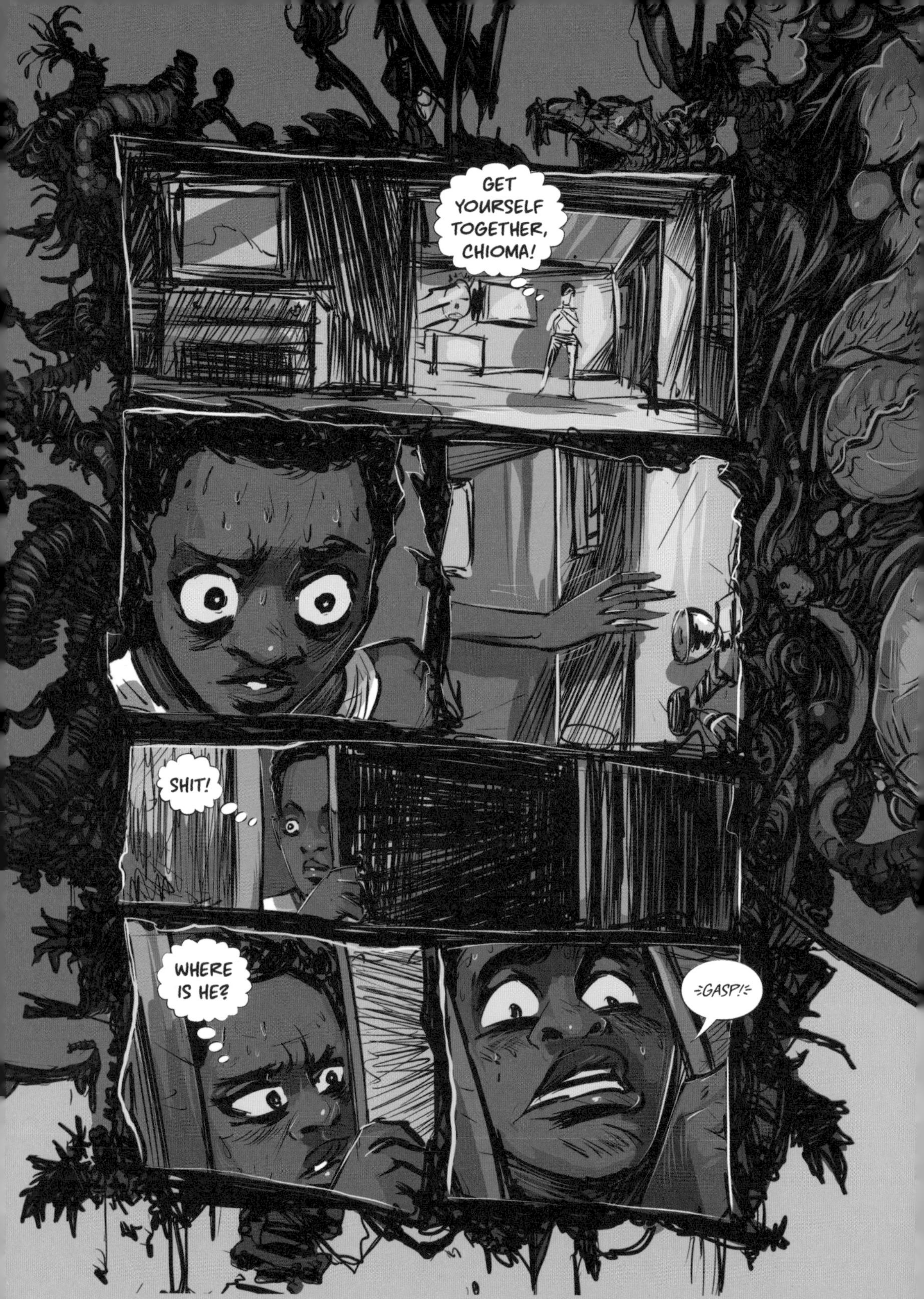
GET YOURSELF TOGETHER, CHIOMA!
SHIT!
WHERE IS HE?
=GASP!=

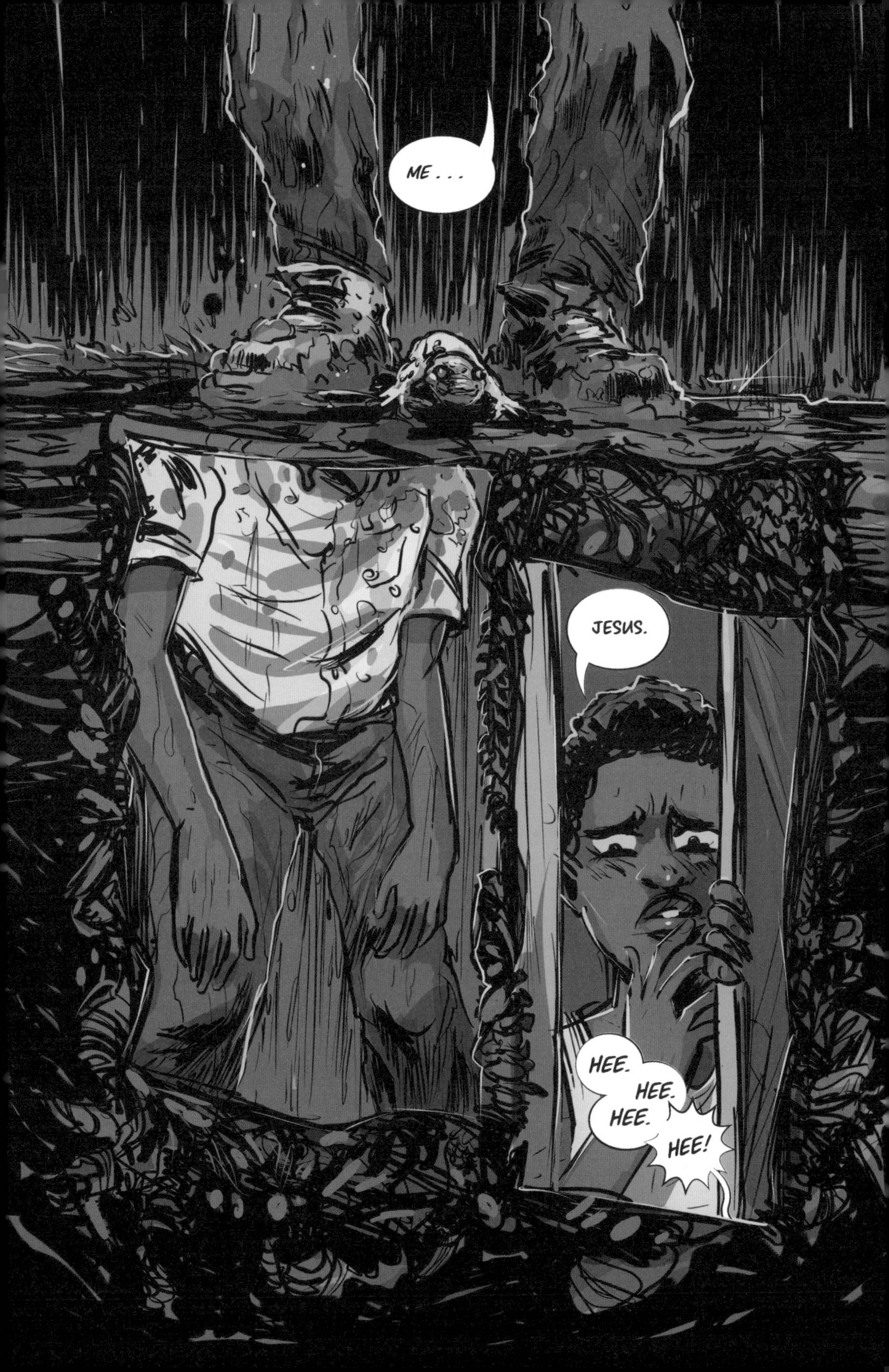
ME . . .
JESUS.
HEE.
HEE.
HEE.
HEE!

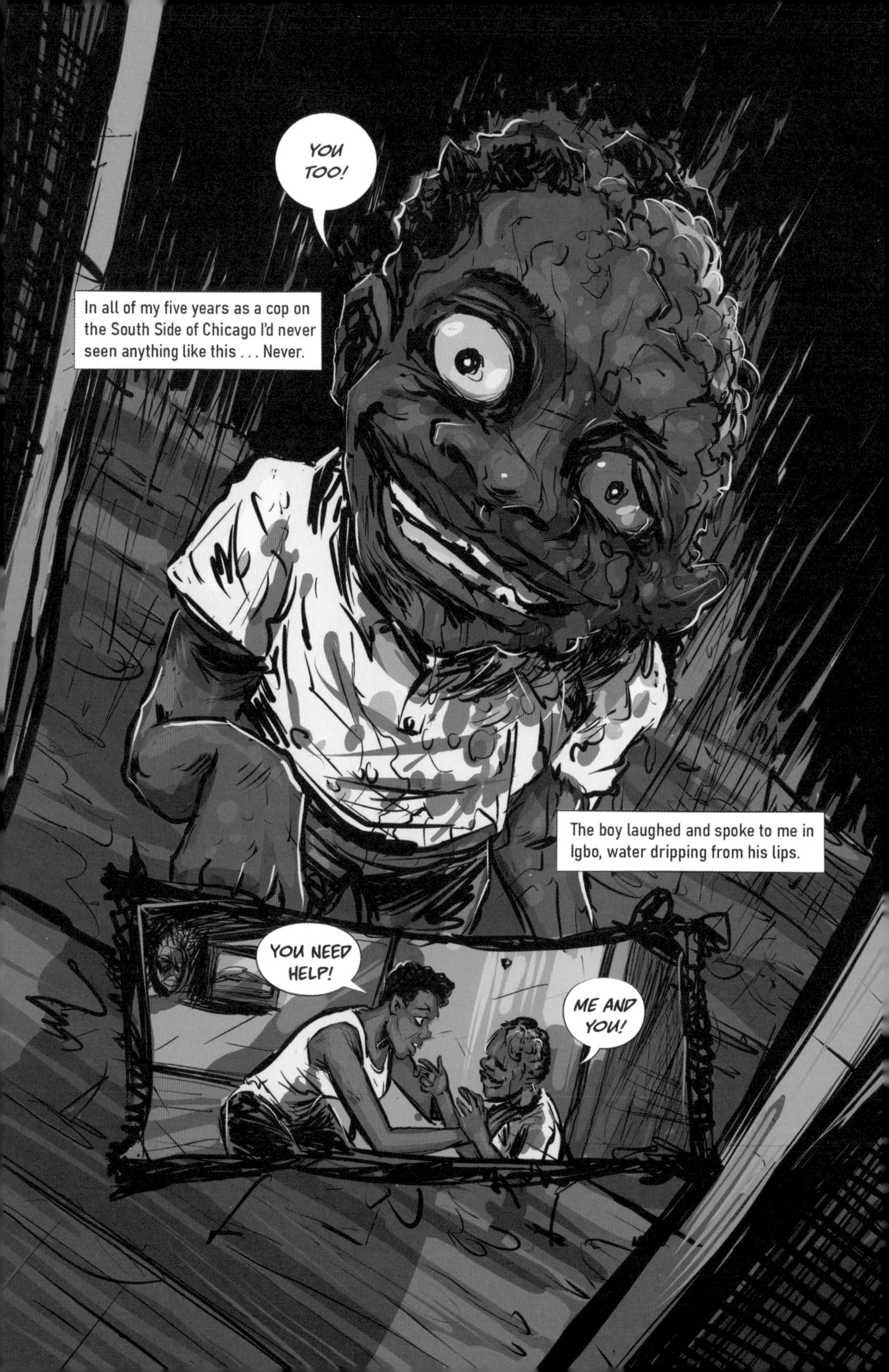
YOU TOO!
In all of my five years as a cop on the South Side of Chicago I'd never seen anything like this . . . Never.
The boy laughed and spoke to me in Igbo, water dripping from his lips.
YOU NEED HELP!
ME AND YOU!

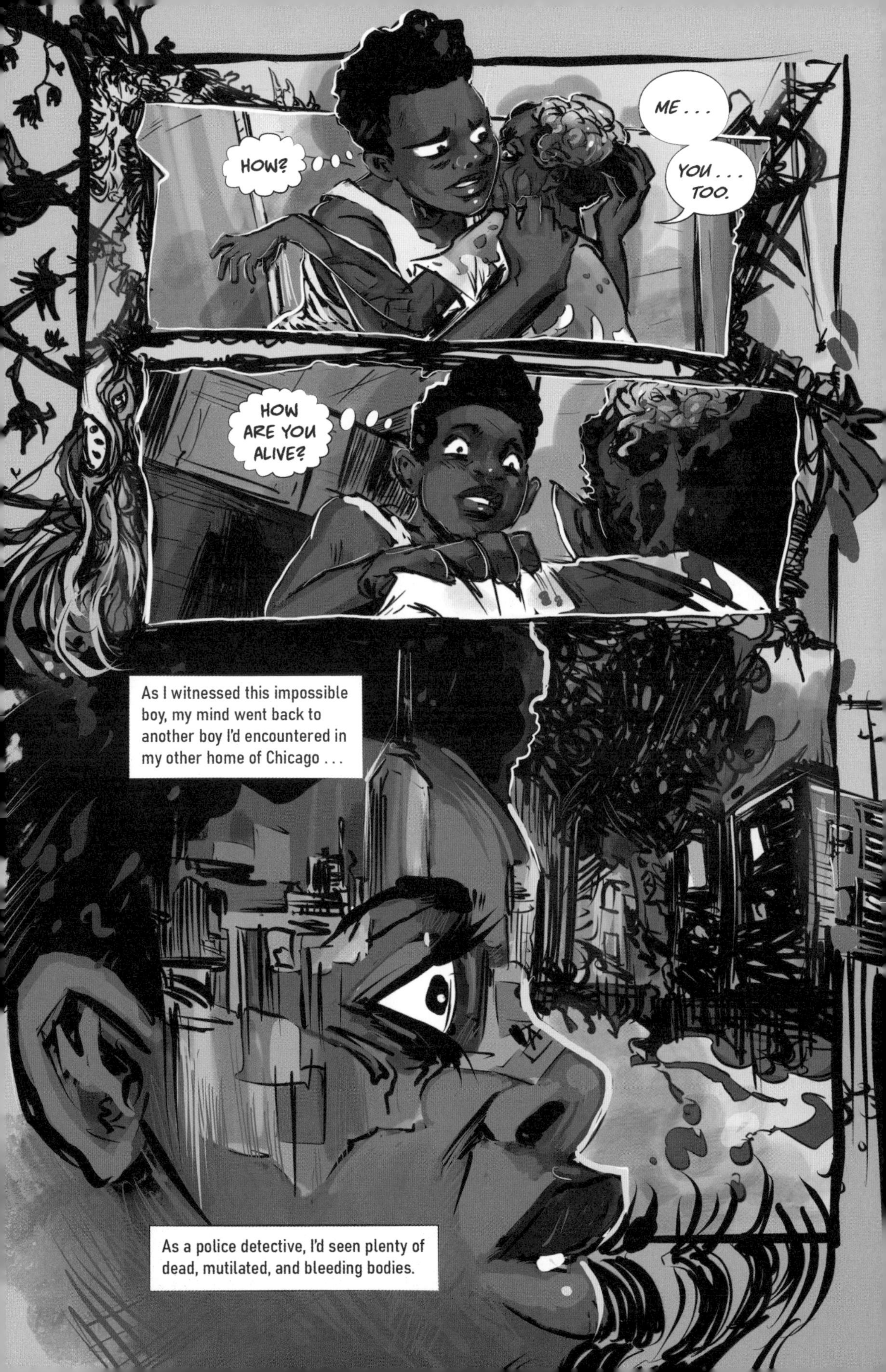
HOW?
ME . . .
YOU . . . TOO.
HOW ARE YOU ALIVE?
As I witnessed this impossible boy, my mind went back to another boy I'd encountered in my other home of Chicago . . .
As a police detective, I'd seen plenty of dead, mutilated, and bleeding bodies.

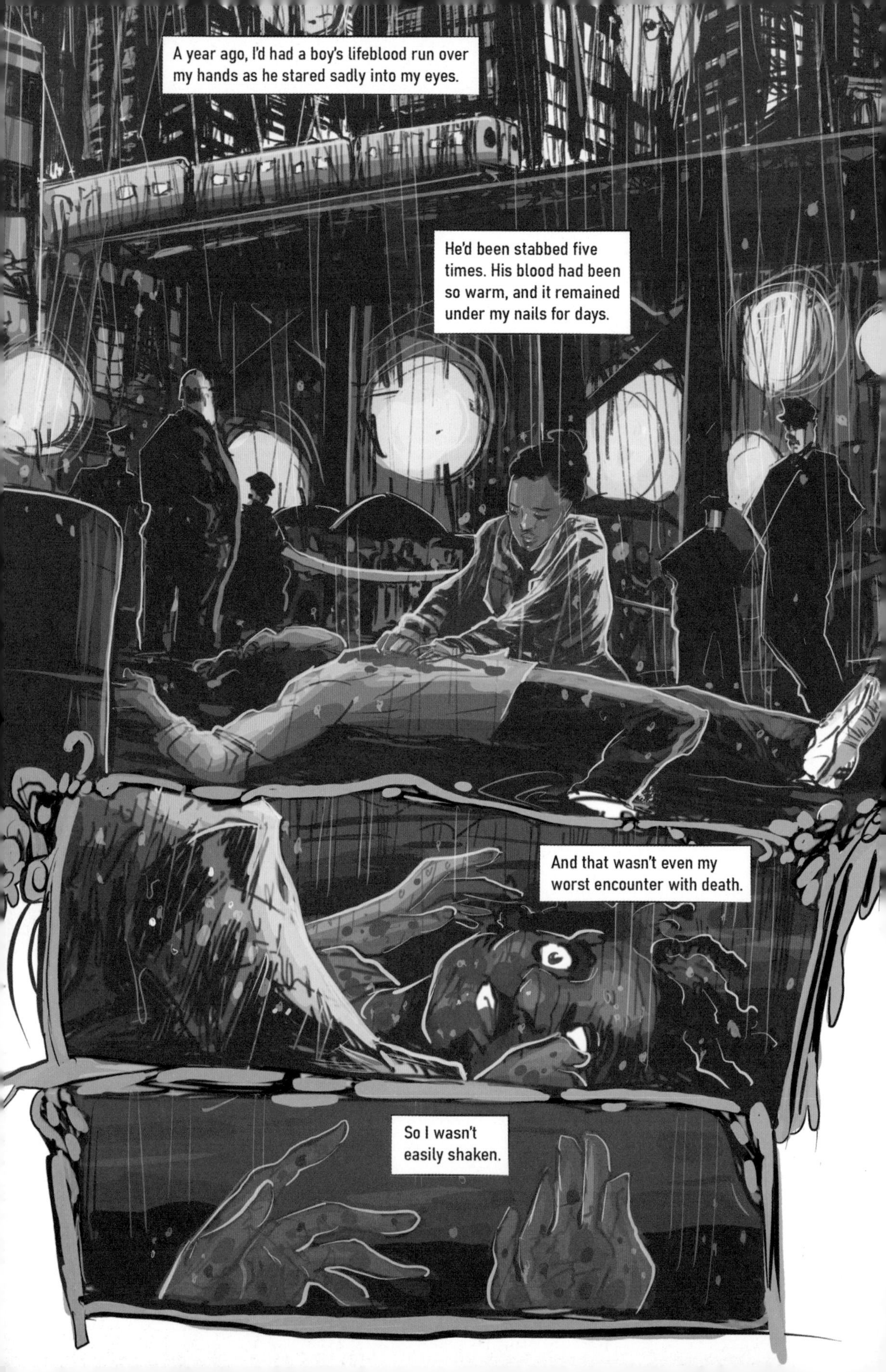
A year ago, I'd had a boy's lifeblood run over my hands as he stared sadly into my eyes.
He'd been stabbed five times. His blood had been so warm, and it remained under my nails for days.
And that wasn't even my worst encounter with death.
So I wasn't easily shaken.

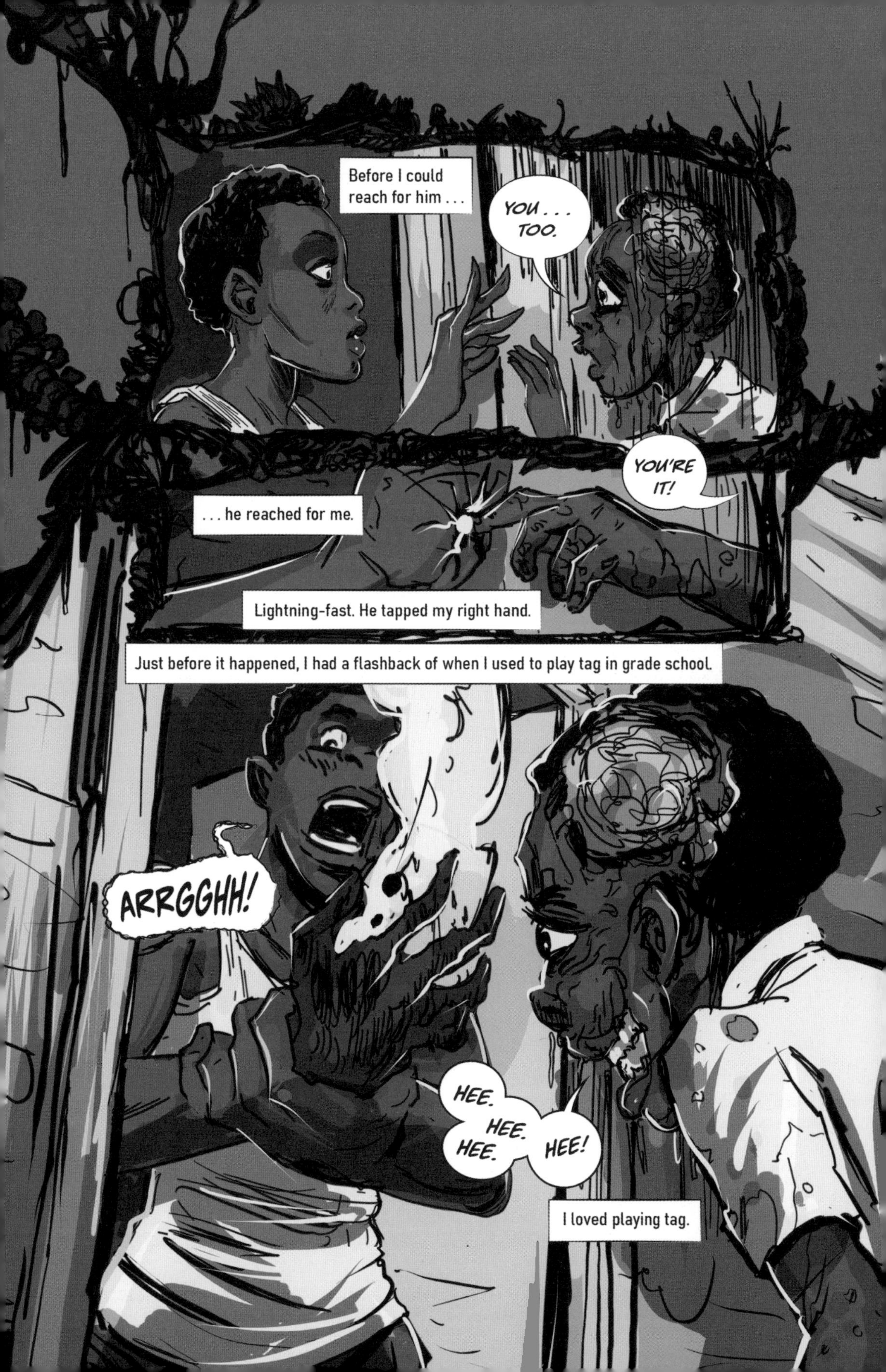
Before I could reach for him . . .
YOU . . . TOO.
. . . he reached for me.
YOU'RE IT!
Lightning-fast. He tapped my right hand.
Just before it happened, I had a flashback of when I used to play tag in grade school.
ARRGGHH!
HEE.
HEE.
HEE.
HEE!
I loved playing tag.

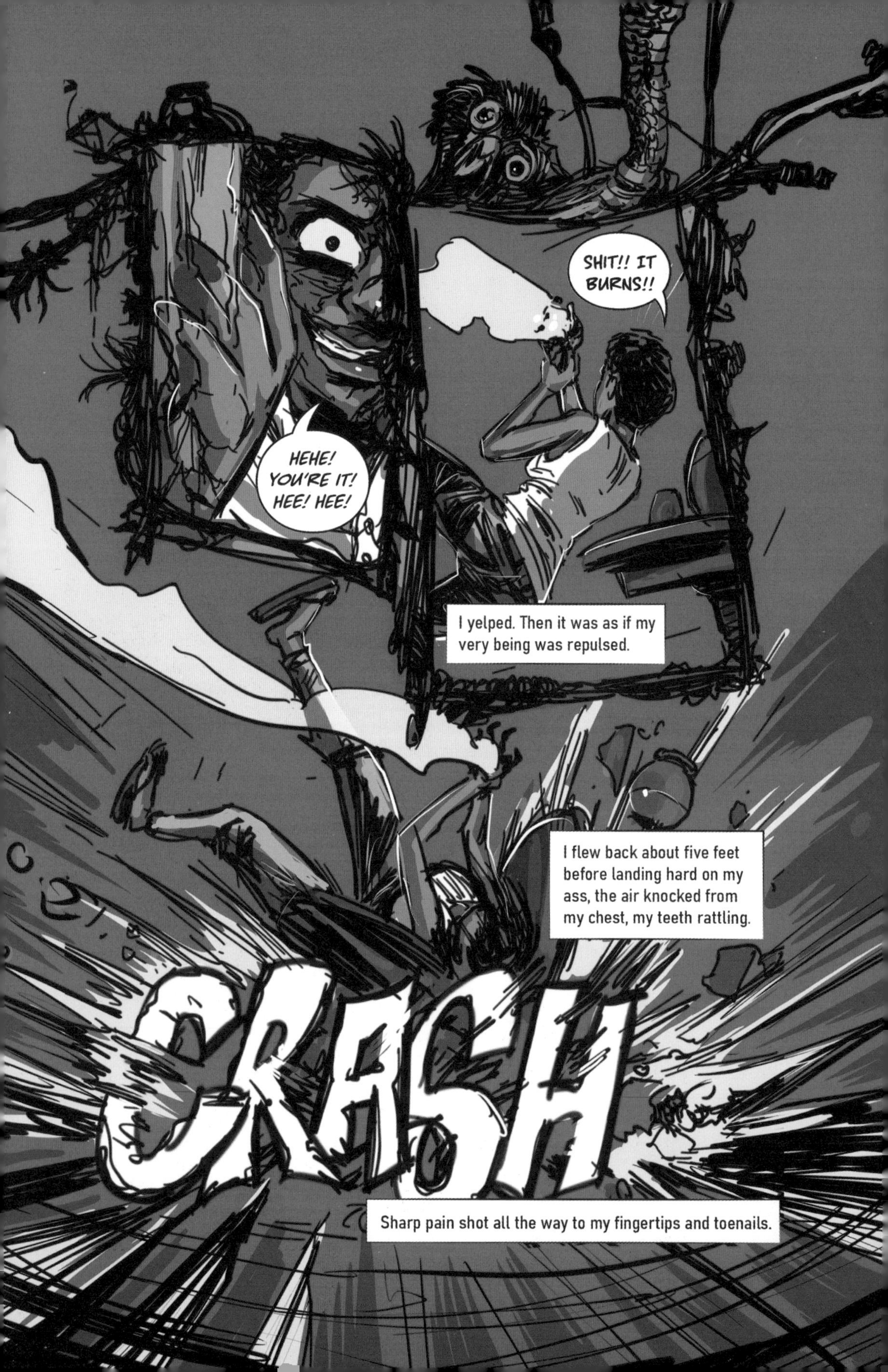
SHIT!! IT BURNS!!
HEHE! YOU'RE IT! HEE! HEE!
I yelped. Then it was as if my very being was repulsed.
I flew back about five feet before landing hard on my ass, the air knocked from my chest, my teeth rattling.
CRASH
Sharp pain shot all the way to my fingertips and toenails.

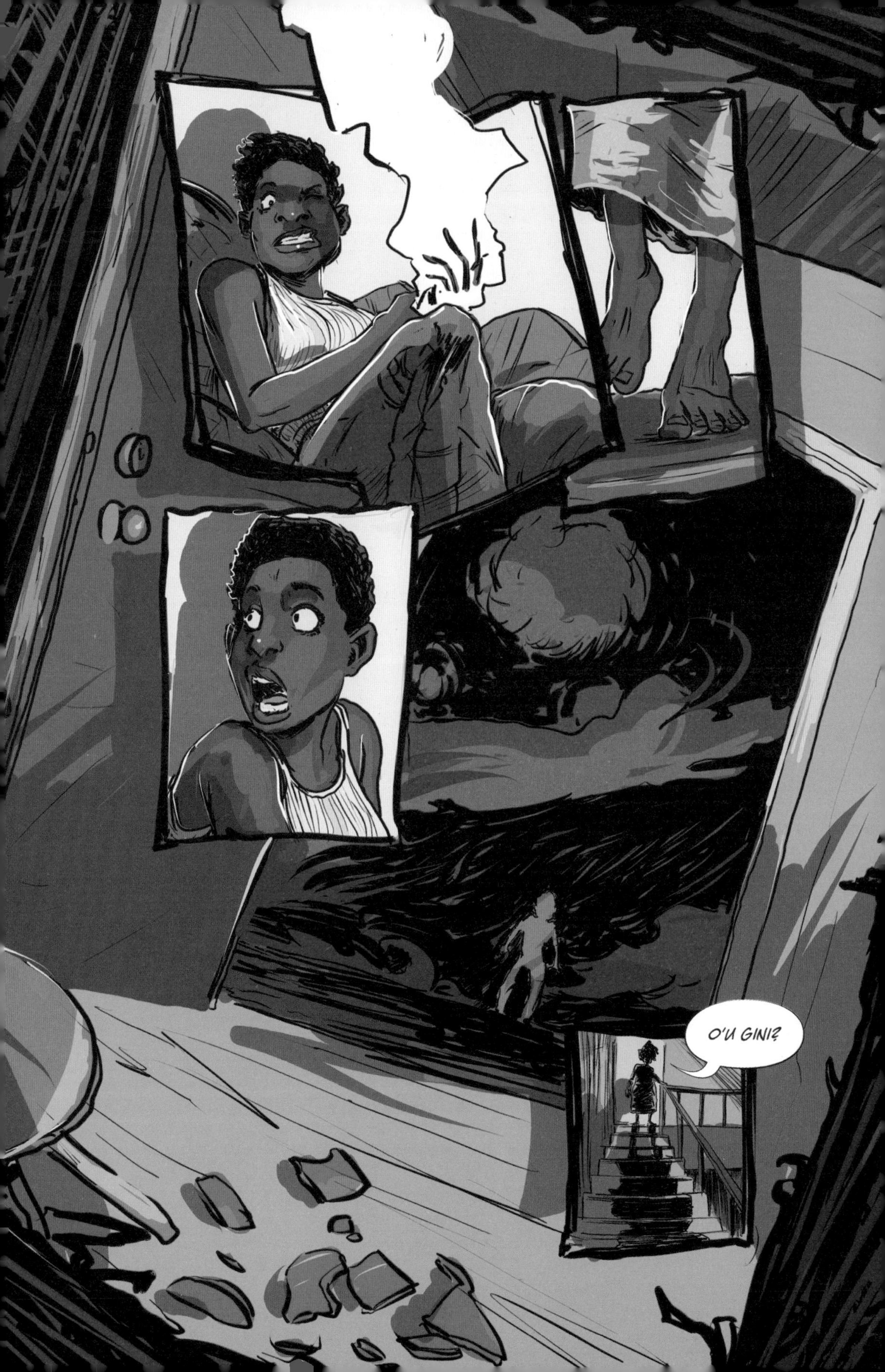
O'U GINI?

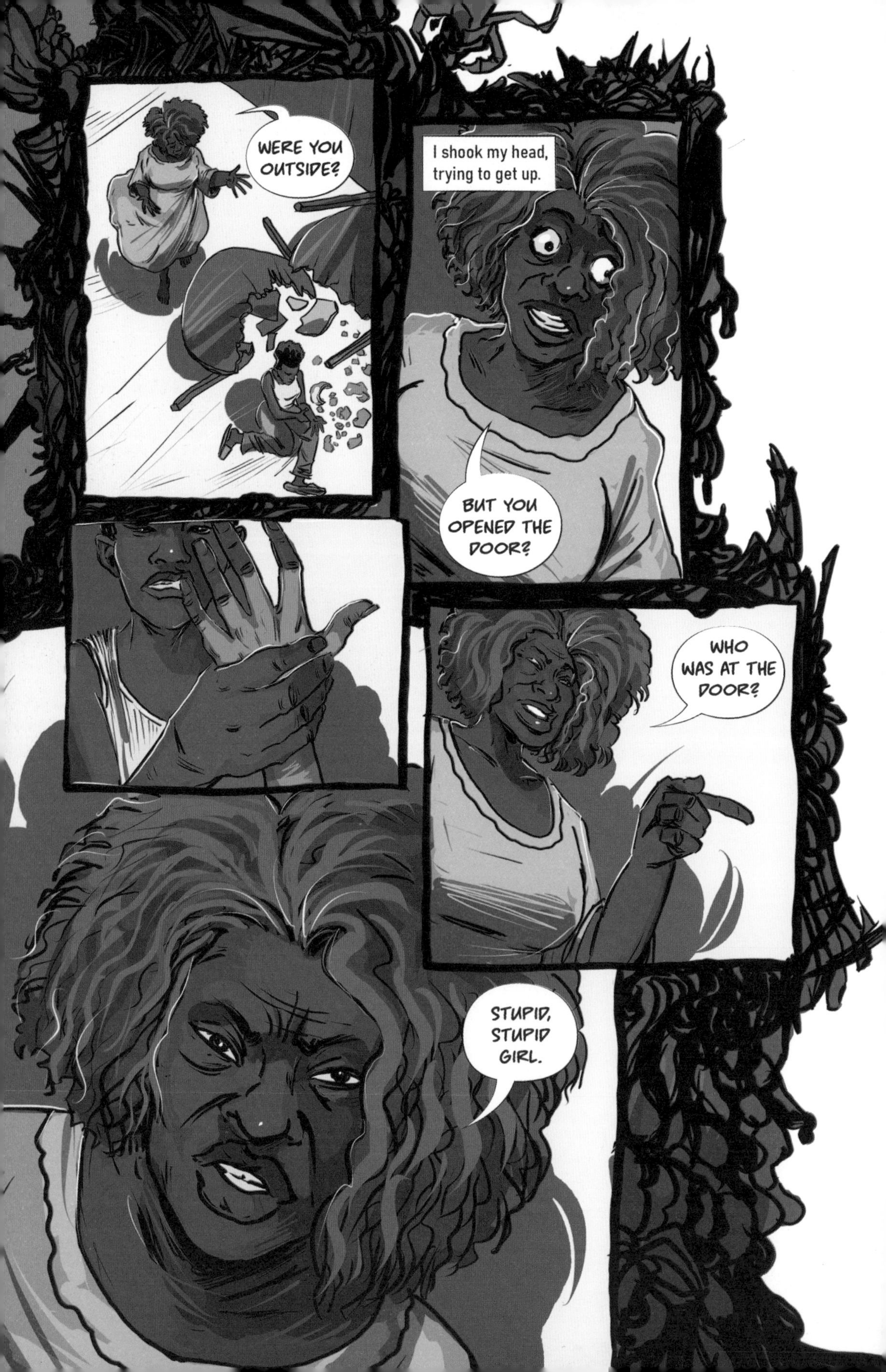
WERE YOU OUTSIDE?
I shook my head, trying to get up.
BUT YOU OPENED THE DOOR?
WHO WAS AT THE DOOR?
STUPID, STUPID GIRL.

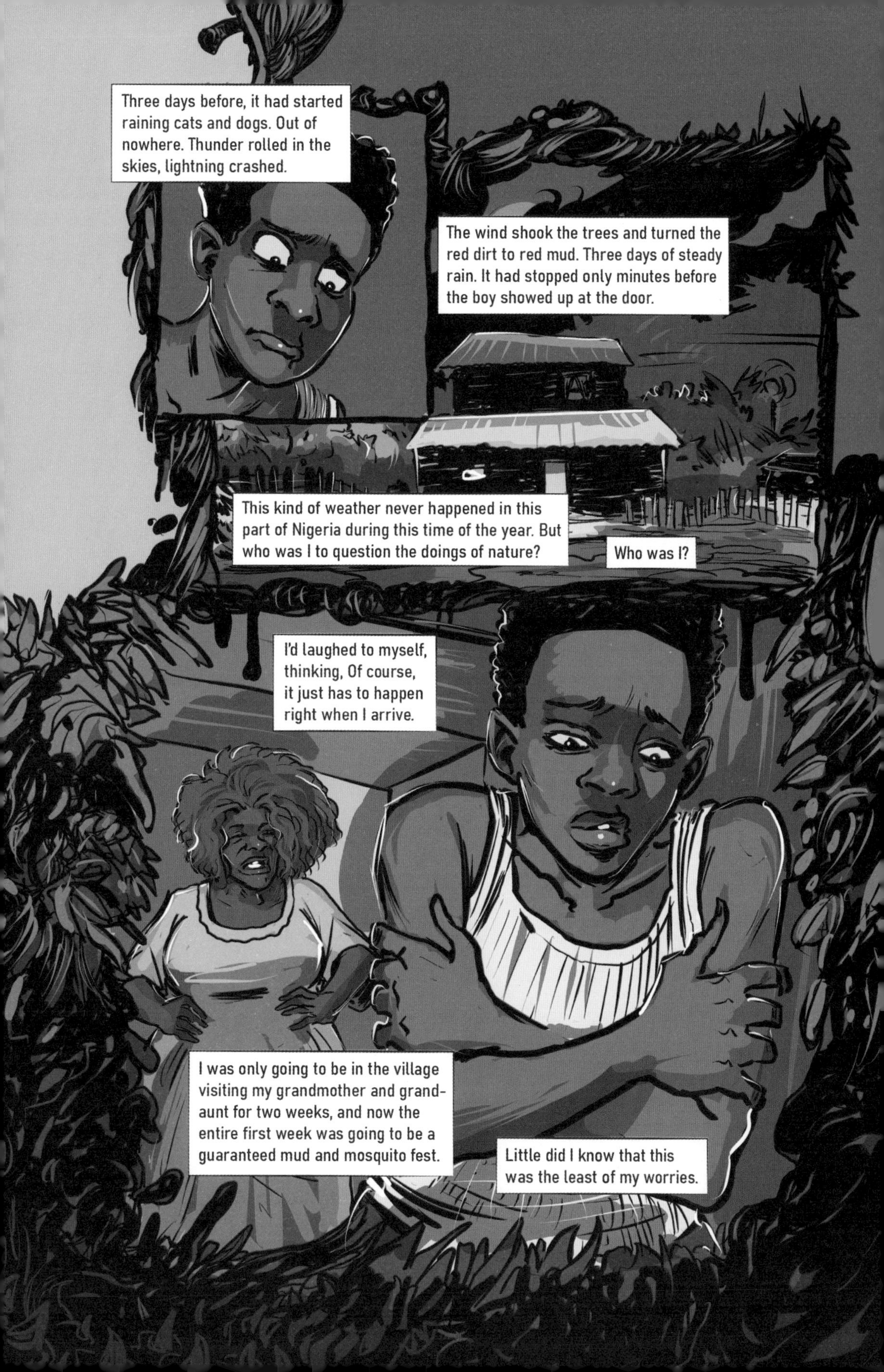

Three days before, it had started raining cats and dogs. Out of nowhere. Thunder rolled in the skies, lightning crashed.
The wind shook the trees and turned the red dirt to red mud. Three days of steady rain. It had stopped only minutes before the boy showed up at the door.
This kind of weather never happened in this part of Nigeria during this time of the year. But who was I to question the doings of nature?
Who was I?
I'd laughed to myself, thinking, Of course, it just has to happen right when I arrive.
I was only going to be in the village visiting my grandmother and grand-aunt for two weeks, and now the entire first week was going to be a guaranteed mud and mosquito fest.
Little did I know that this was the least of my worries.

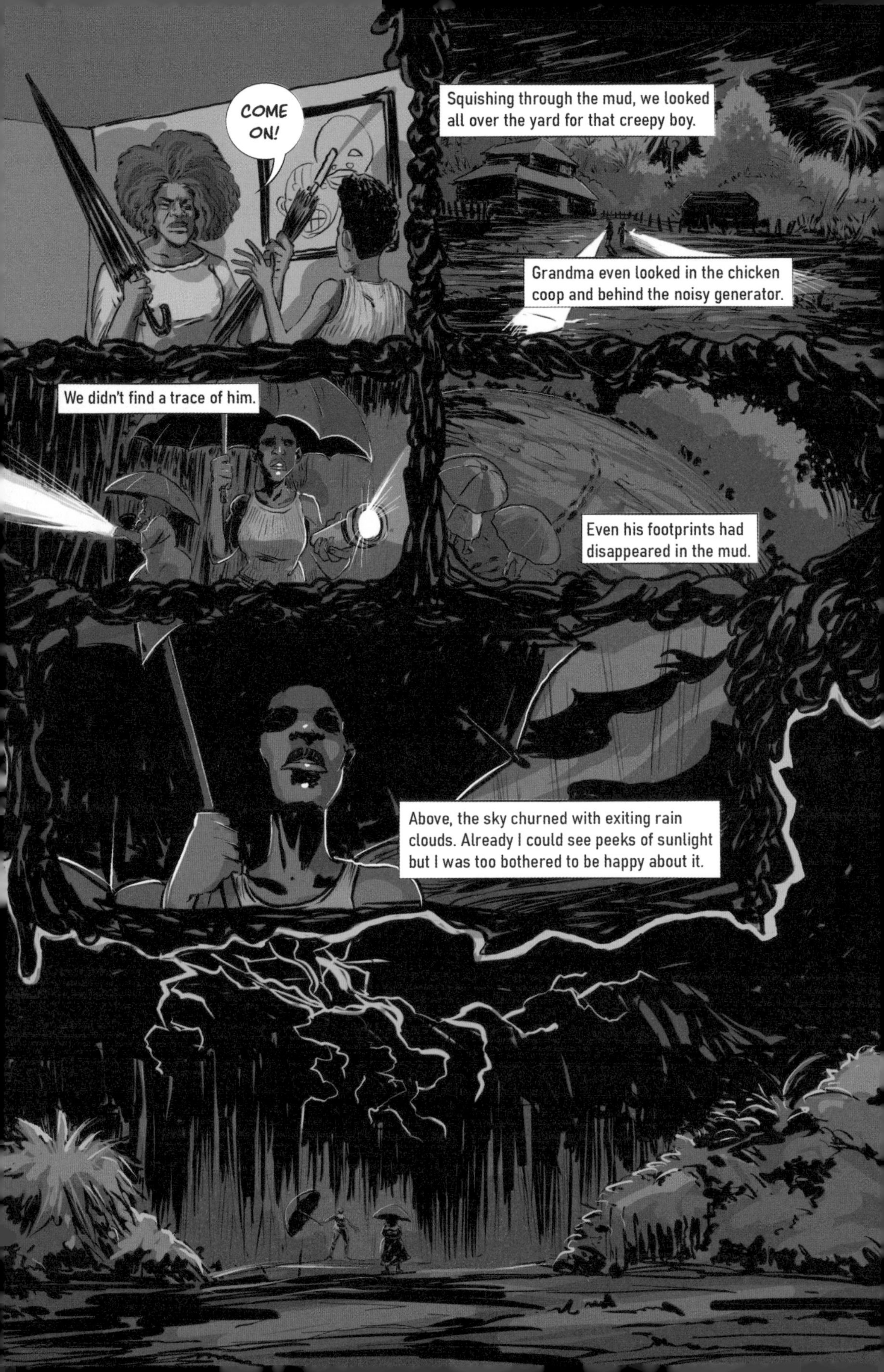
COME ON!
Squishing through the mud, we looked all over the yard for that creepy boy.
Grandma even looked in the chicken coop and behind the noisy generator.
We didn't find a trace of him.
Even his footprints had disappeared in the mud.
Above, the sky churned with exiting rain clouds. Already I could see peeks of sunlight but I was too bothered to be happy about it.

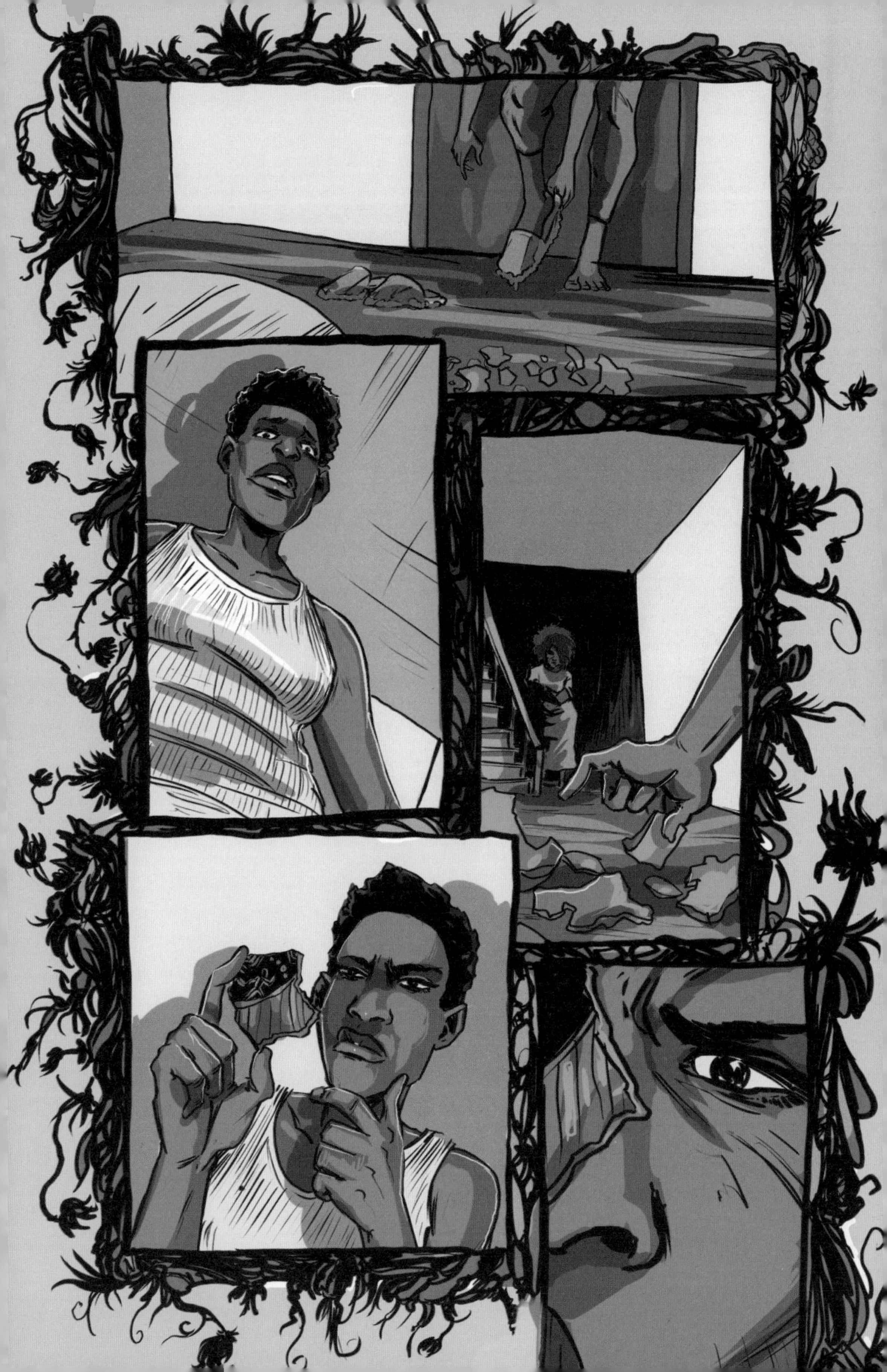

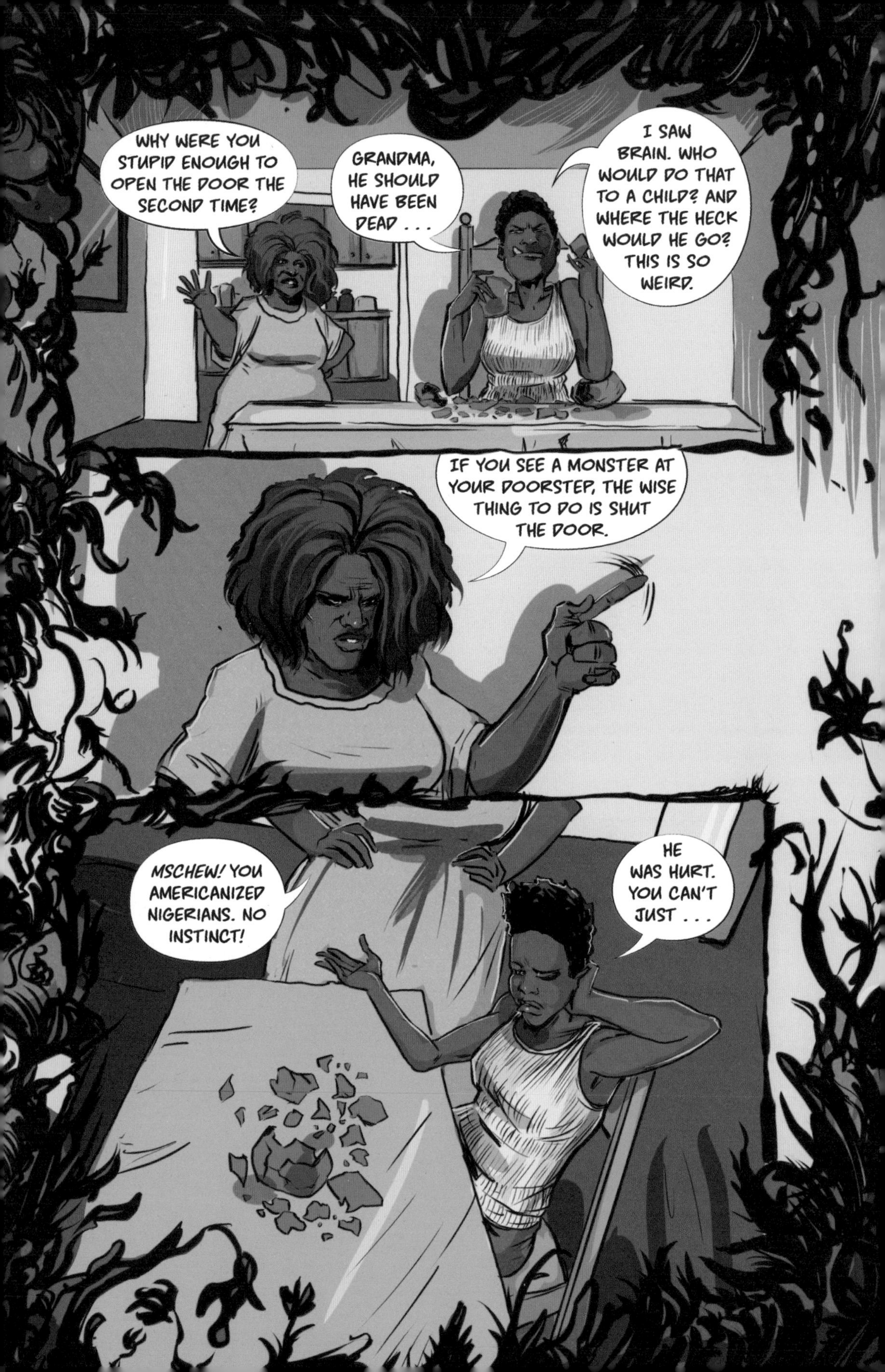
WHY WERE YOU STUPID ENOUGH TO OPEN THE DOOR THE SECOND TIME?
GRANDMA, HE SHOULD HAVE BEEN DEAD . . .
I SAW BRAIN. WHO WOULD DO THAT TO A CHILD? AND WHERE THE HECK WOULD HE GO? THIS IS SO WEIRD.
IF YOU SEE A MONSTER AT YOUR DOORSTEP, THE WISE THING TO DO IS SHUT THE DOOR.
MSCHEW! YOU AMERICANIZED NIGERIANS. NO INSTINCT!
HE WAS HURT. YOU CAN'T JUST . . .

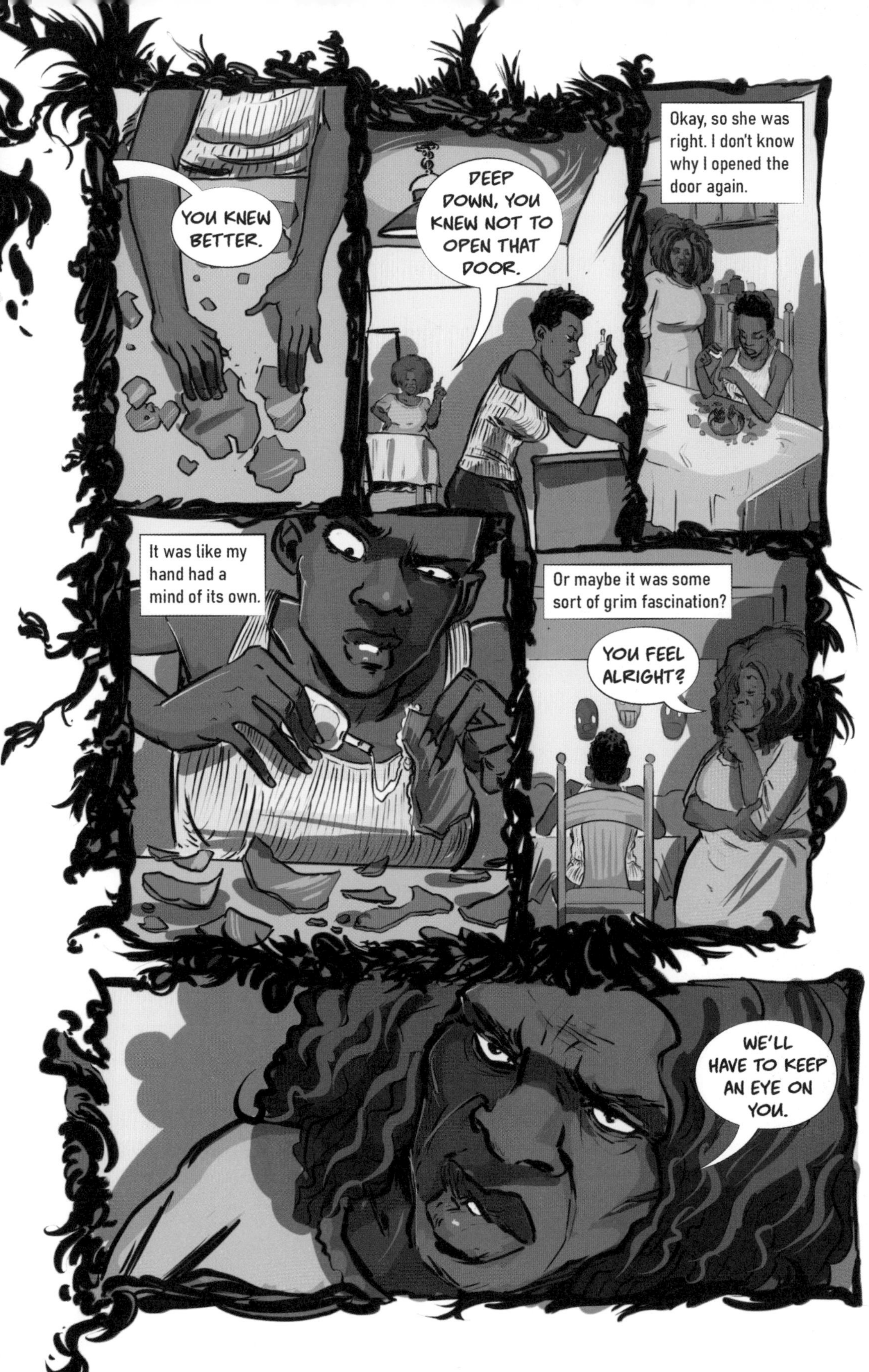
YOU KNEW BETTER.
DEEP DOWN, YOU KNEW NOT TO OPEN THAT DOOR.
Okay, so she was right. I don't know why I opened the door again.
It was like my hand had a mind of its own.
Or maybe it was some sort of grim fascination?
YOU FEEL ALRIGHT?
WE'LL HAVE TO KEEP AN EYE ON YOU.

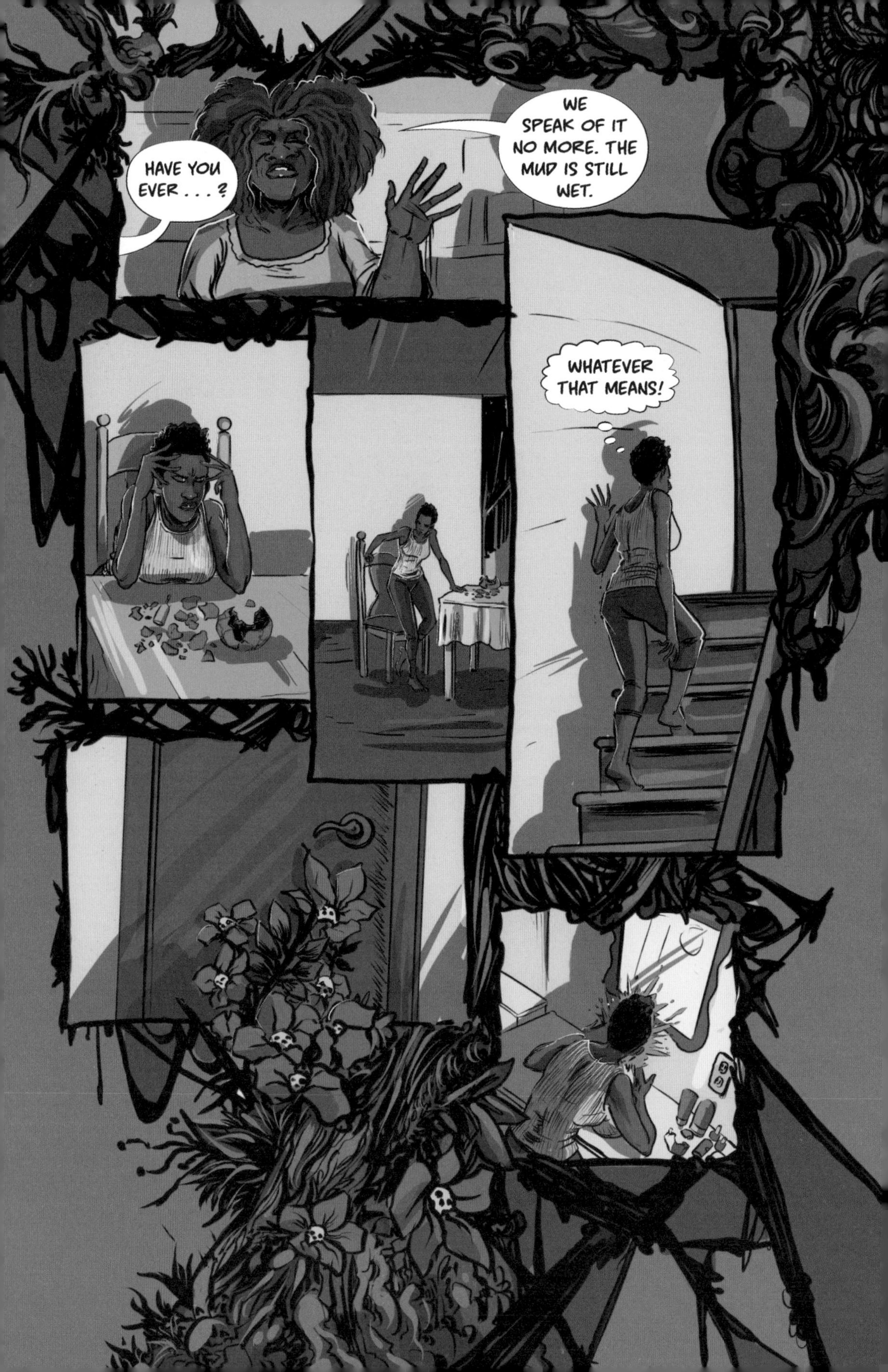
HAVE YOU EVER . . . ?
WE SPEAK OF IT NO MORE. THE MUD IS STILL WET.
WHATEVER THAT MEANS!

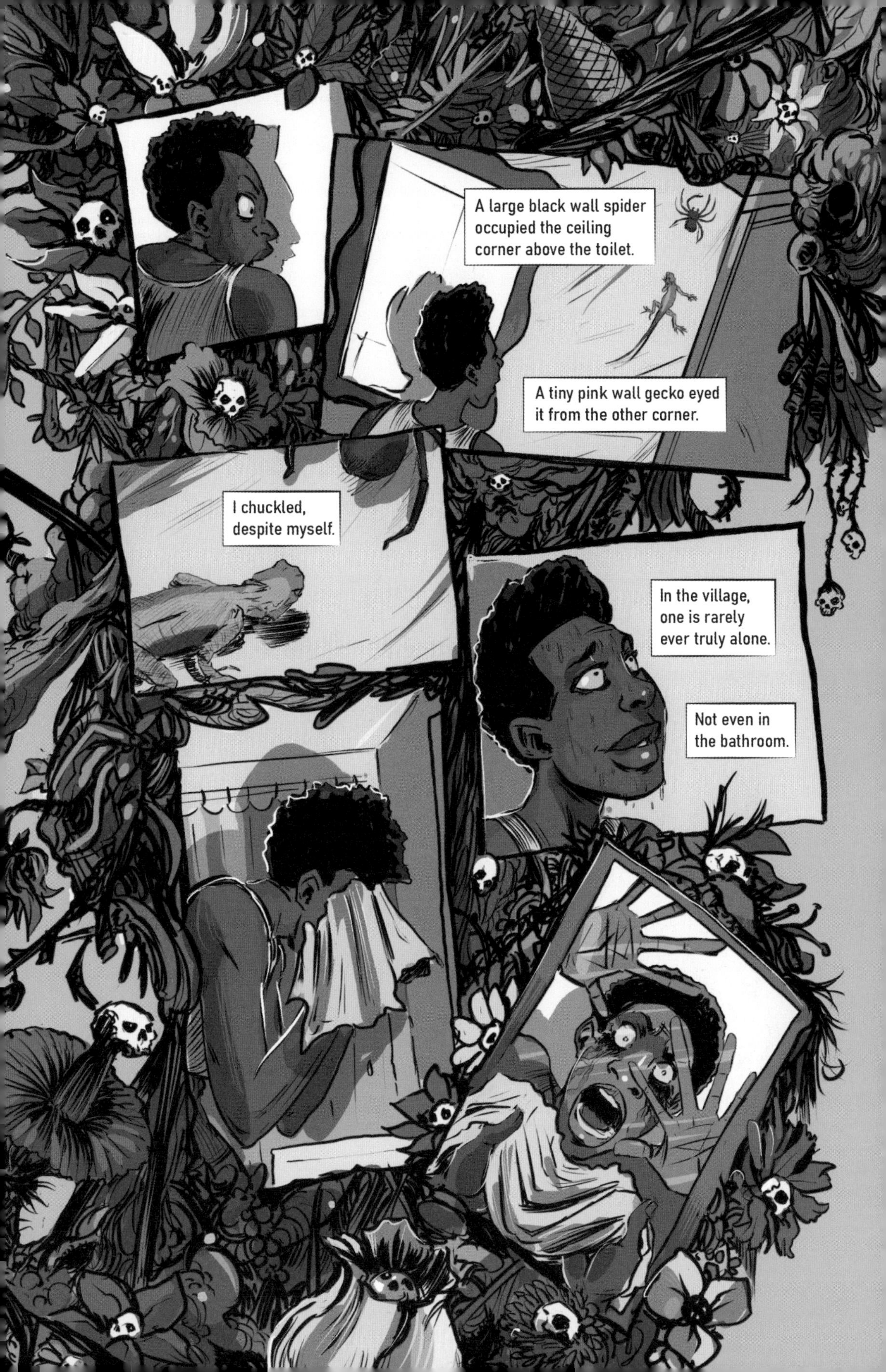
A large black wall spider occupied the ceiling corner above the toilet.
A tiny pink wall gecko eyed it from the other corner.
I chuckled, despite myself.
In the village, one is rarely ever truly alone.
Not even in the bathroom.

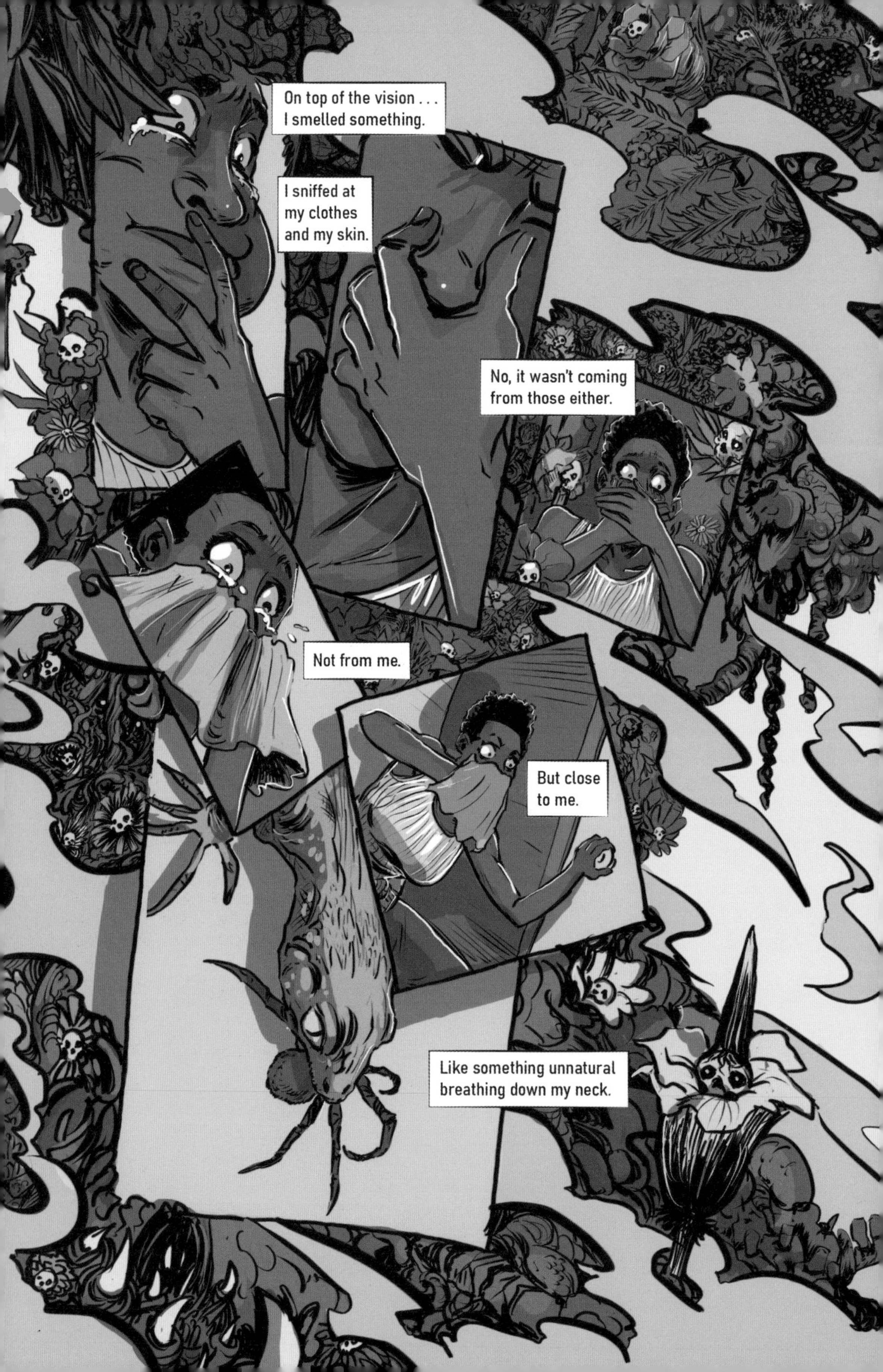
On top of the vision . . . I smelled something.
I sniffed at my clothes and my skin.
No, it wasn't coming from those either.
Not from me.
But close to me.
Like something unnatural breathing down my neck.

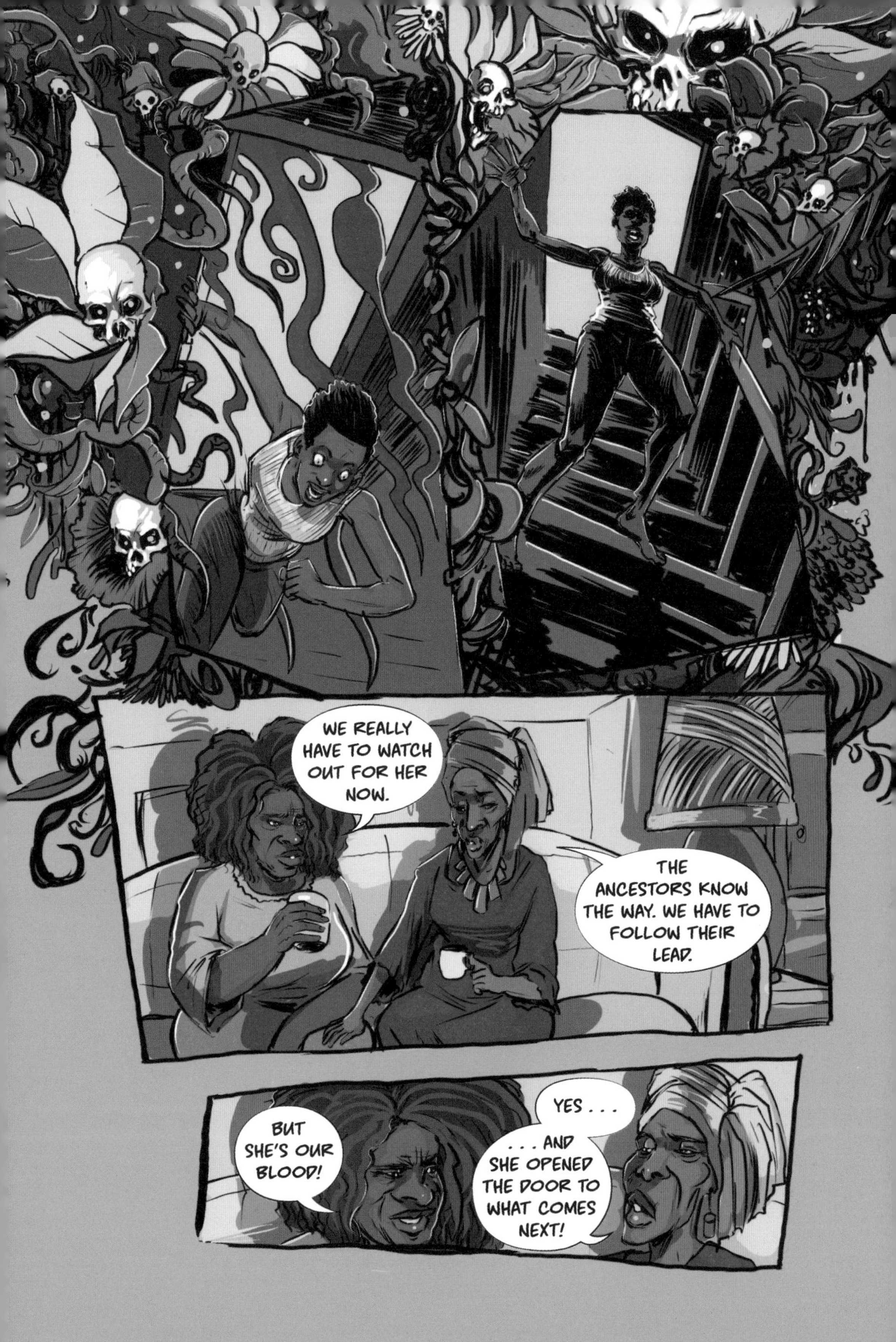
WE REALLY HAVE TO WATCH OUT FOR HER NOW.
THE ANCESTORS KNOW THE WAY. WE HAVE TO FOLLOW THEIR LEAD.
BUT SHE'S OUR BLOOD!
YES . . .
. . . AND SHE OPENED THE DOOR TO WHAT COMES NEXT!

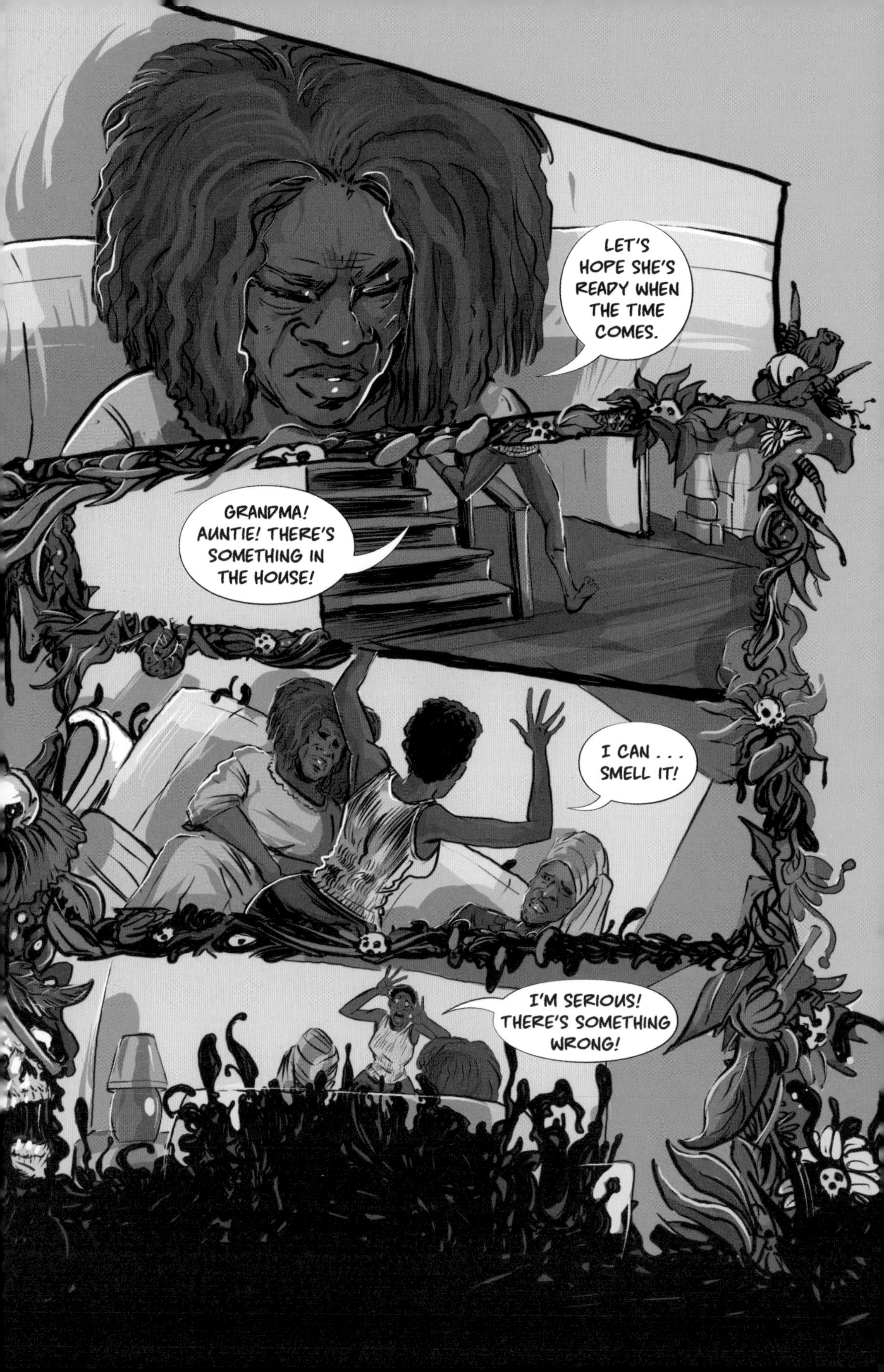
LET'S HOPE SHE'S READY WHEN THE TIME COMES.
GRANDMA! AUNTIE! THERE'S SOMETHING IN THE HOUSE!
I CAN . . . SMELL IT!
I'M SERIOUS! THERE'S SOMETHING WRONG!

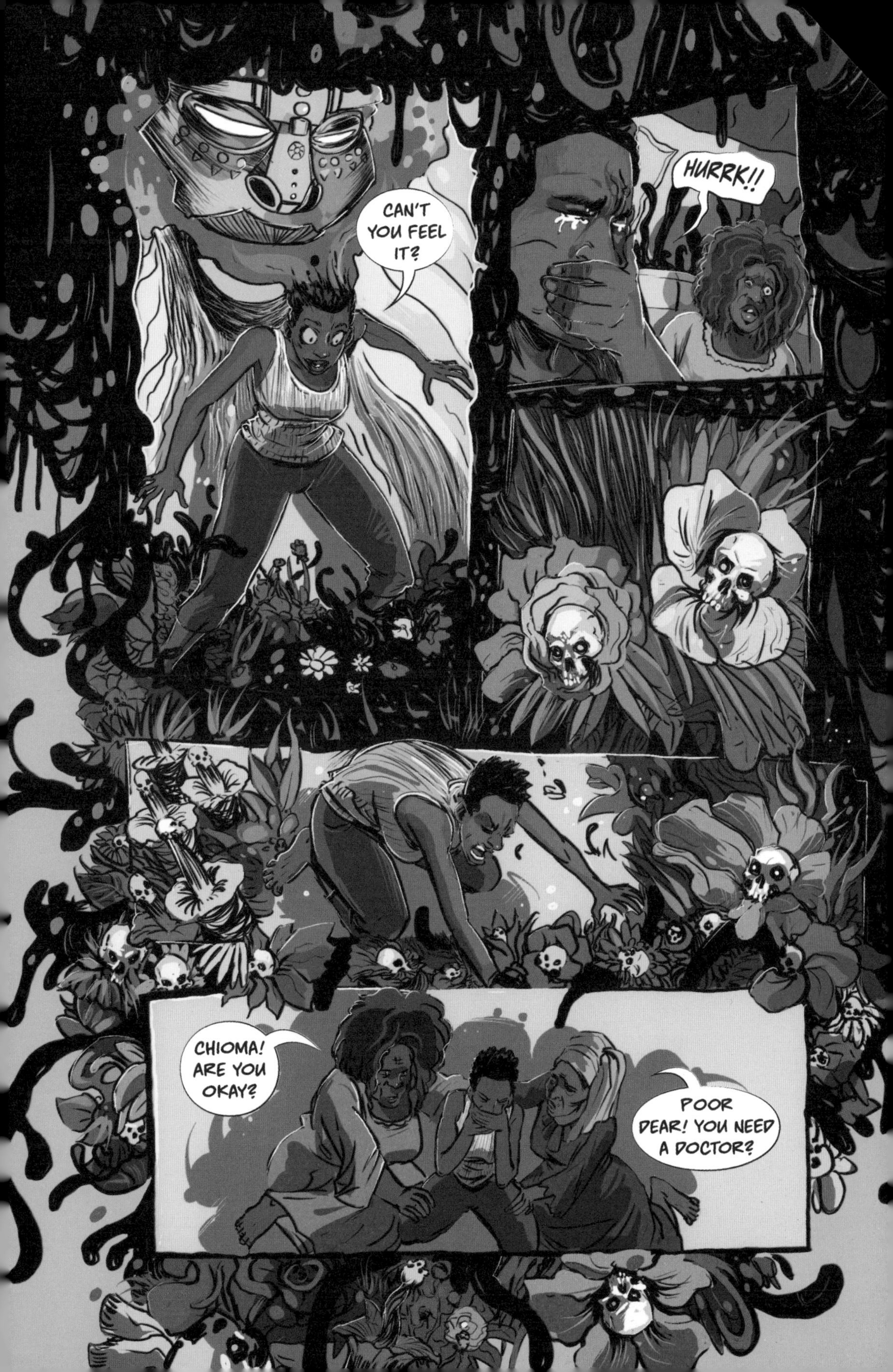
CAN'T YOU FEEL IT?
HURRK!!
CHIOMA! ARE YOU OKAY?
POOR DEAR! YOU NEED A DOCTOR?

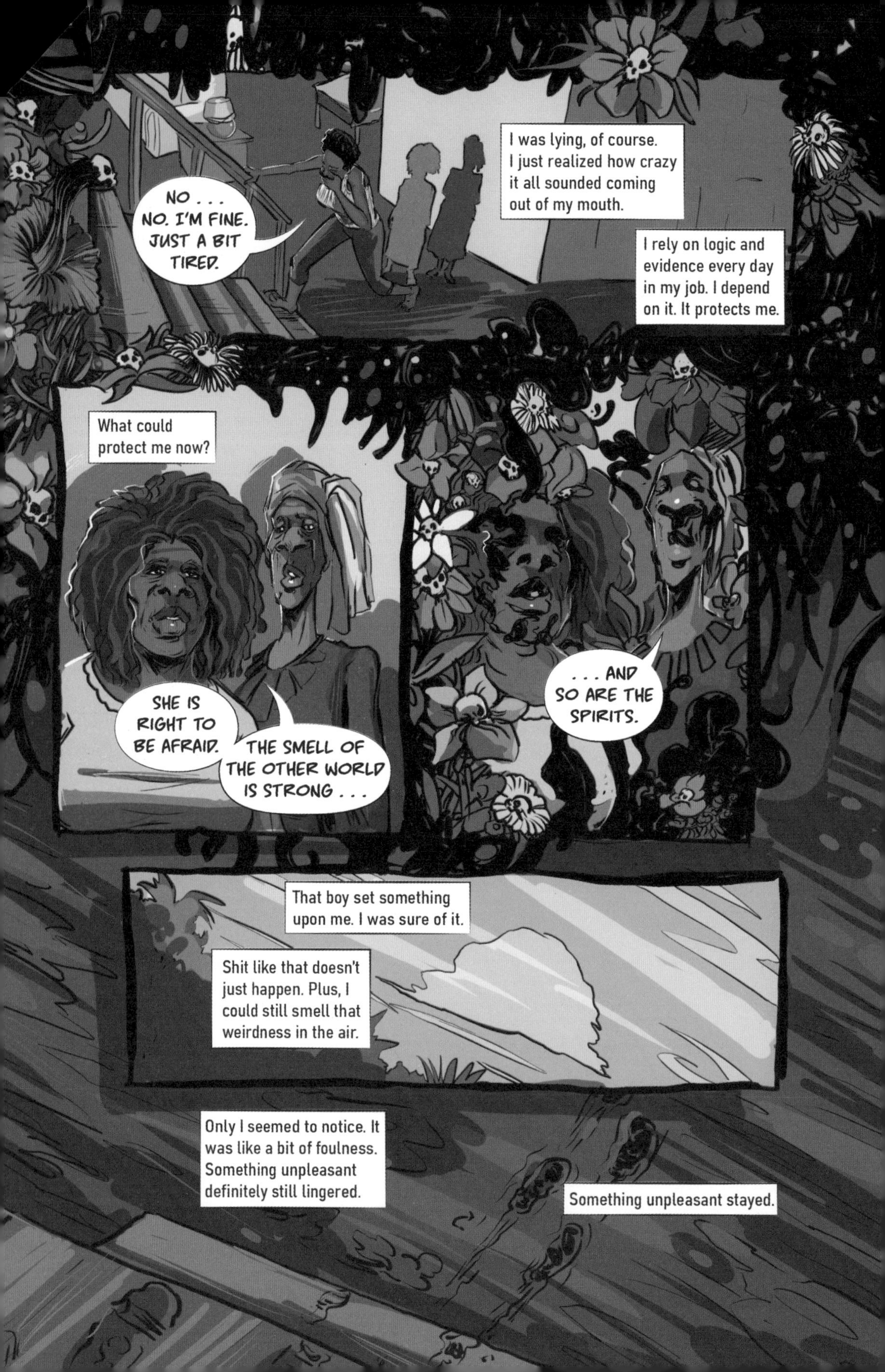
NO . . . NO. I'M FINE. JUST A BIT TIRED.
I was lying, of course. I just realized how crazy it all sounded coming out of my mouth.
I rely on logic and evidence every day in my job. I depend on it. It protects me.
What could protect me now?
SHE IS RIGHT TO BE AFRAID.
THE SMELL OF THE OTHER WORLD IS STRONG . . .
. . . AND SO ARE THE SPIRITS.
That boy set something upon me. I was sure of it.
Shit like that doesn't just happen. Plus, I could still smell that weirdness in the air.
Only I seemed to notice. It was like a bit of foulness. Something unpleasant definitely still lingered.
Something unpleasant stayed.

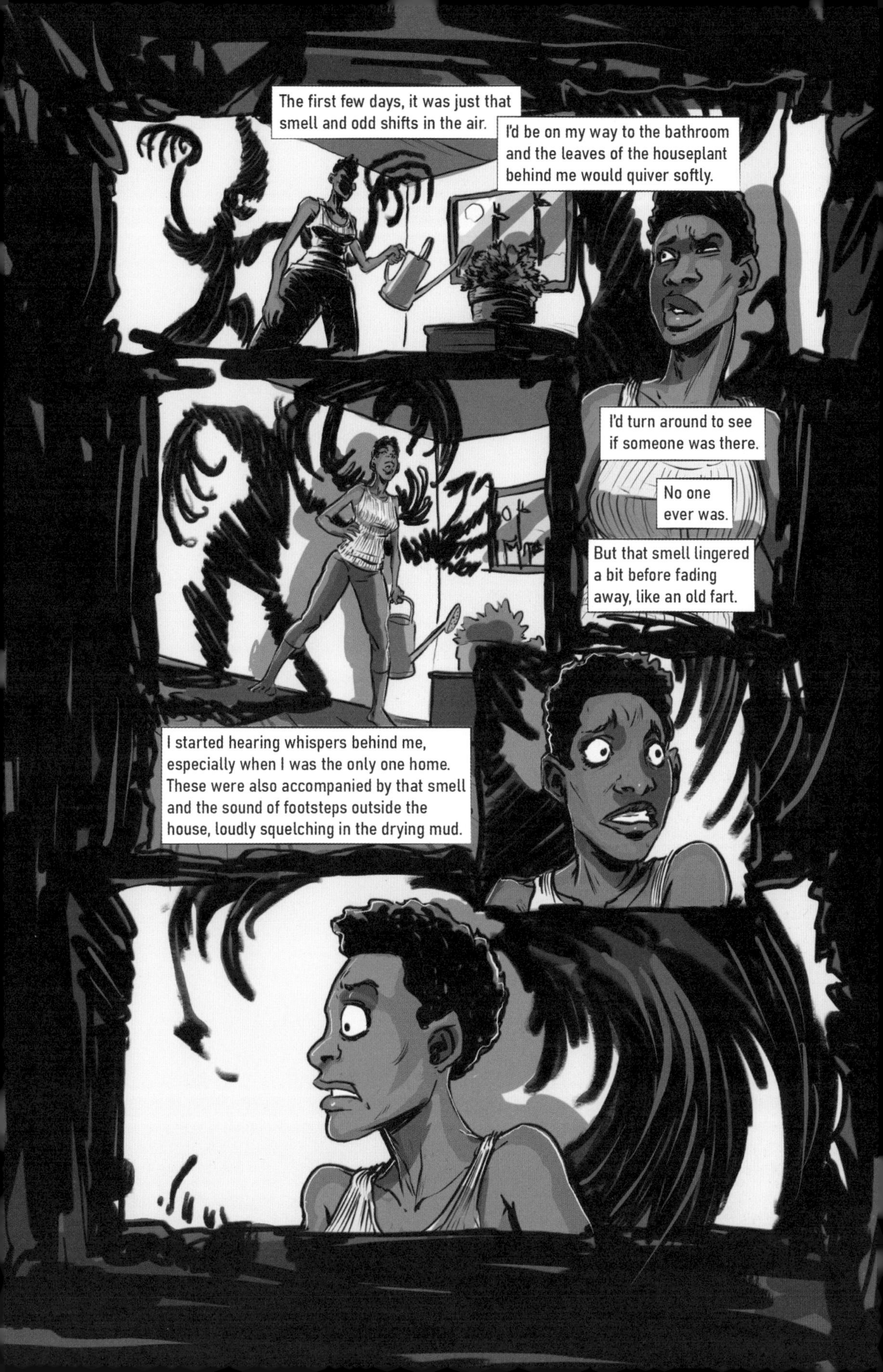
The first few days, it was just that smell and odd shifts in the air.
I'd be on my way to the bathroom and the leaves of the houseplant behind me would quiver softly.
I'd turn around to see if someone was there.
No one ever was.
But that smell lingered a bit before fading away, like an old fart.
I started hearing whispers behind me, especially when I was the only one home. These were also accompanied by that smell and the sound of footsteps outside the house, loudly squelching in the drying mud.

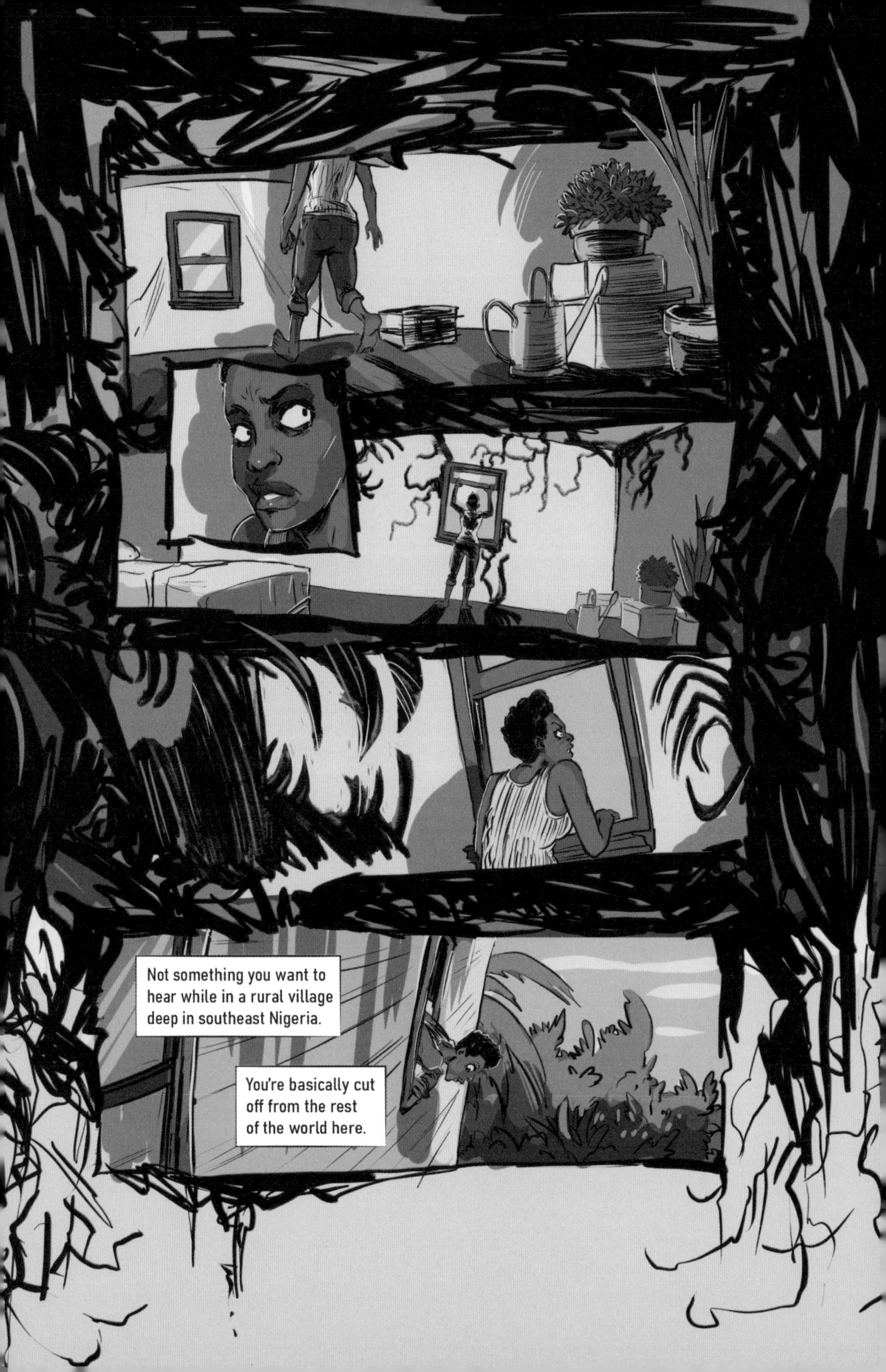
Not something you want to hear while in a rural village deep in southeast Nigeria.
You're basically cut off from the rest of the world here.

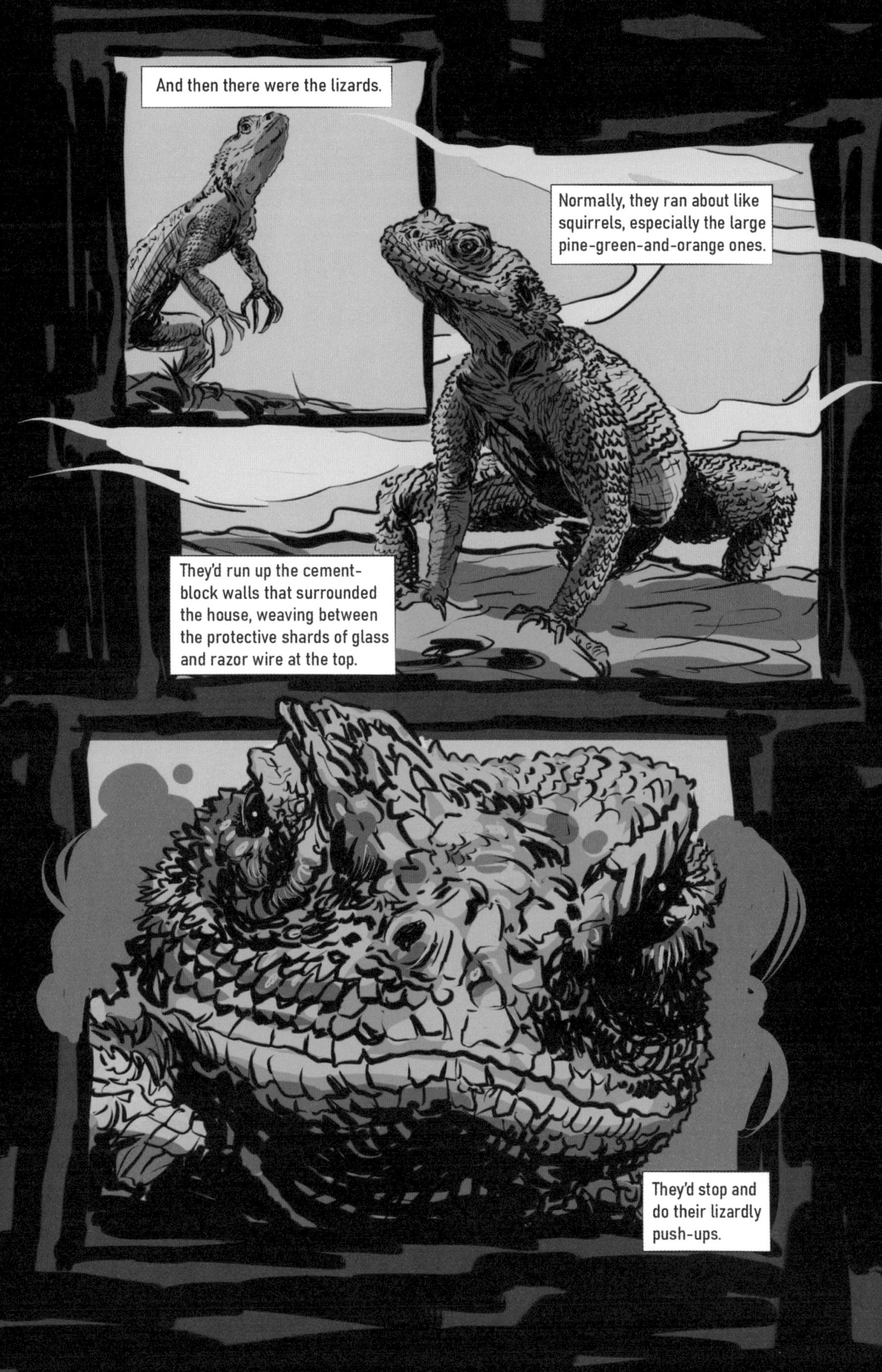
And then there were the lizards.
Normally, they ran about like squirrels, especially the large pine-green-and-orange ones.
They'd run up the cement-block walls that surrounded the house, weaving between the protective shards of glass and razor wire at the top.
They'd stop and do their lizardly push-ups.

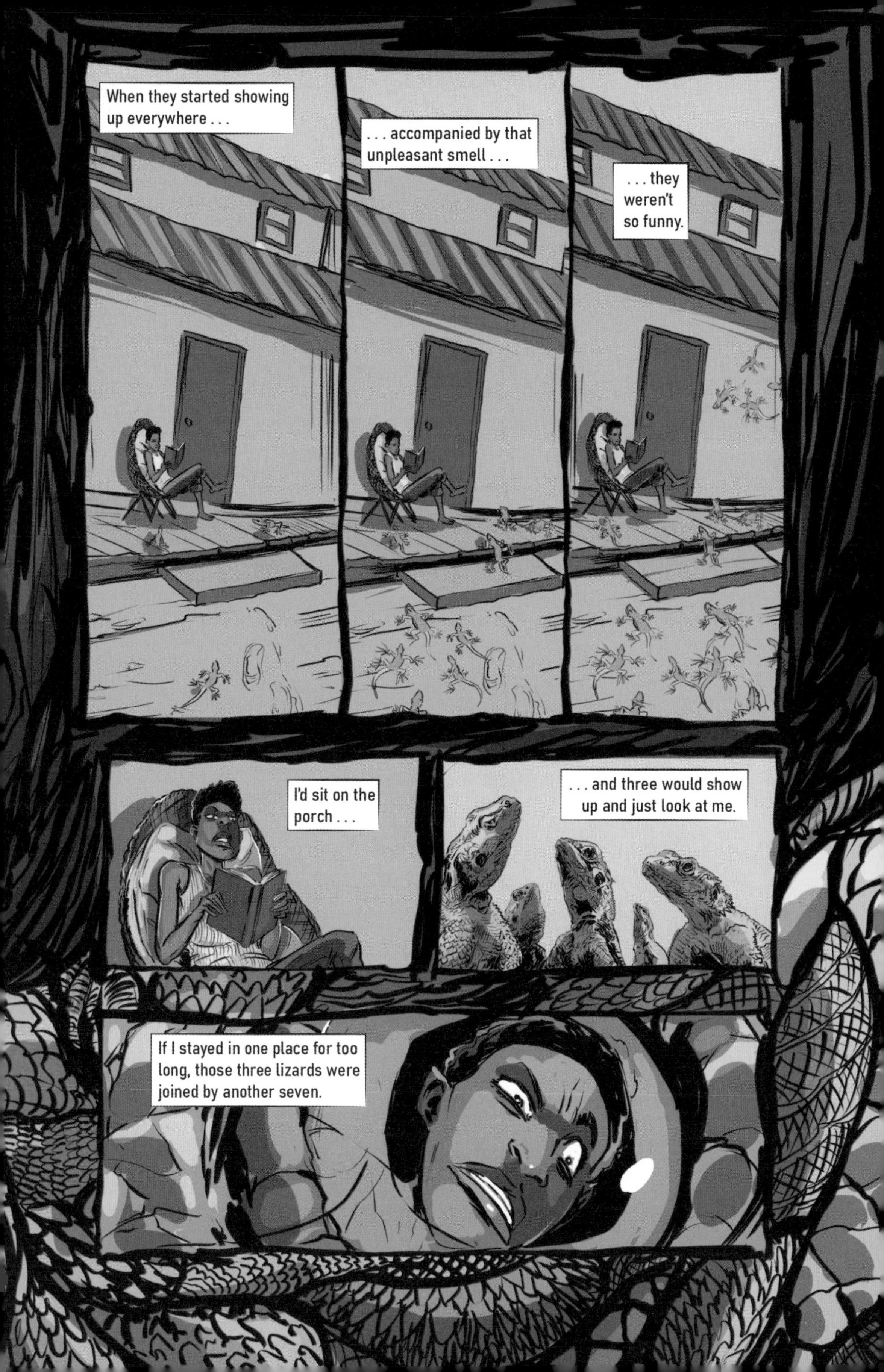
When they started showing up everywhere . . .
. . . accompanied by that unpleasant smell . . .
. . . they weren't so funny.
I'd sit on the porch . . .
. . . and three would show up and just look at me.
If I stayed in one place for too long, those three lizards were joined by another seven.

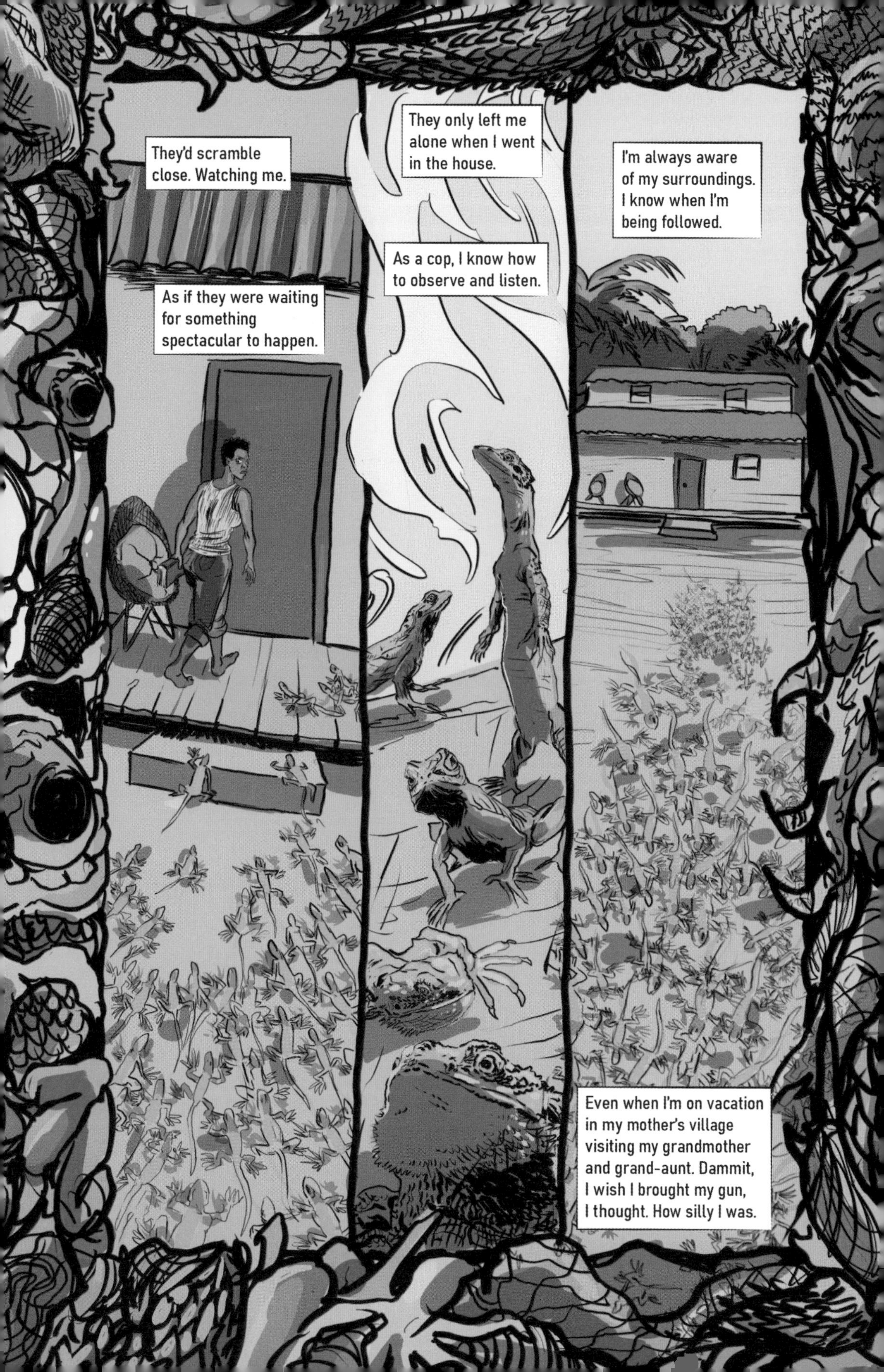
They'd scramble close. Watching me.
As if they were waiting for something spectacular to happen.
They only left me alone when I went in the house.
As a cop, I know how to observe and listen.
I'm always aware of my surroundings. I know when I'm being followed.
Even when I'm on vacation in my mother's village visiting my grandmother and grand-aunt. Dammit, I wish I brought my gun, I thought. How silly I was.

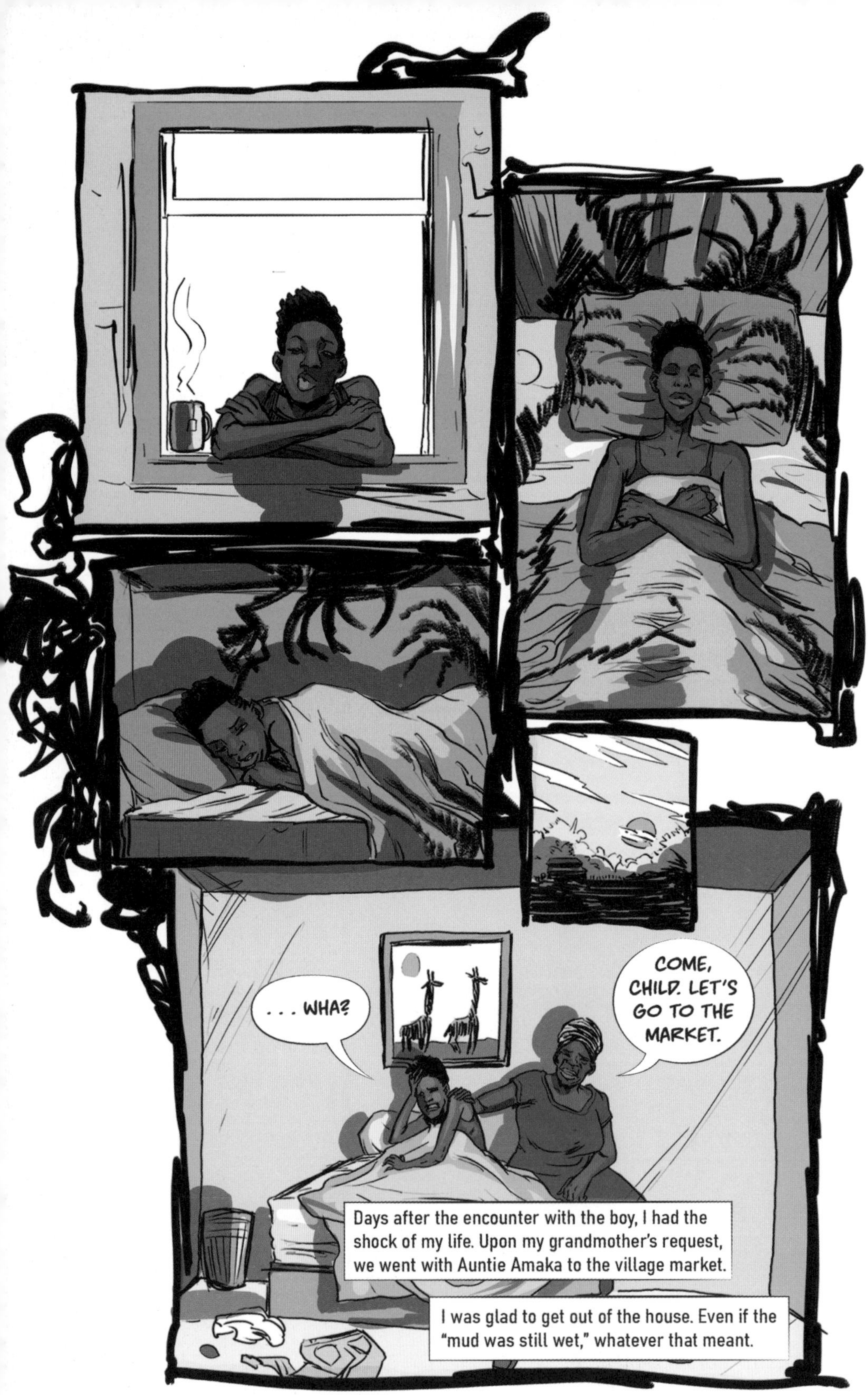

. . . WHA?
COME, CHILD. LET'S GO TO THE MARKET.
Days after the encounter with the boy, I had the shock of my life. Upon my grandmother's request, we went with Auntie Amaka to the village market.
I was glad to get out of the house. Even if the "mud was still wet," whatever that meant.

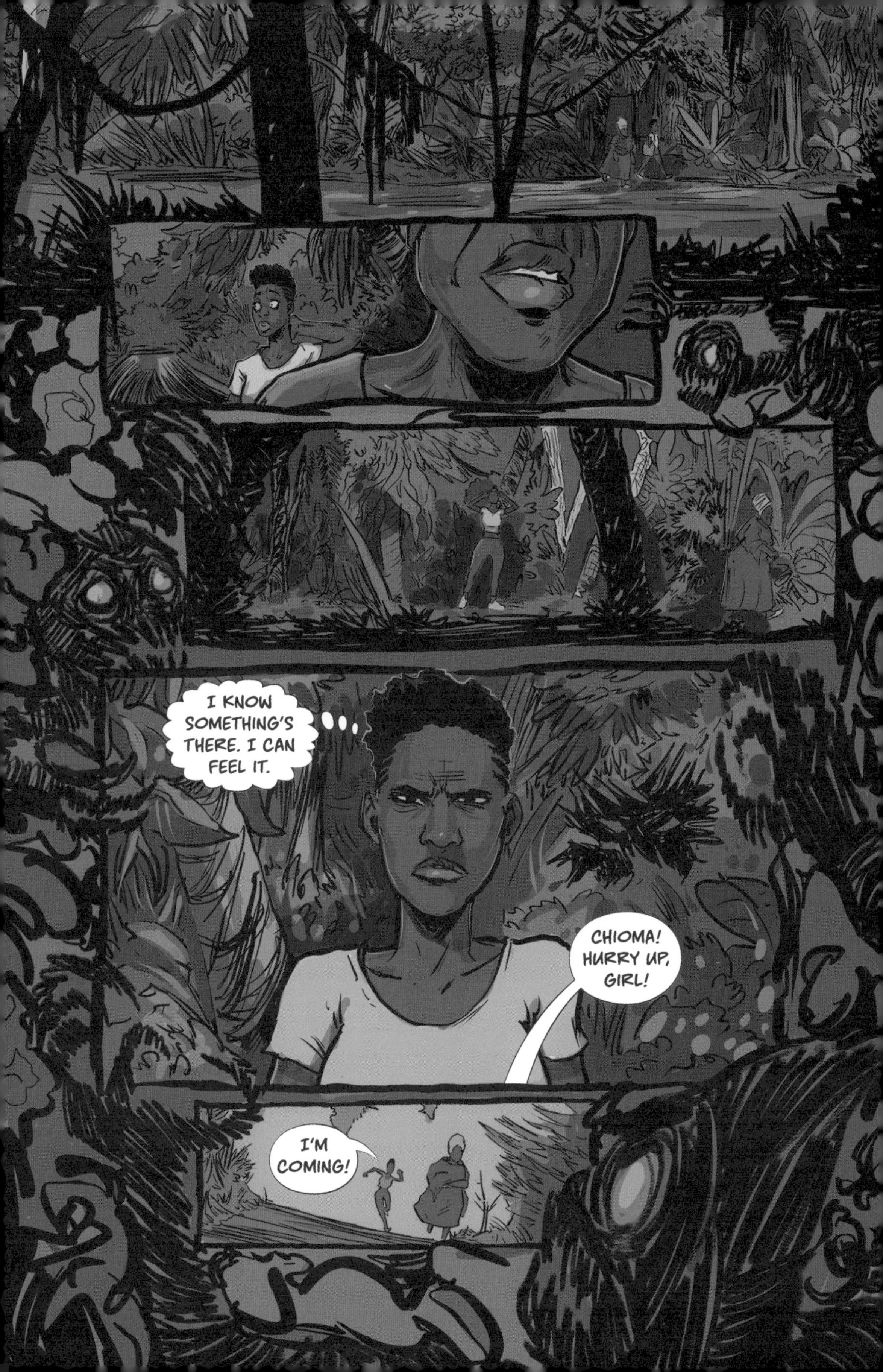
I KNOW SOMETHING'S THERE. I CAN FEEL IT.
CHIOMA! HURRY UP, GIRL!
I'M COMING!

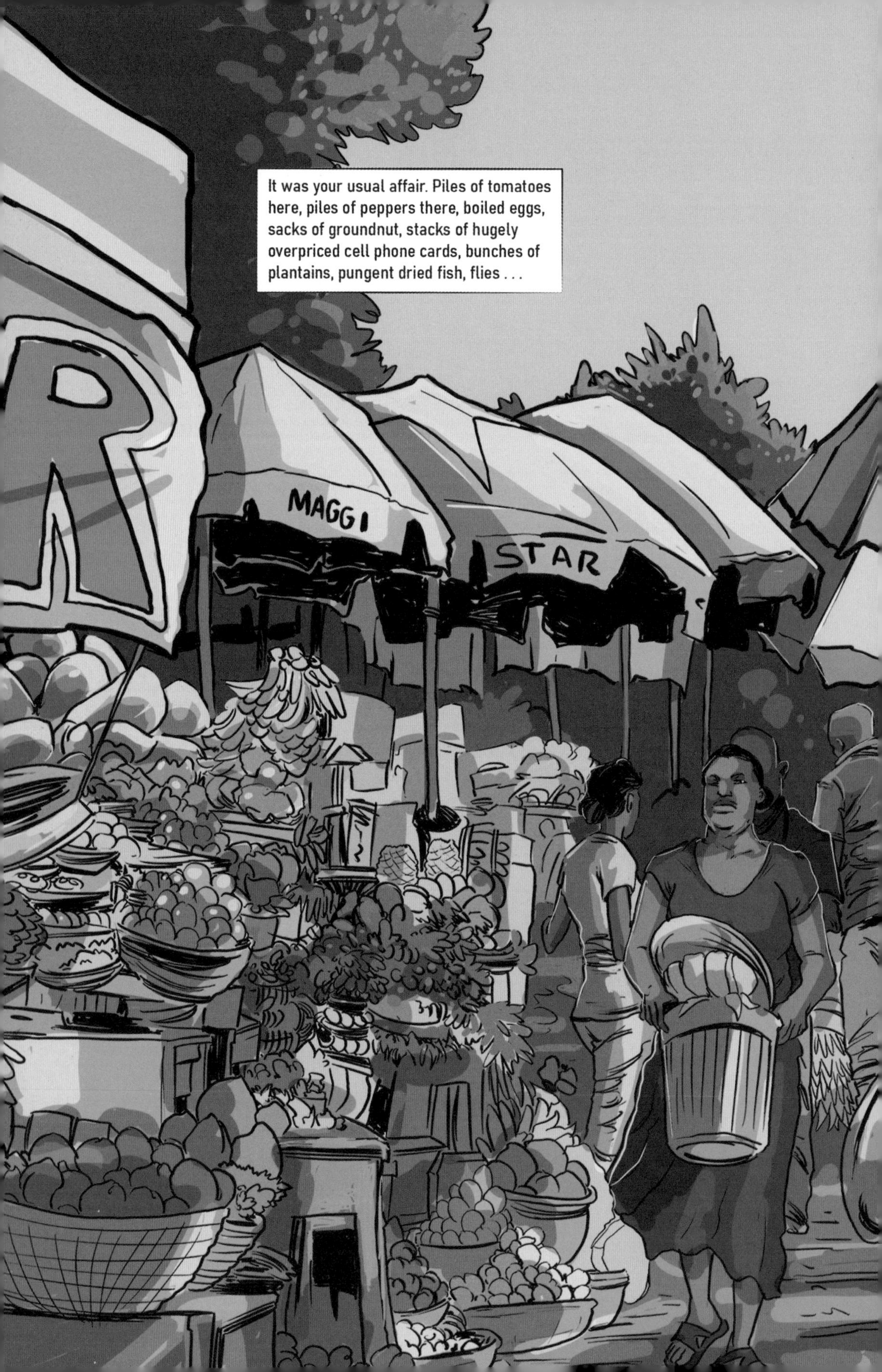
It was your usual affair. Piles of tomatoes here, piles of peppers there, boiled eggs, sacks of groundnut, stacks of hugely overpriced cell phone cards, bunches of plantains, pungent dried fish, flies . . .
MAGGI
STAR

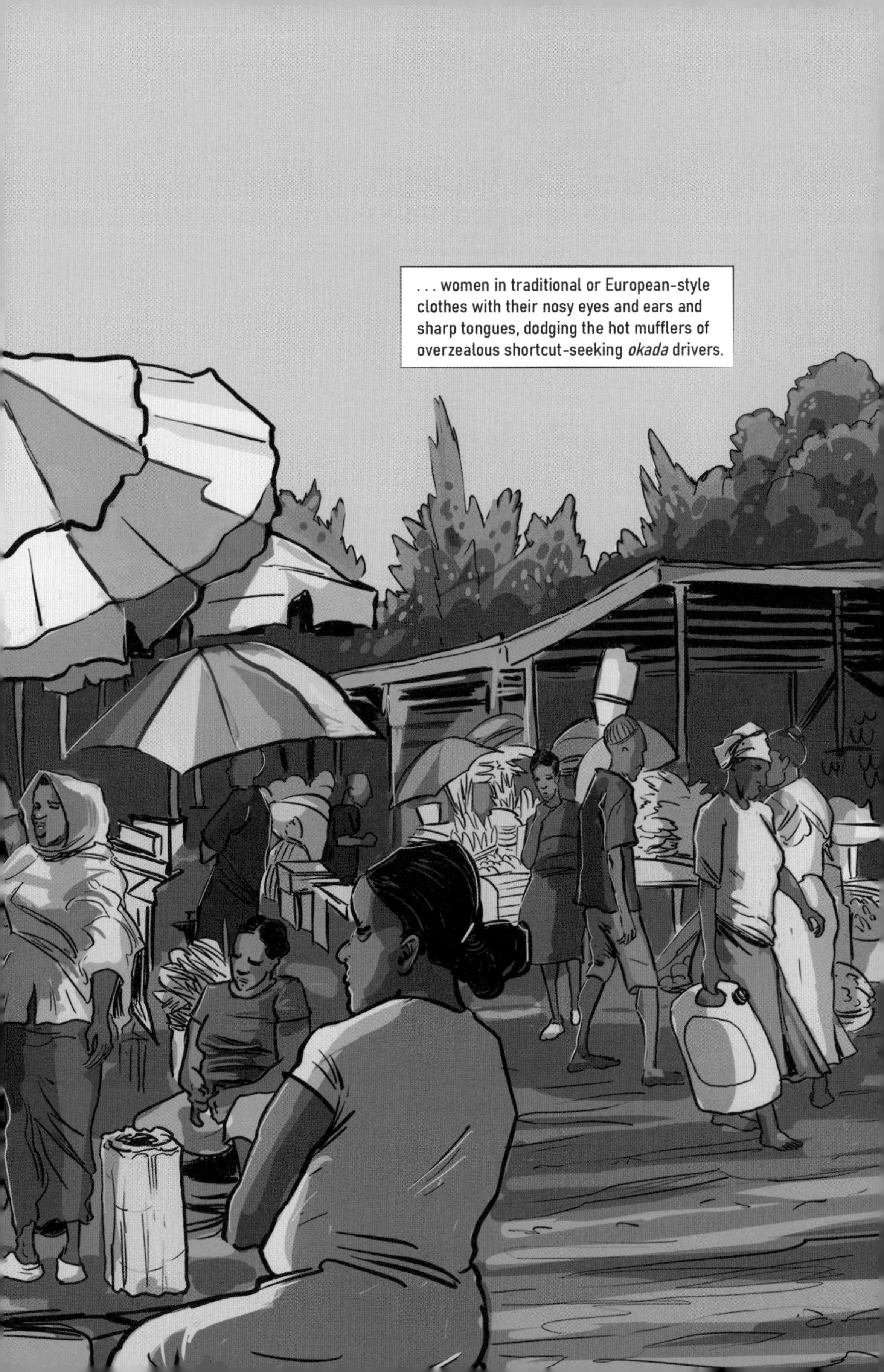
. . . women in traditional or European-style clothes with their nosy eyes and ears and sharp tongues, dodging the hot mufflers of overzealous shortcut-seeking *okada* drivers.

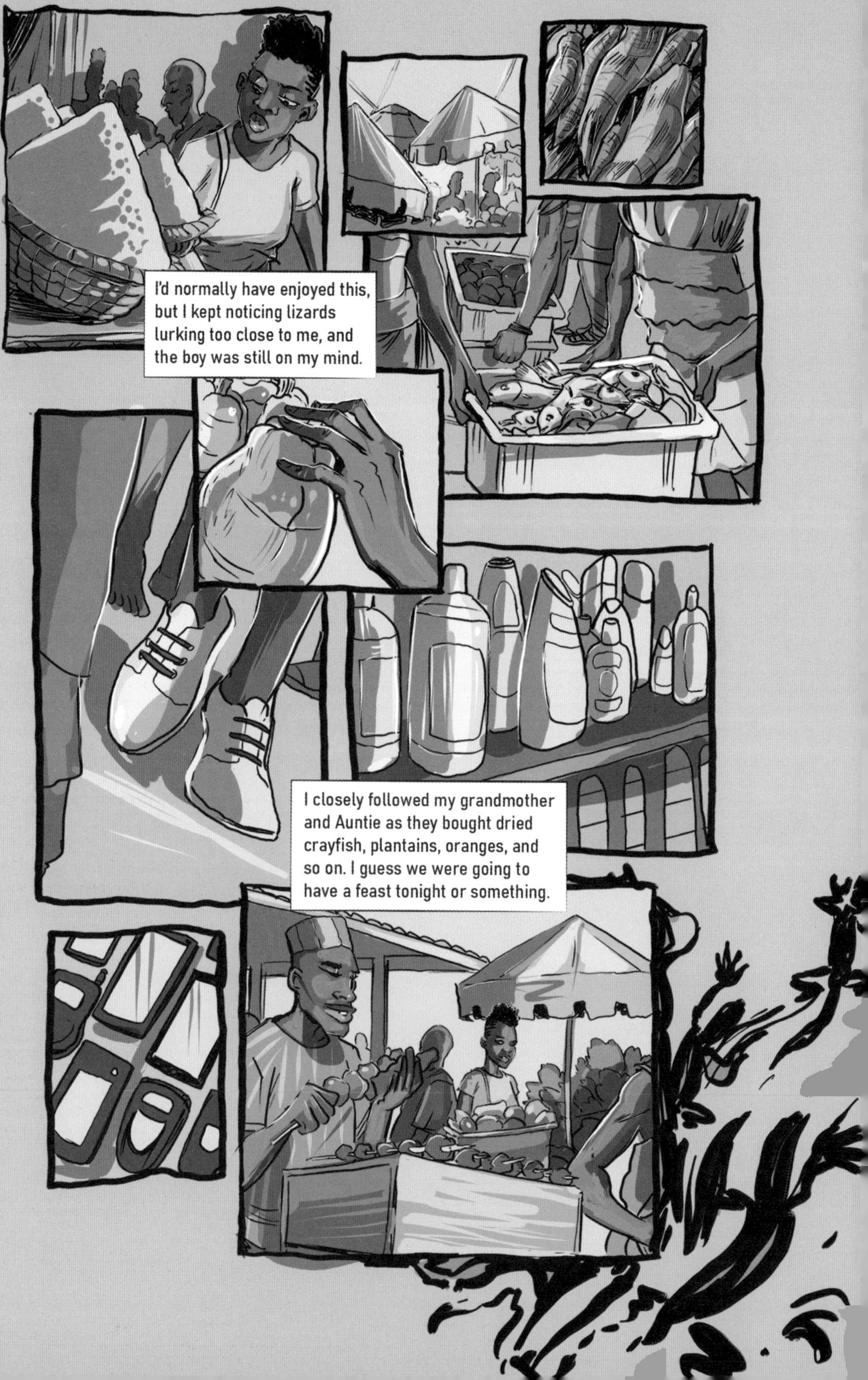
I'd normally have enjoyed this, but I kept noticing lizards lurking too close to me, and the boy was still on my mind.
I closely followed my grandmother and Auntie as they bought dried crayfish, plantains, oranges, and so on. I guess we were going to have a feast tonight or something.

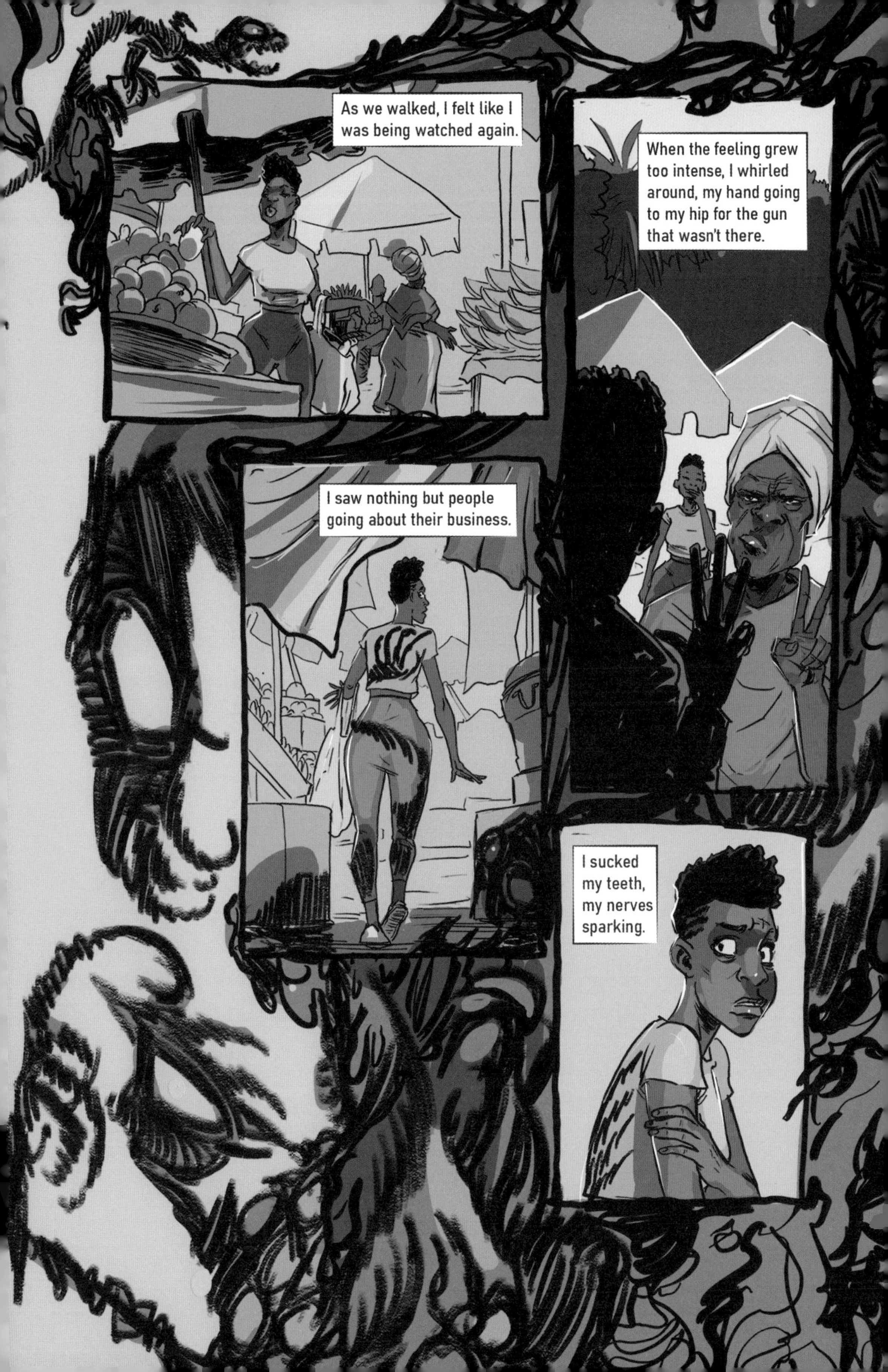

As we walked, I felt like I was being watched again.
When the feeling grew too intense, I whirled around, my hand going to my hip for the gun that wasn't there.
I saw nothing but people going about their business.
I sucked my teeth, my nerves sparking.

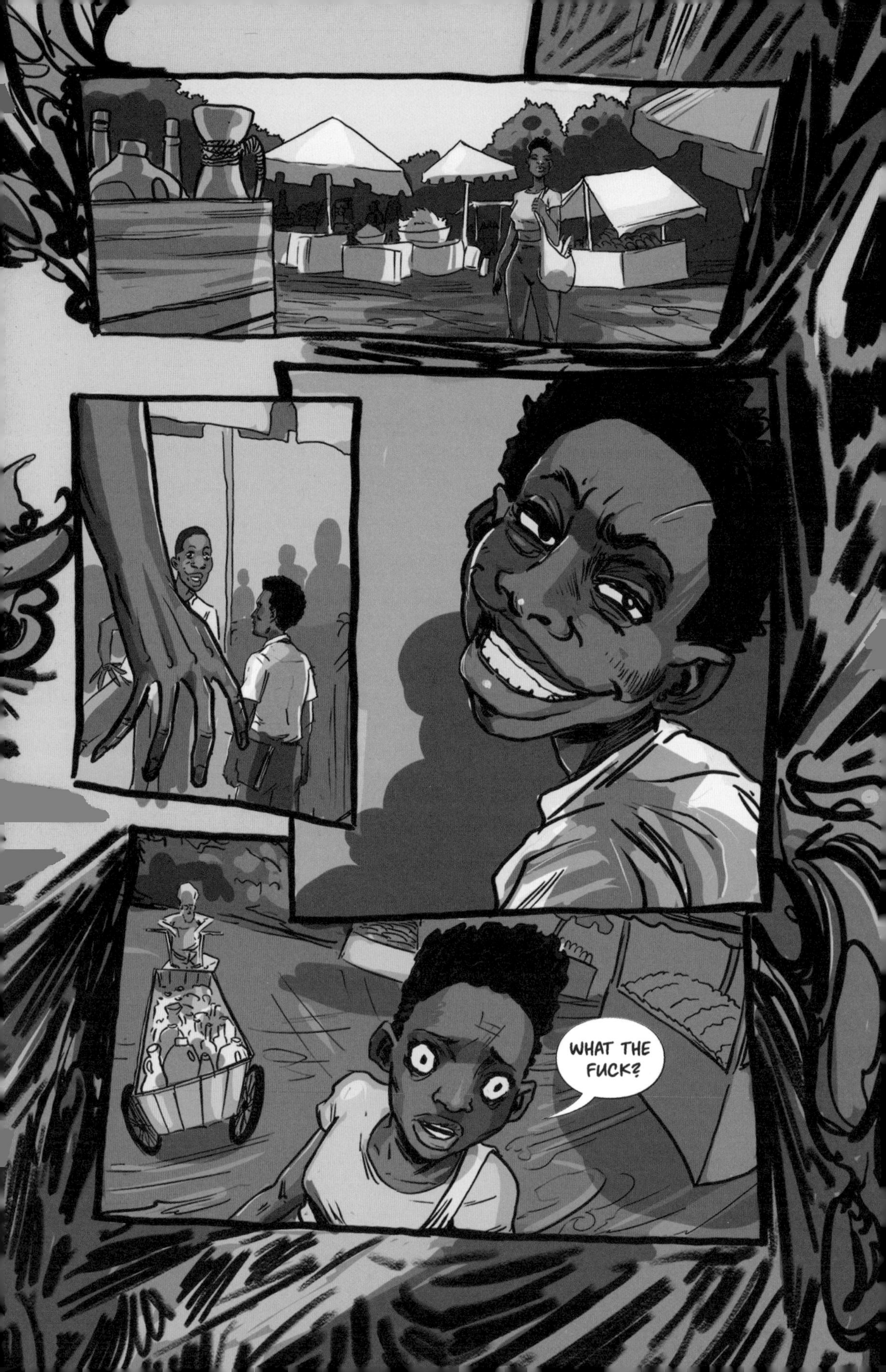
WHAT THE FUCK?

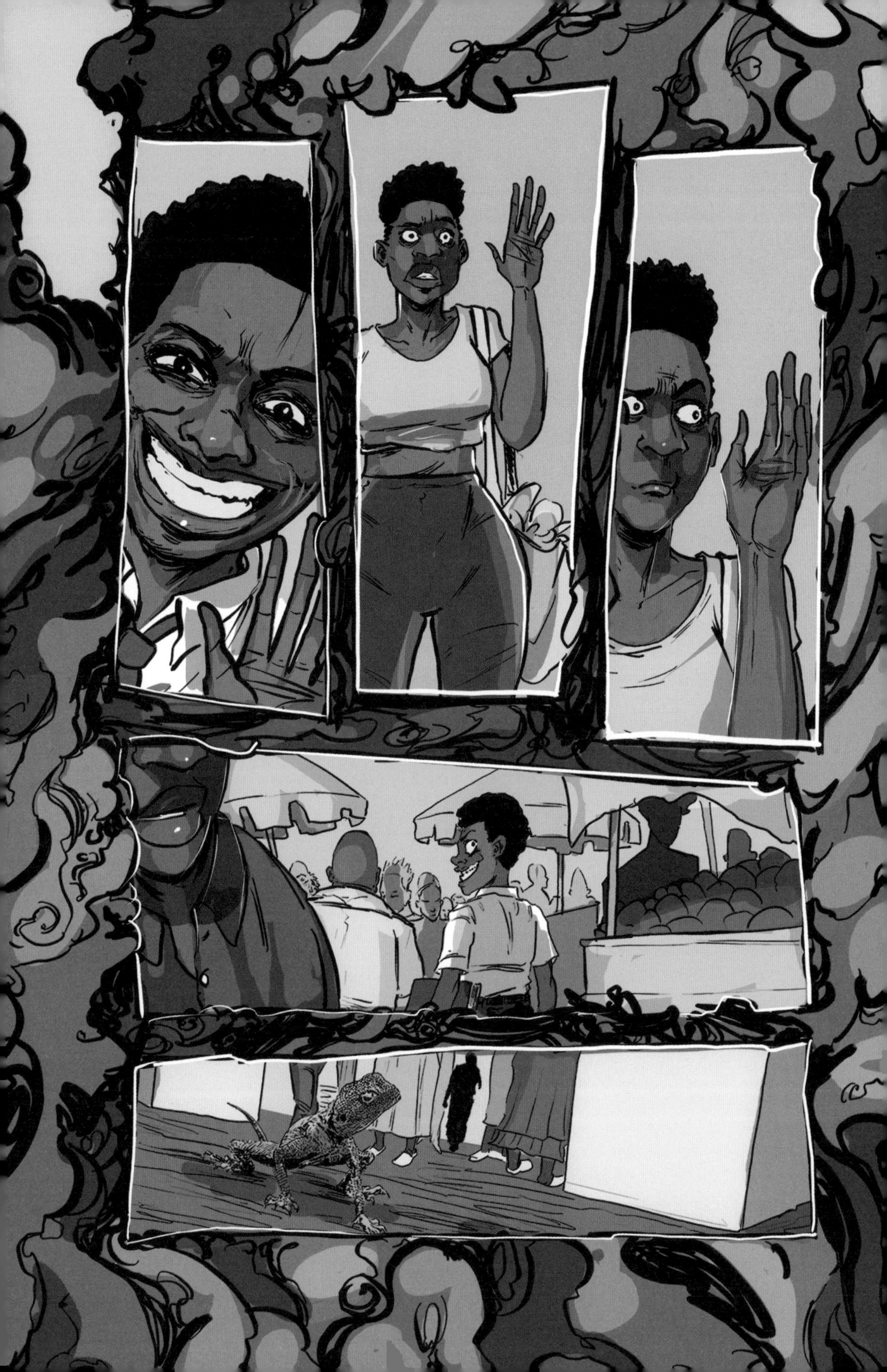

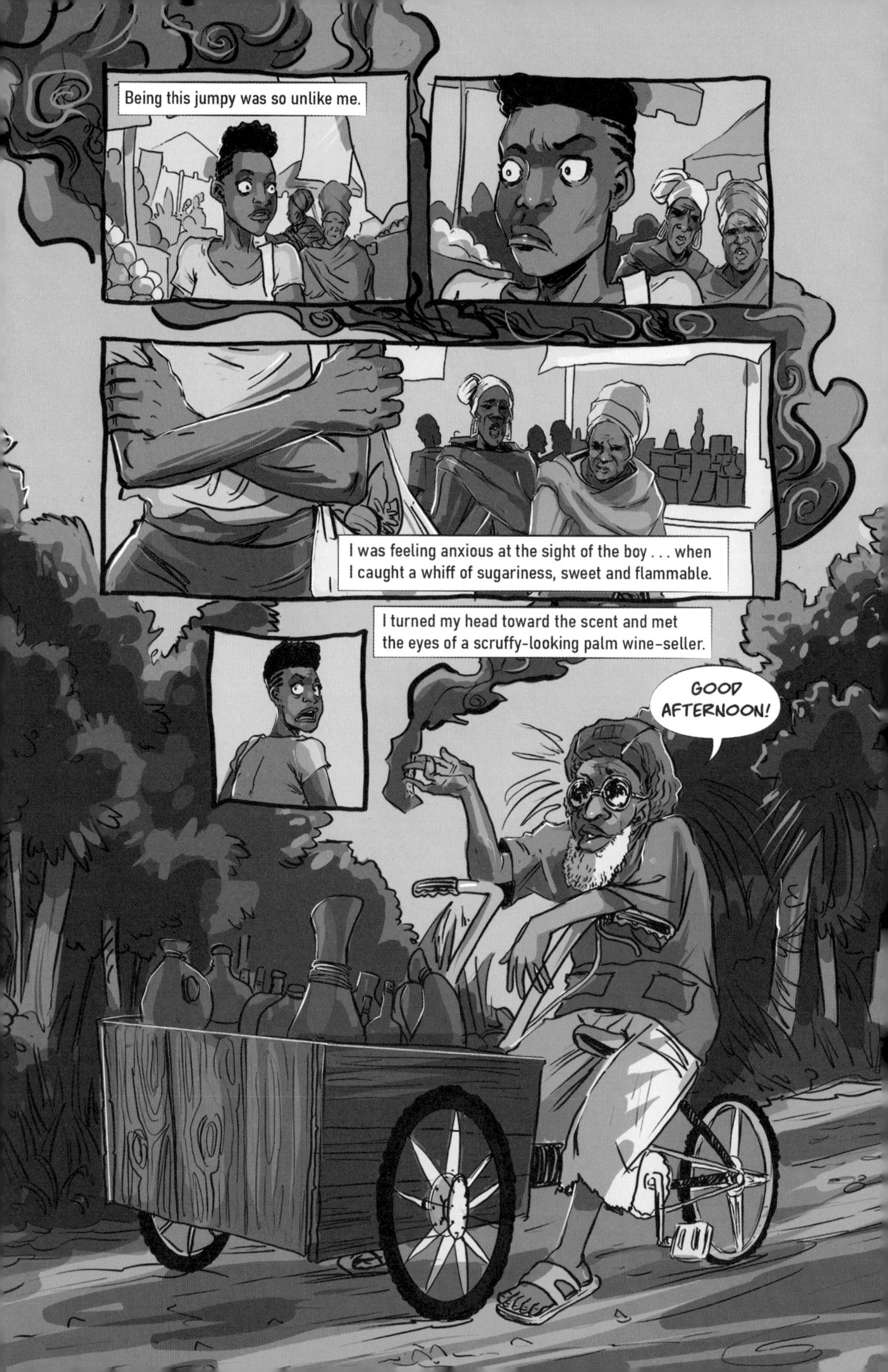
Being this jumpy was so unlike me.
I was feeling anxious at the sight of the boy . . . when I caught a whiff of sugariness, sweet and flammable.
I turned my head toward the scent and met the eyes of a scruffy-looking palm wine-seller.
GOOD AFTERNOON!

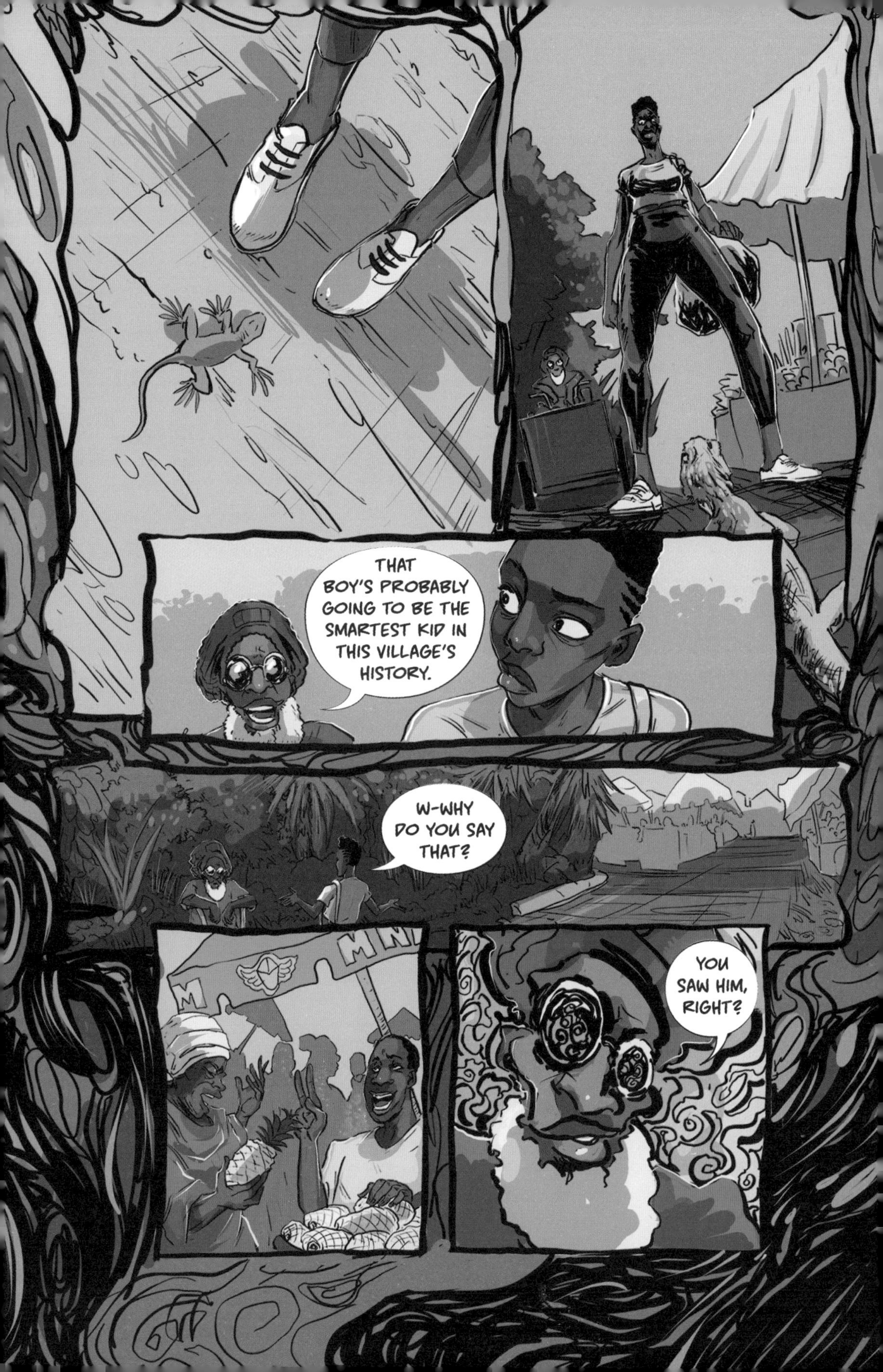
THAT BOY'S PROBABLY GOING TO BE THE SMARTEST KID IN THIS VILLAGE'S HISTORY.
W-WHY DO YOU SAY THAT?
YOU SAW HIM, RIGHT?

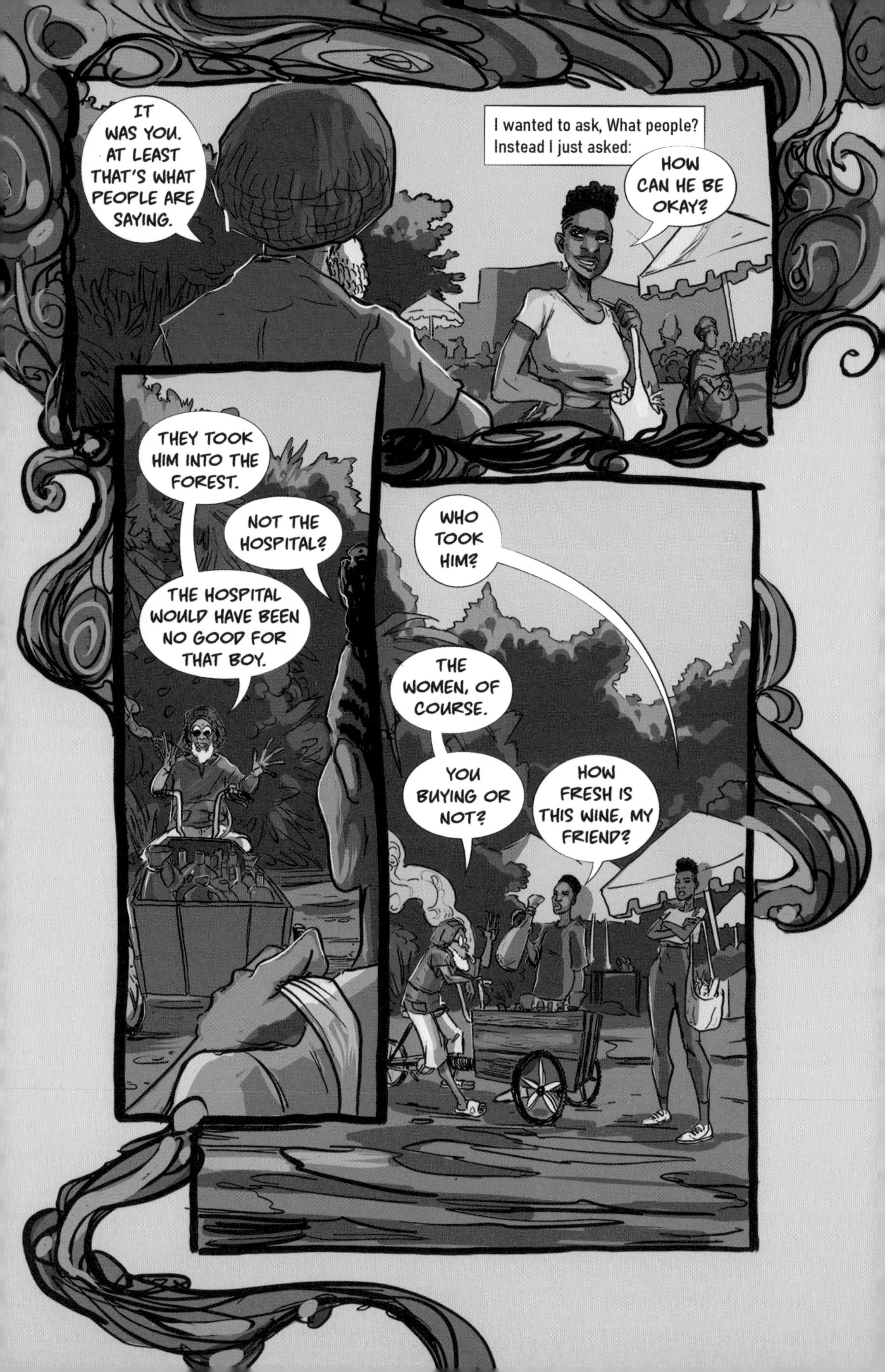
IT WAS YOU. AT LEAST THAT'S WHAT PEOPLE ARE SAYING.
I wanted to ask, What people? Instead I just asked:
HOW CAN HE BE OKAY?
THEY TOOK HIM INTO THE FOREST.
NOT THE HOSPITAL?
THE HOSPITAL WOULD HAVE BEEN NO GOOD FOR THAT BOY.
WHO TOOK HIM?
THE WOMEN, OF COURSE.
YOU BUYING OR NOT?
HOW FRESH IS THIS WINE, MY FRIEND?

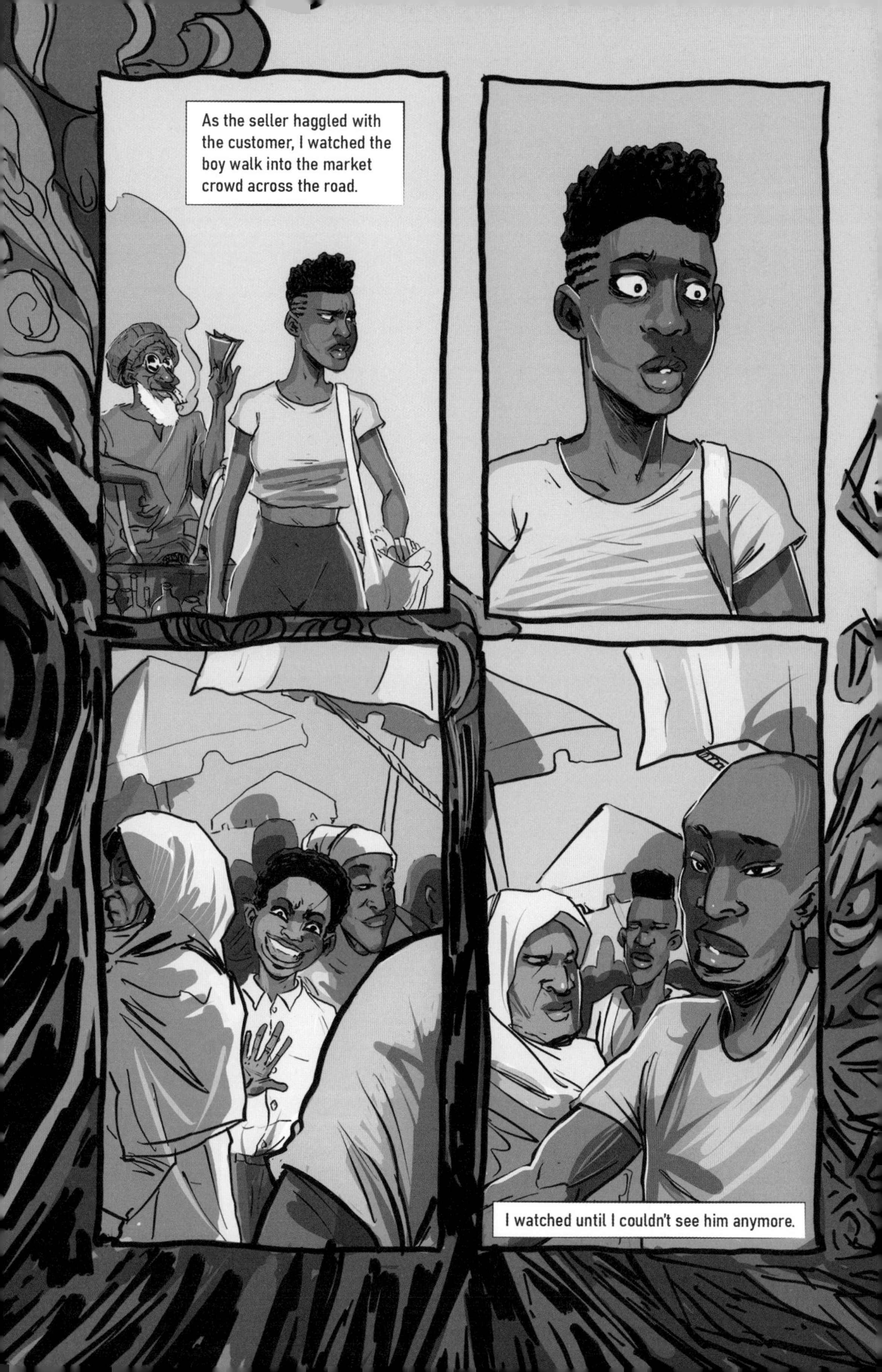
As the seller haggled with the customer, I watched the boy walk into the market crowd across the road.
I watched until I couldn't see him anymore.

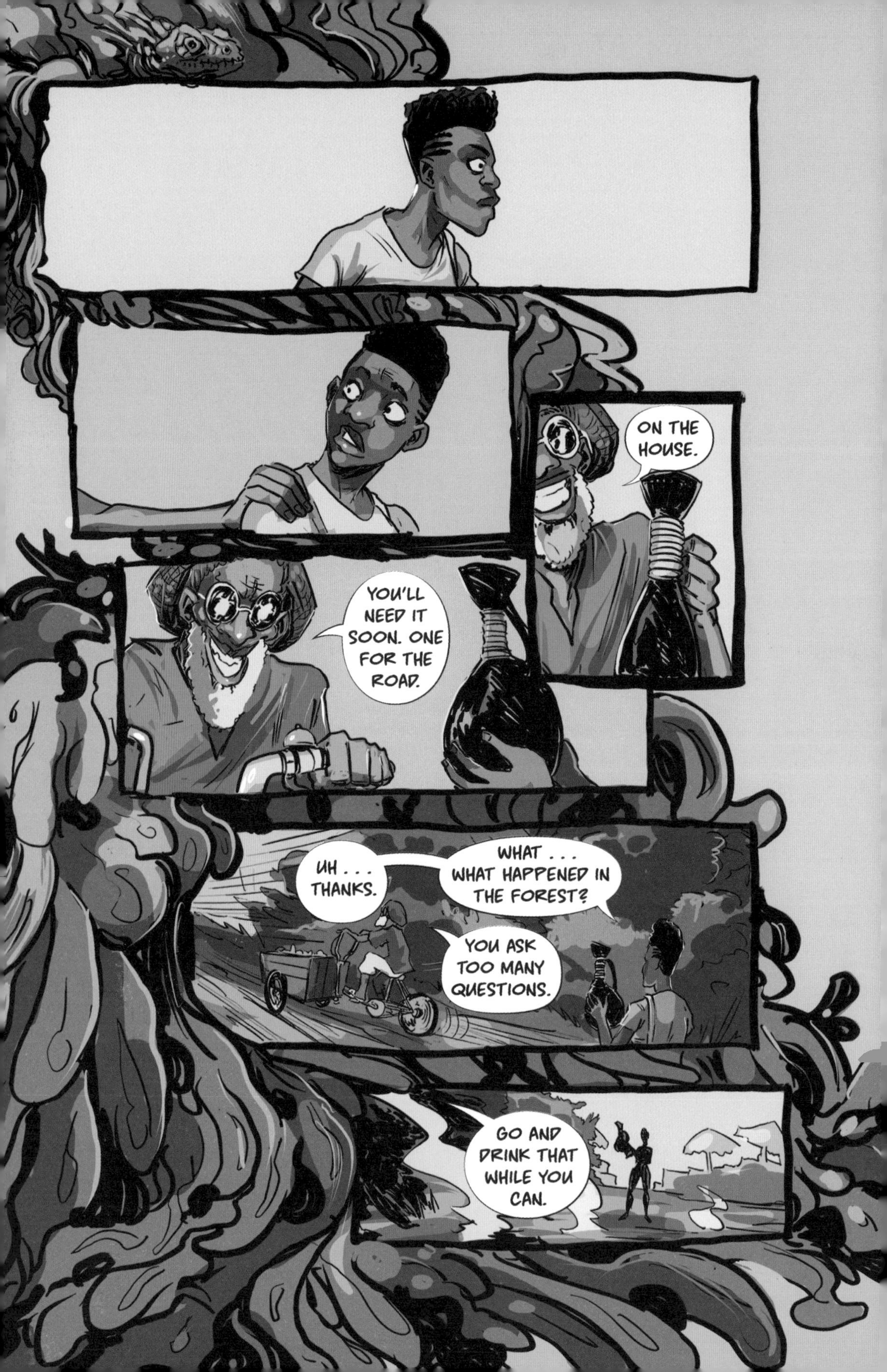
ON THE HOUSE.
YOU'LL NEED IT SOON. ONE FOR THE ROAD.
UH . . . THANKS.
WHAT . . . WHAT HAPPENED IN THE FOREST?
YOU ASK TOO MANY QUESTIONS.
GO AND DRINK THAT WHILE YOU CAN.

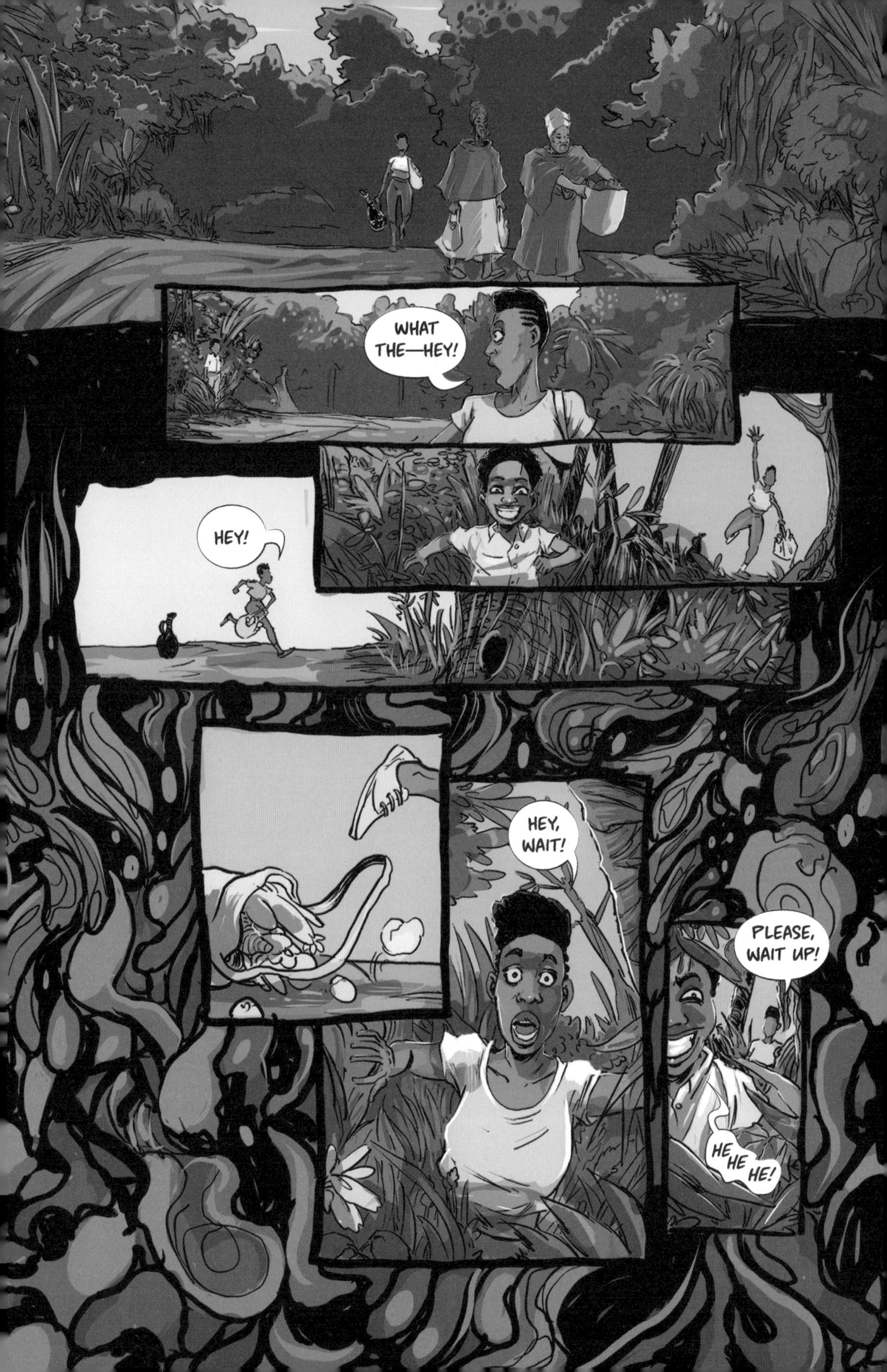
WHAT THE—HEY!
HEY!
HEY, WAIT!
PLEASE, WAIT UP!
HE HE HE!

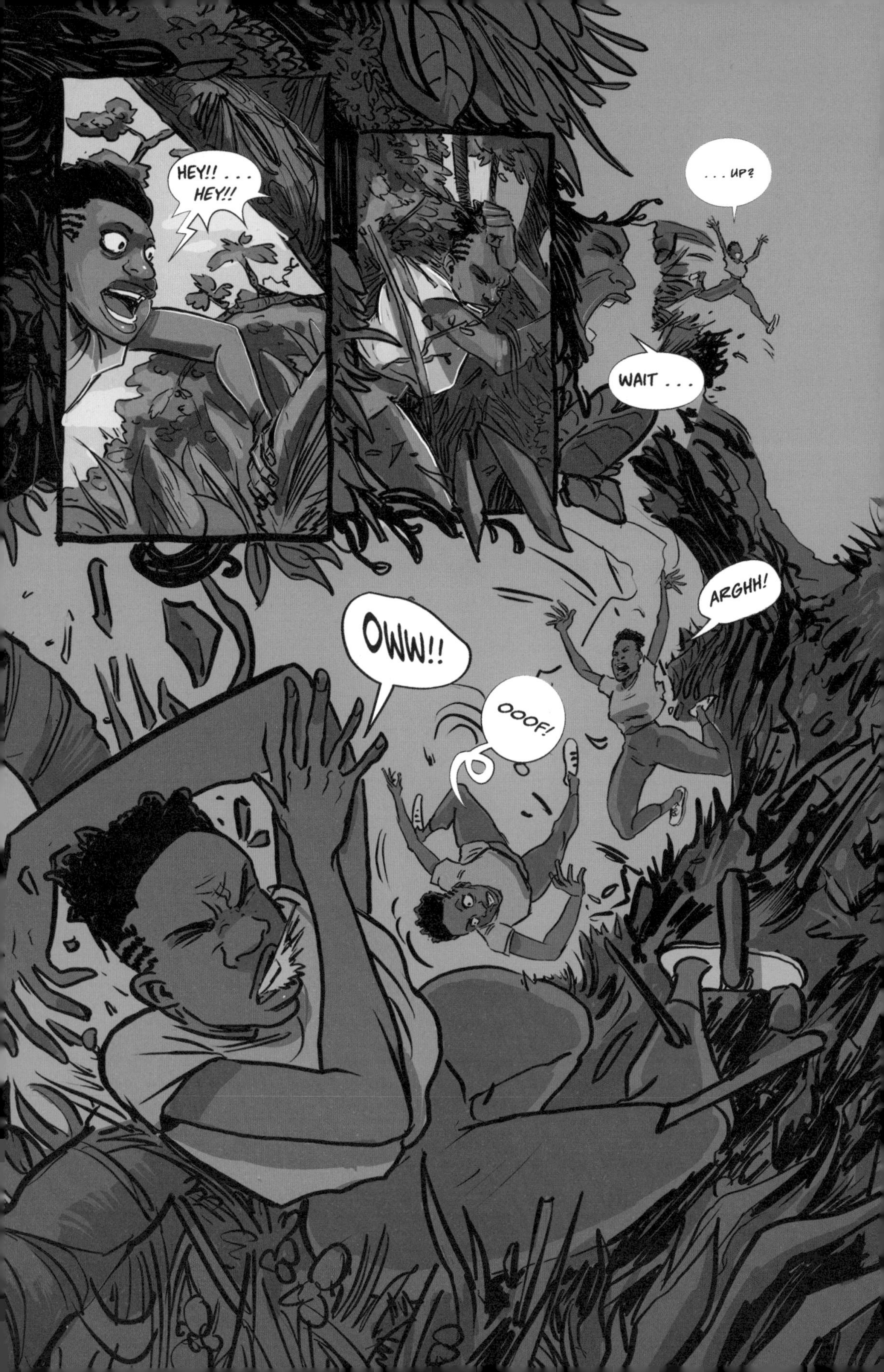
HEY!! . . .
HEY!!
. . . UP?
WAIT . . .
ARGHH!
OWW!!
OOOF!

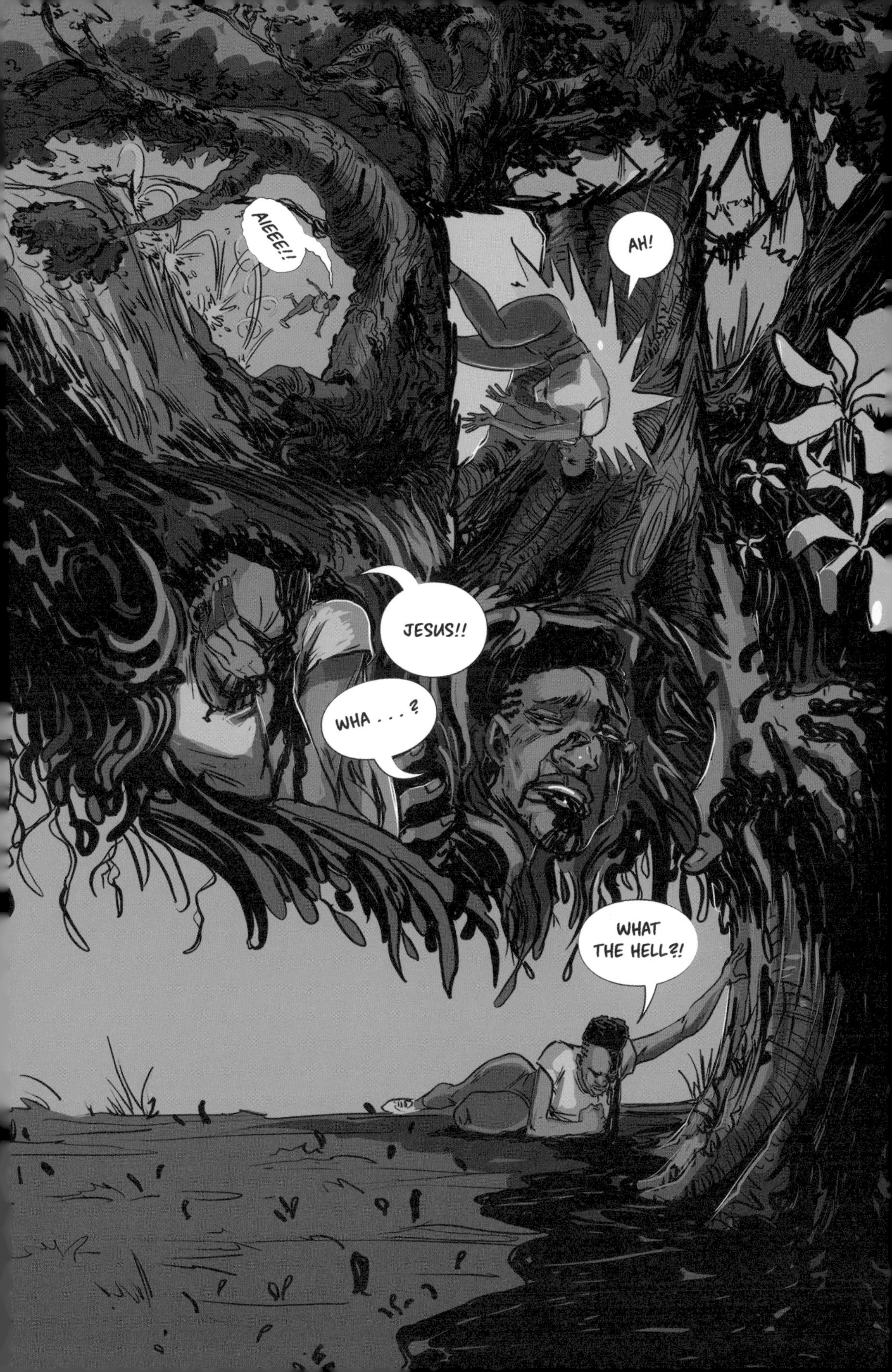
AIEEE!!
AH!
JESUS!!
WHA . . . ?
WHAT THE HELL?!

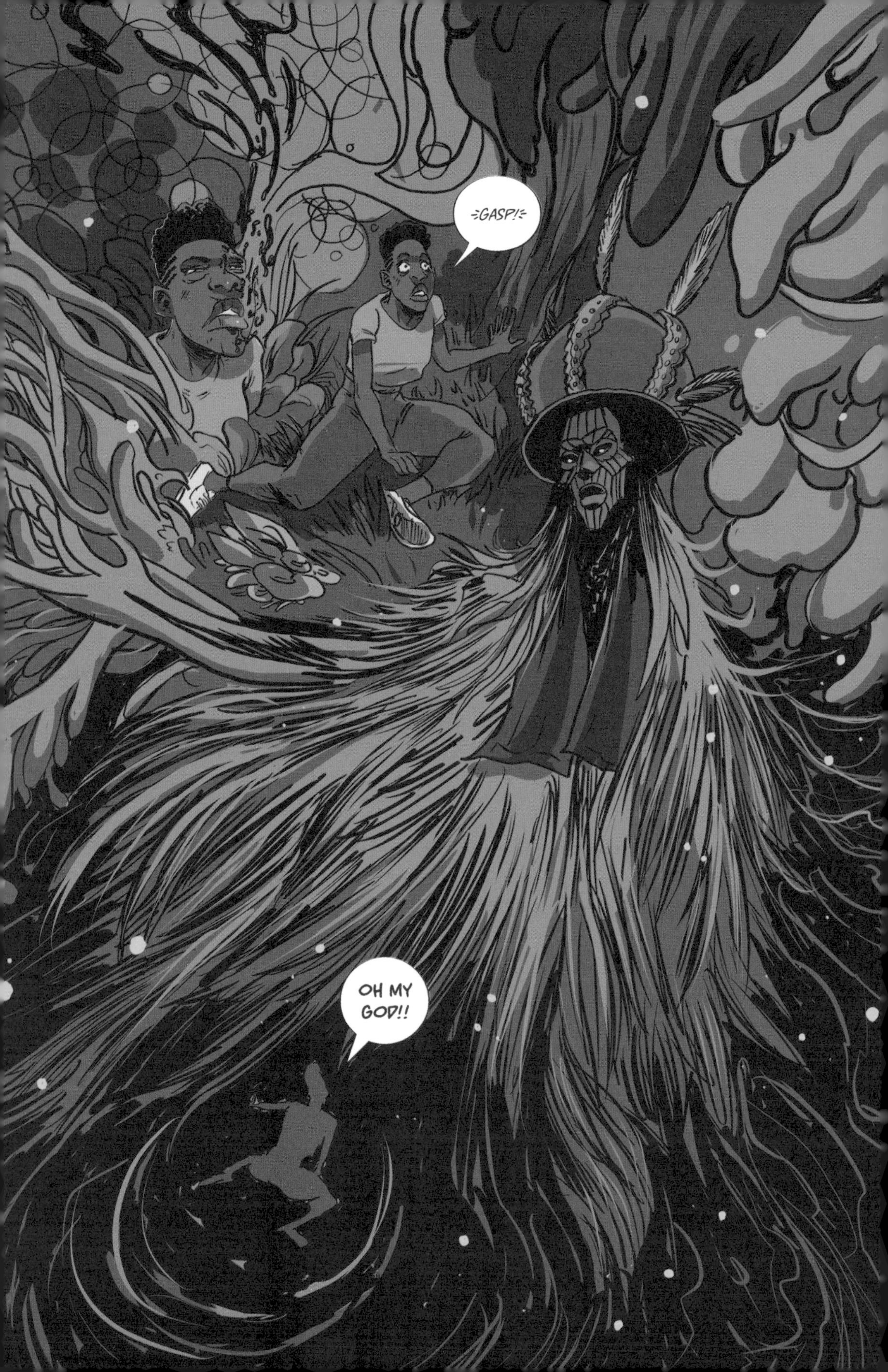
GASP!
OH MY GOD!!

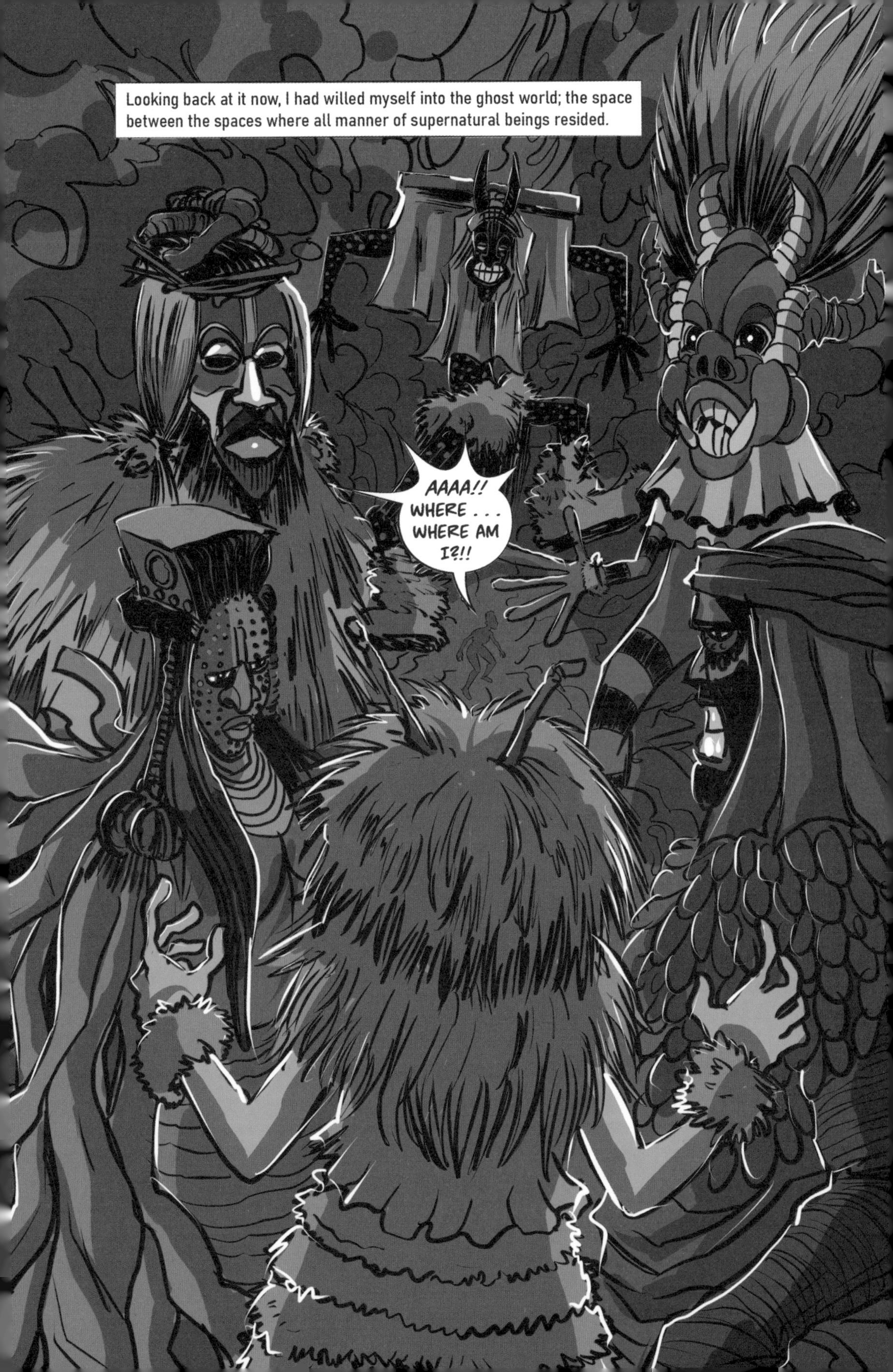
Looking back at it now, I had willed myself into the ghost world; the space between the spaces where all manner of supernatural beings resided.
AAAA!! WHERE . . . WHERE AM I?!!

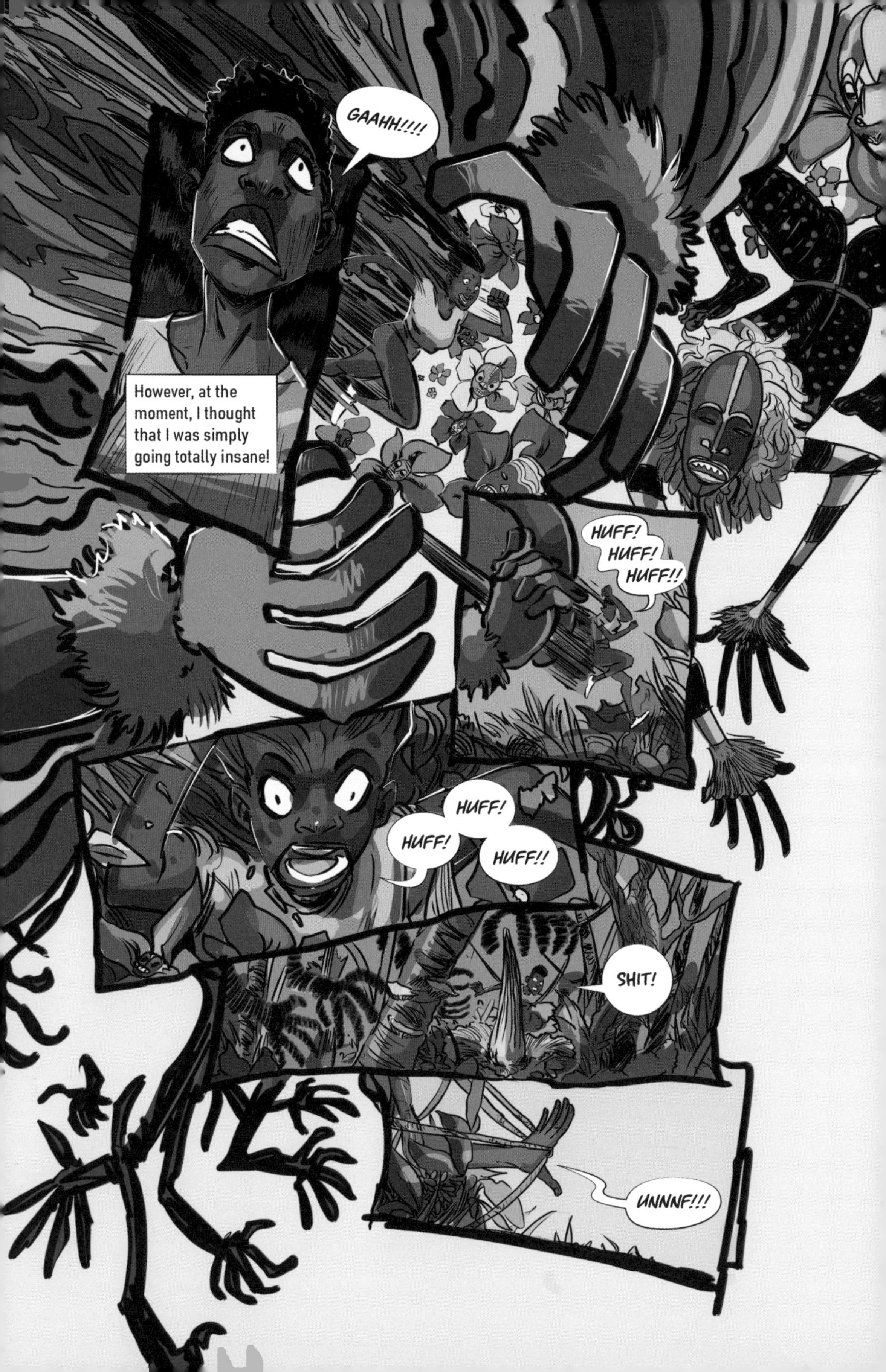

GAAHH!!!!
However, at the moment, I thought that I was simply going totally insane!
HUFF! HUFF! HUFF!!
HUFF!
HUFF!
HUFF!!
SHIT!
UNNNF!!!

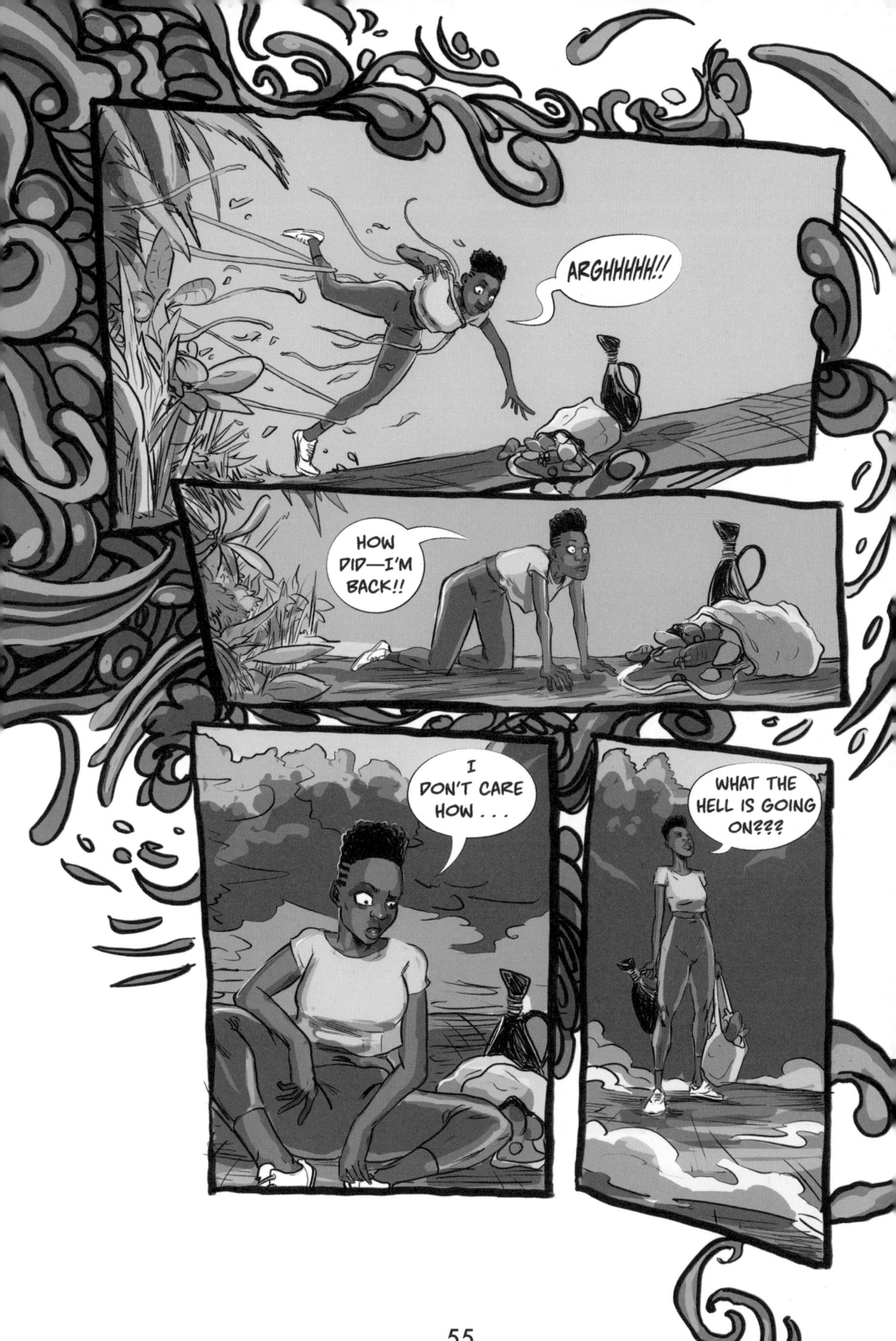
ARGHHHHH!!
HOW DID—I'M BACK!!
I DON'T CARE HOW . . .
WHAT THE HELL IS GOING ON???

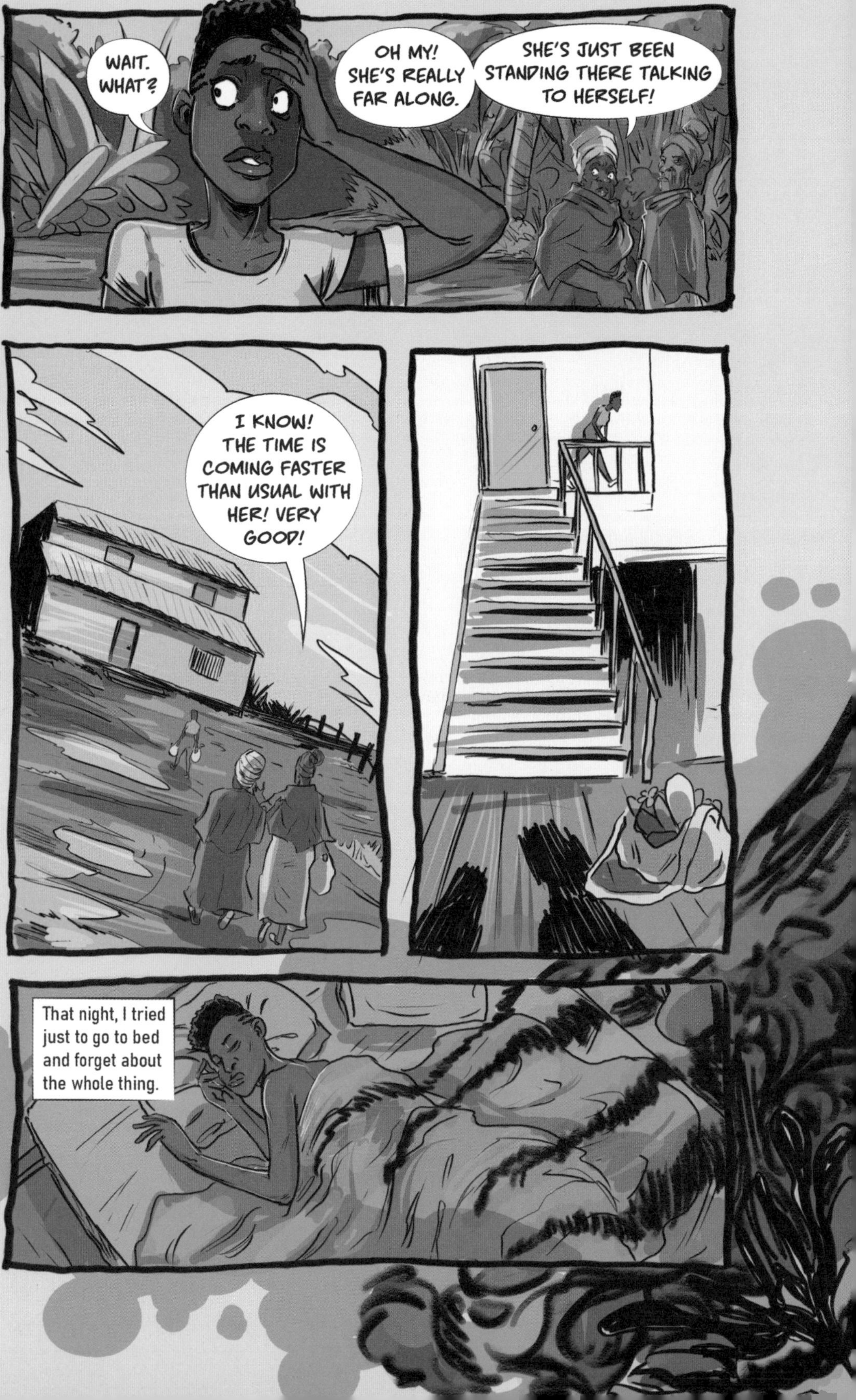
WAIT. WHAT?
OH MY! SHE'S REALLY FAR ALONG.
SHE'S JUST BEEN STANDING THERE TALKING TO HERSELF!
I KNOW! THE TIME IS COMING FASTER THAN USUAL WITH HER! VERY GOOD!
That night, I tried just to go to bed and forget about the whole thing.

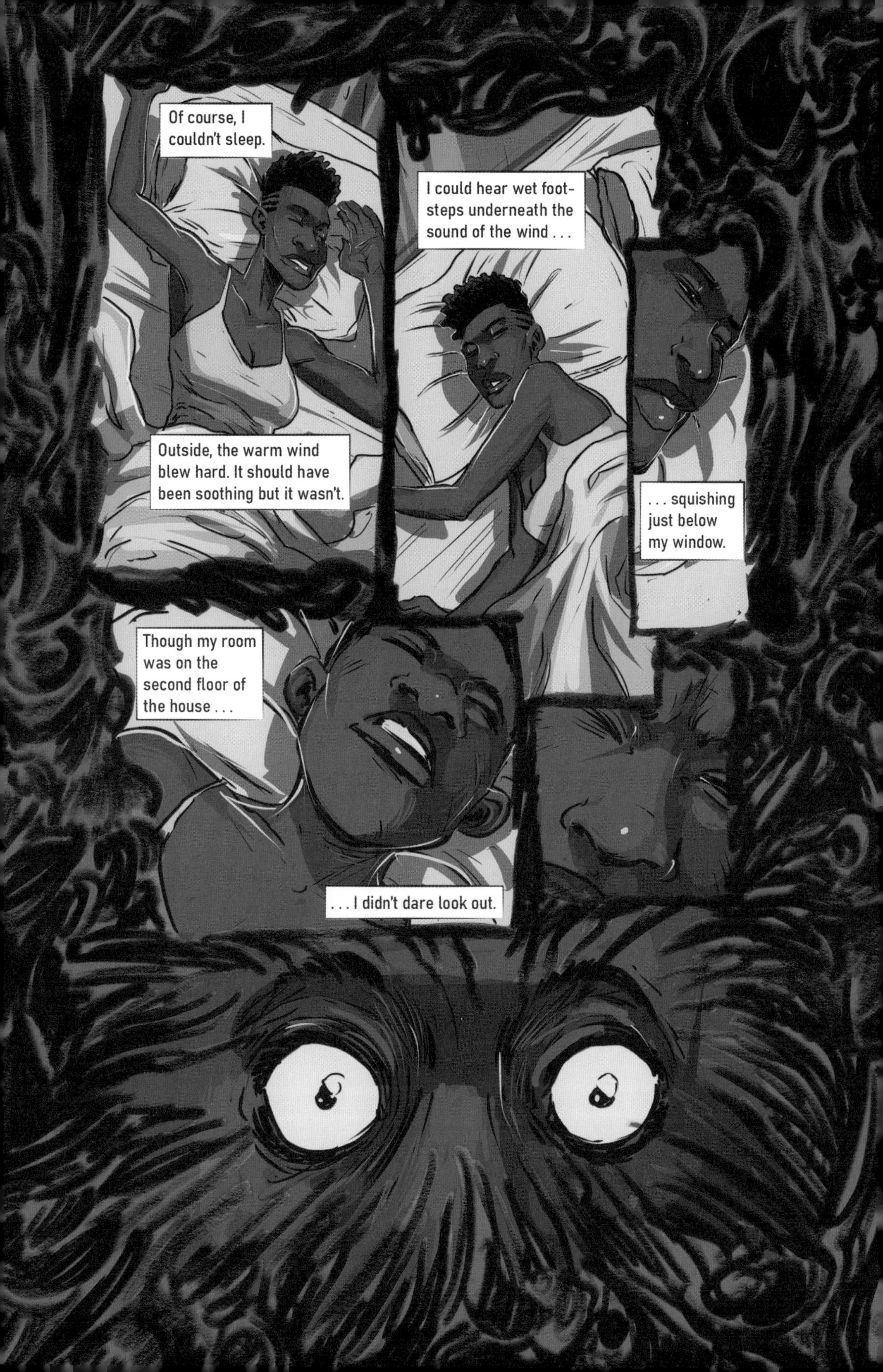
Of course, I couldn't sleep.
Outside, the warm wind blew hard. It should have been soothing but it wasn't.
I could hear wet foot-steps underneath the sound of the wind . . .
. . . squishing just below my window.
Though my room was on the second floor of the house . . .
. . . I didn't dare look out.

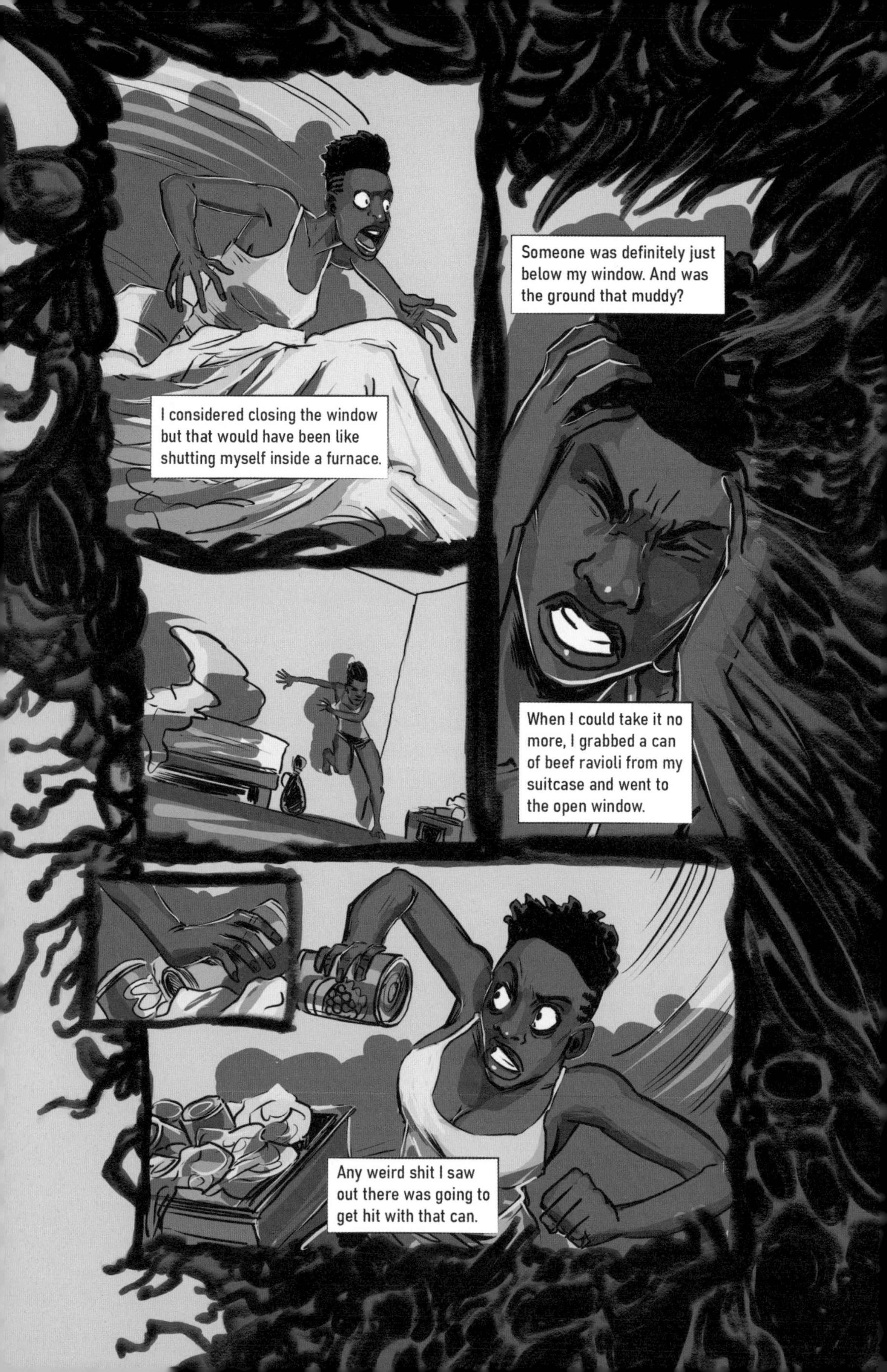
I considered closing the window but that would have been like shutting myself inside a furnace.
Someone was definitely just below my window. And was the ground that muddy?
When I could take it no more, I grabbed a can of beef ravioli from my suitcase and went to the open window.
Any weird shit I saw out there was going to get hit with that can.

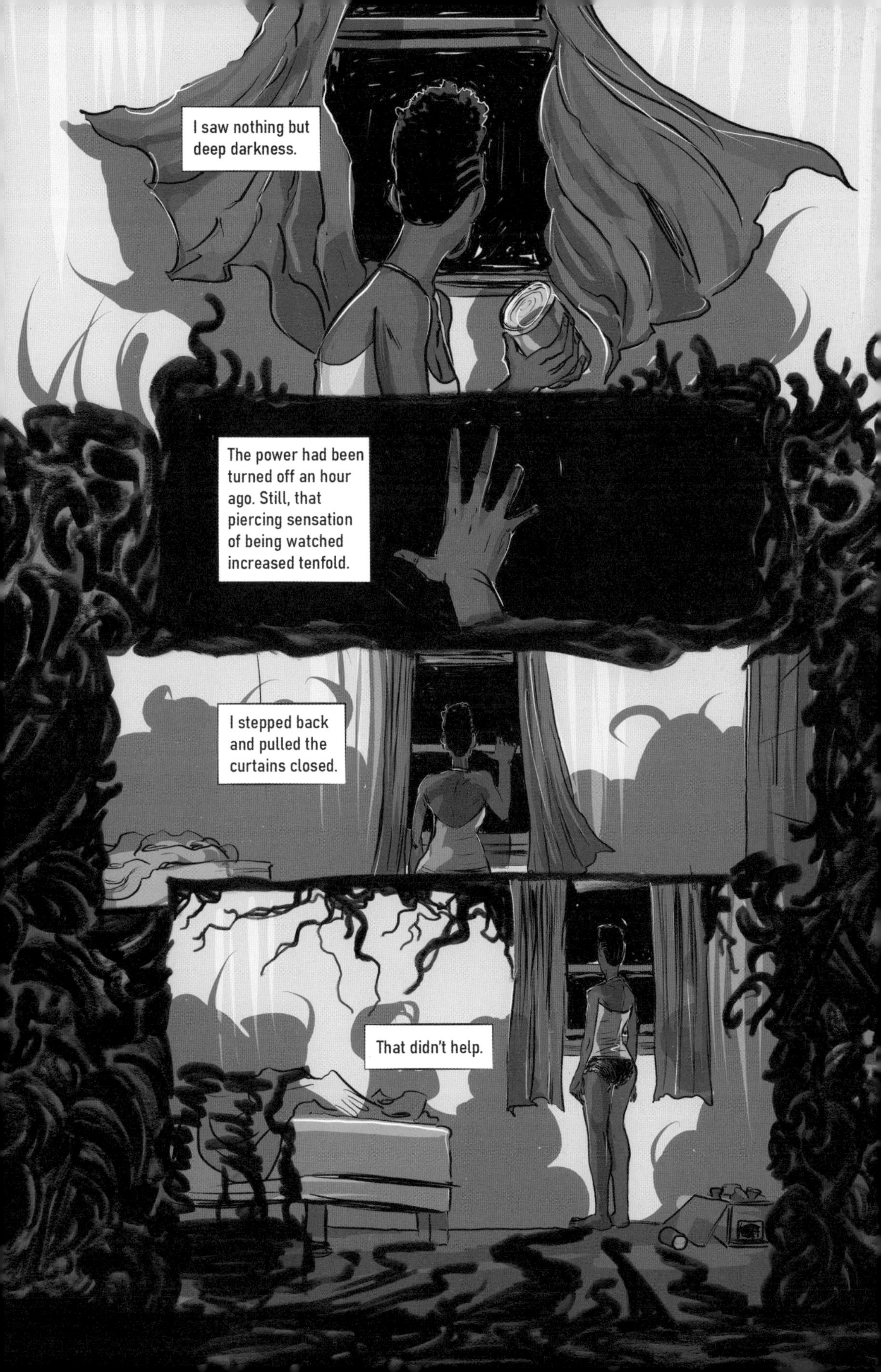
I saw nothing but deep darkness.
The power had been turned off an hour ago. Still, that piercing sensation of being watched increased tenfold.
I stepped back and pulled the curtains closed.
That didn't help.

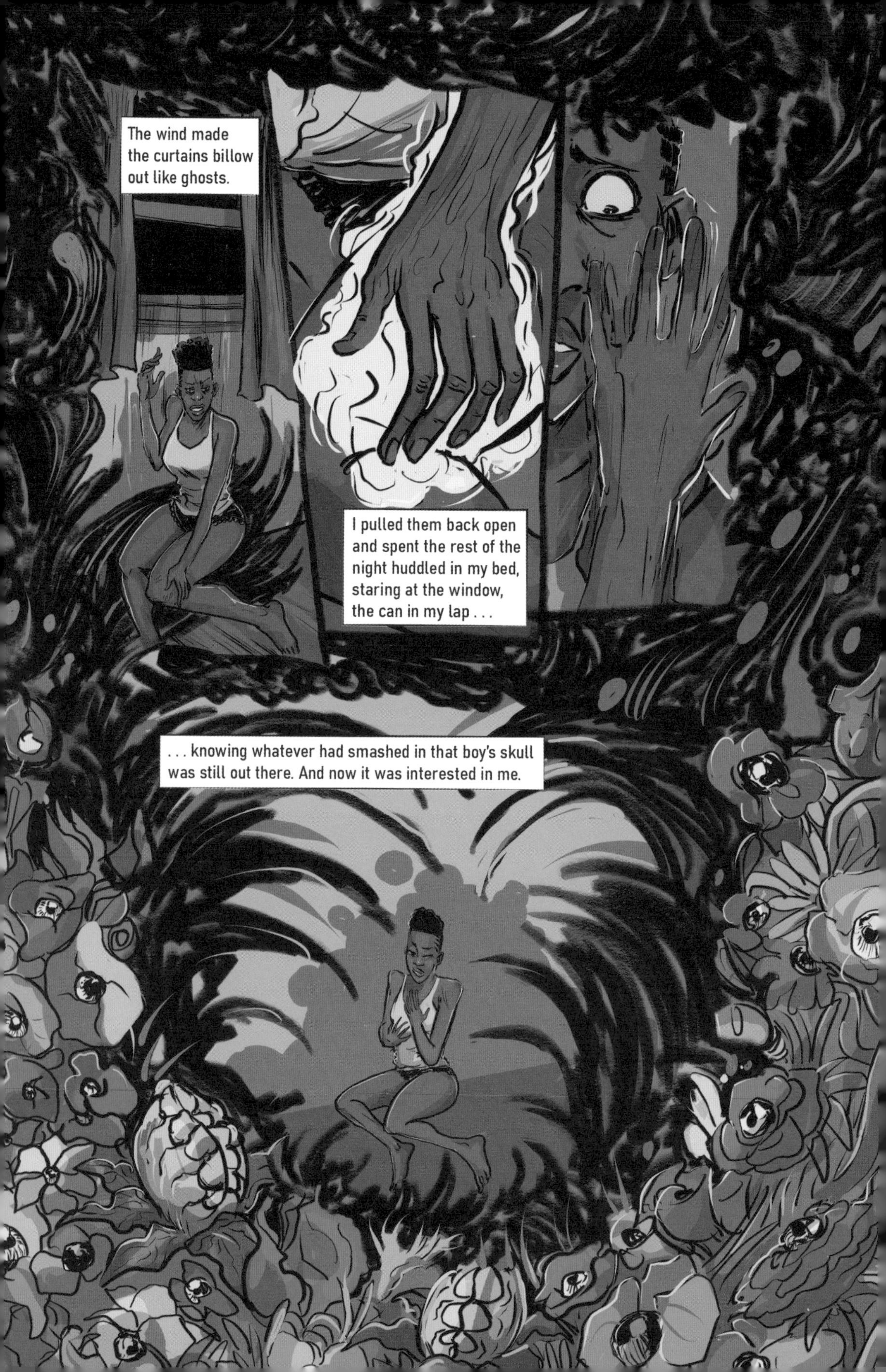
The wind made the curtains billow out like ghosts.
I pulled them back open and spent the rest of the night huddled in my bed, staring at the window, the can in my lap . . .
. . . knowing whatever had smashed in that boy's skull was still out there. And now it was interested in me.

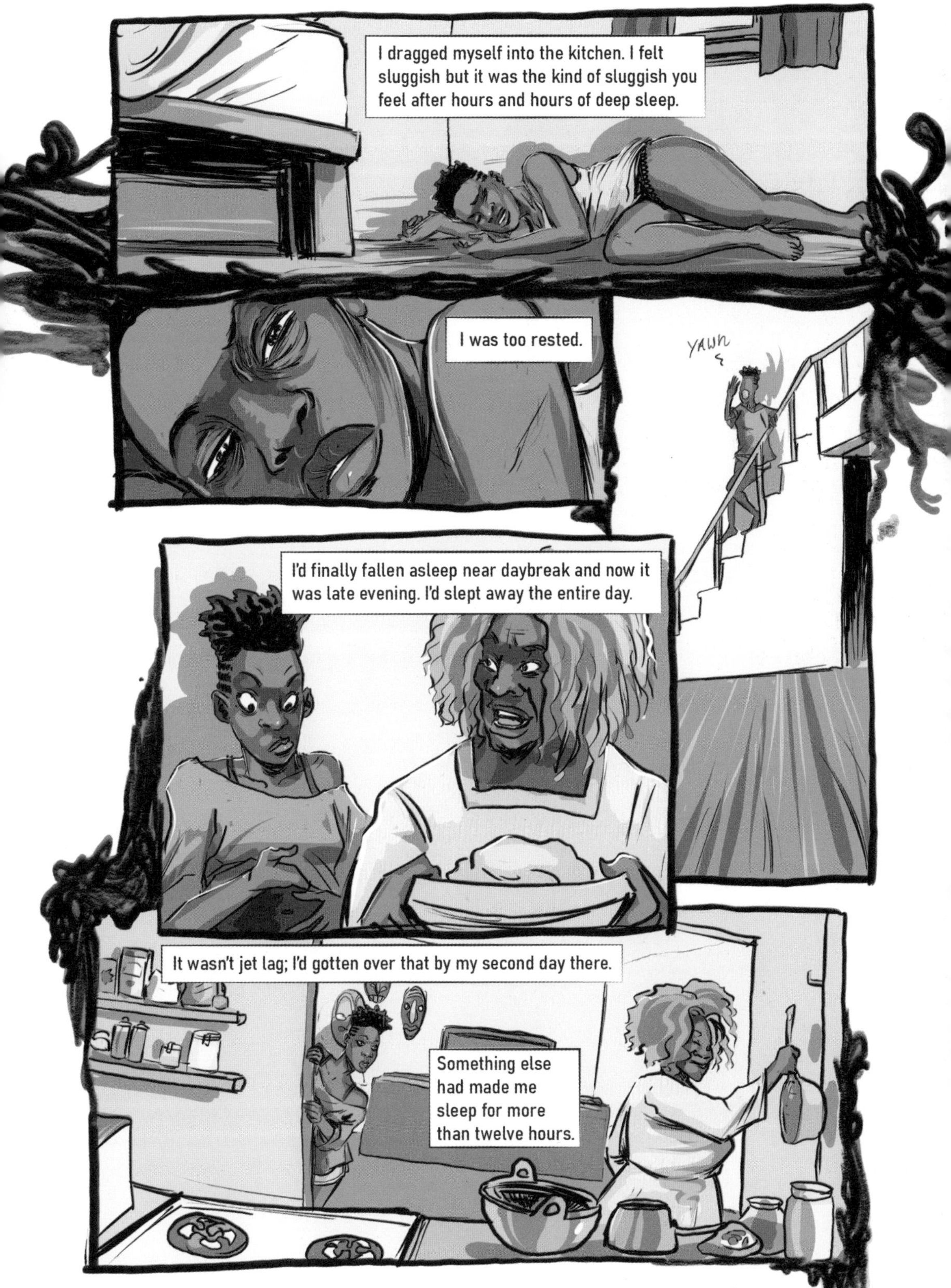

I dragged myself into the kitchen. I felt sluggish but it was the kind of sluggish you feel after hours and hours of deep sleep.
I was too rested.
YAWN
I'd finally fallen asleep near daybreak and now it was late evening. I'd slept away the entire day.
It wasn't jet lag; I'd gotten over that by my second day there.
Something else had made me sleep for more than twelve hours.

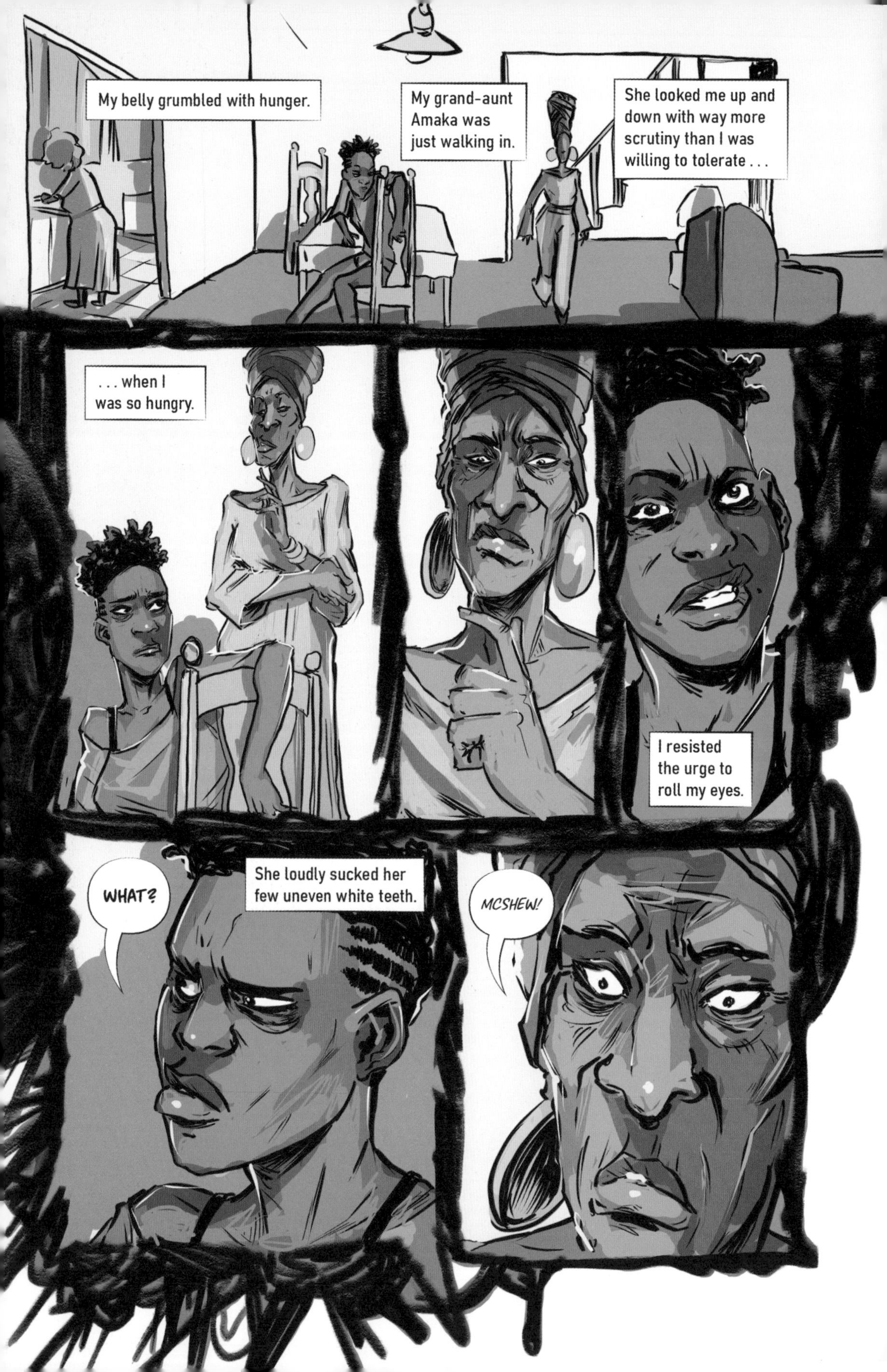
My belly grumbled with hunger.
My grand-aunt Amaka was just walking in.
She looked me up and down with way more scrutiny than I was willing to tolerate . . .
. . . when I was so hungry.
I resisted the urge to roll my eyes.
WHAT?
She loudly sucked her few uneven white teeth.
MCSHEW!

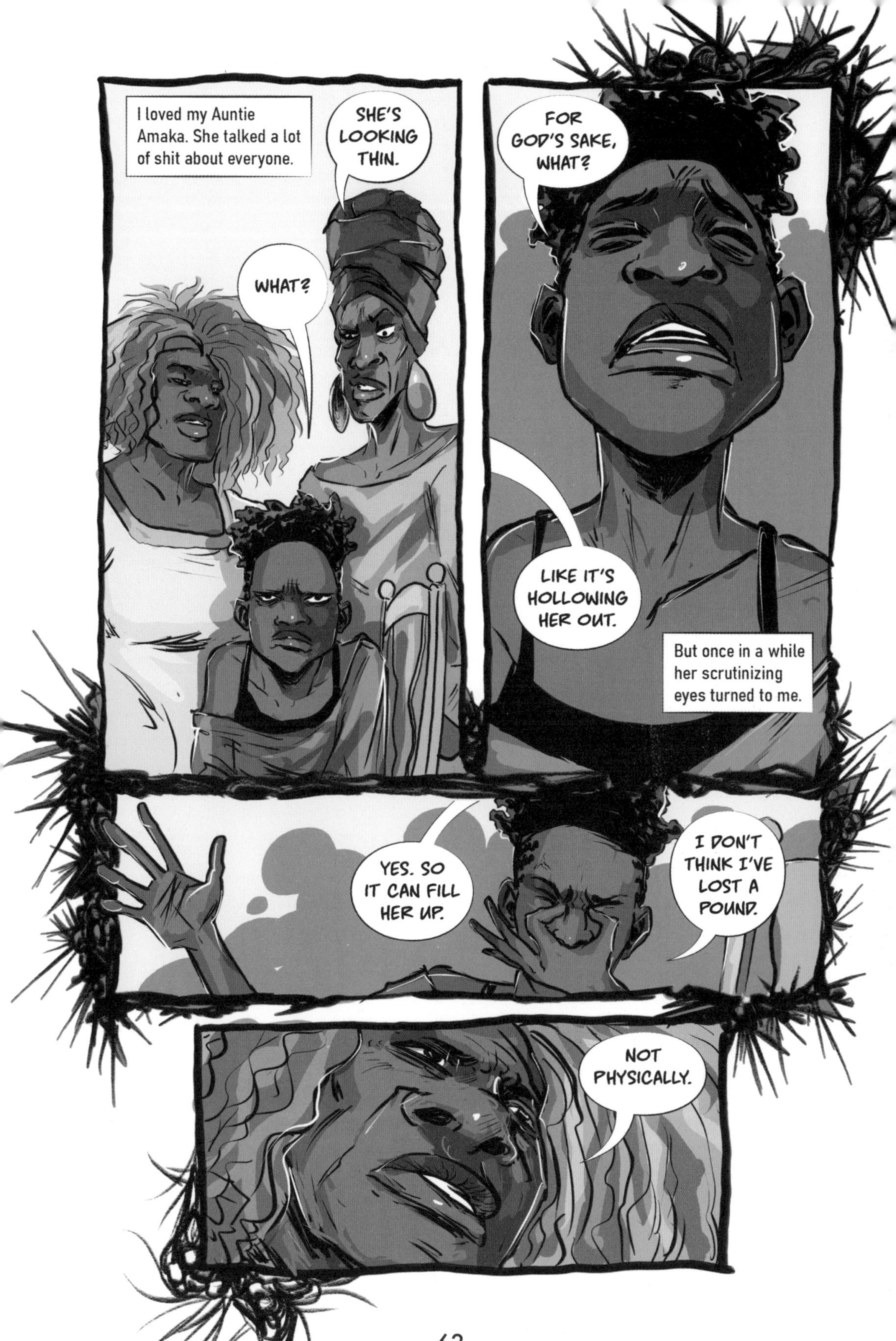

I loved my Auntie Amaka. She talked a lot of shit about everyone.
SHE'S LOOKING THIN.
WHAT?
FOR GOD'S SAKE, WHAT?
LIKE IT'S HOLLOWING HER OUT.
But once in a while her scrutinizing eyes turned to me.
YES. SO IT CAN FILL HER UP.
I DON'T THINK I'VE LOST A POUND.
NOT PHYSICALLY.

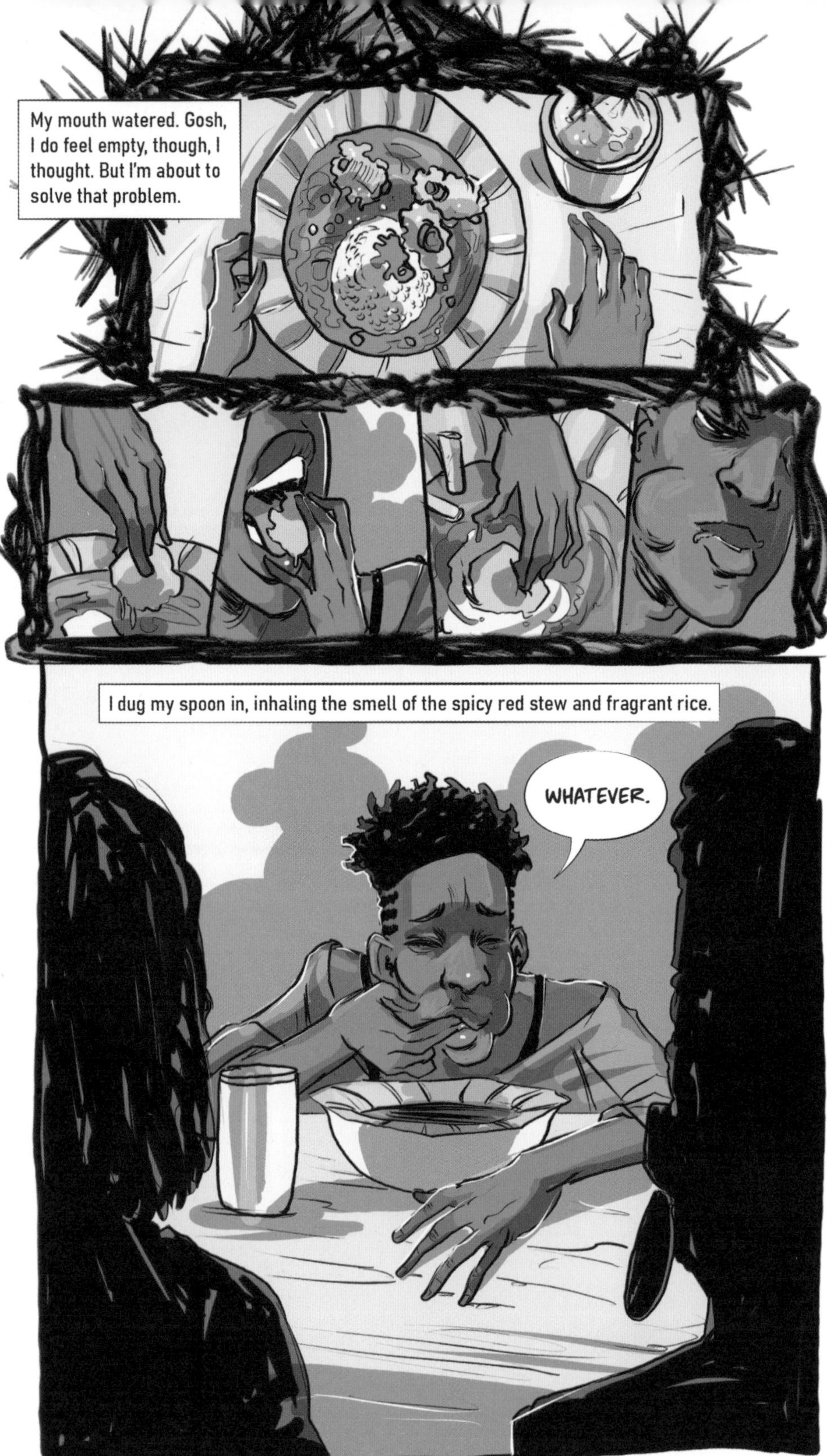
My mouth watered. Gosh, I do feel empty, though, I thought. But I'm about to solve that problem.
I dug my spoon in, inhaling the smell of the spicy red stew and fragrant rice.
WHATEVER.

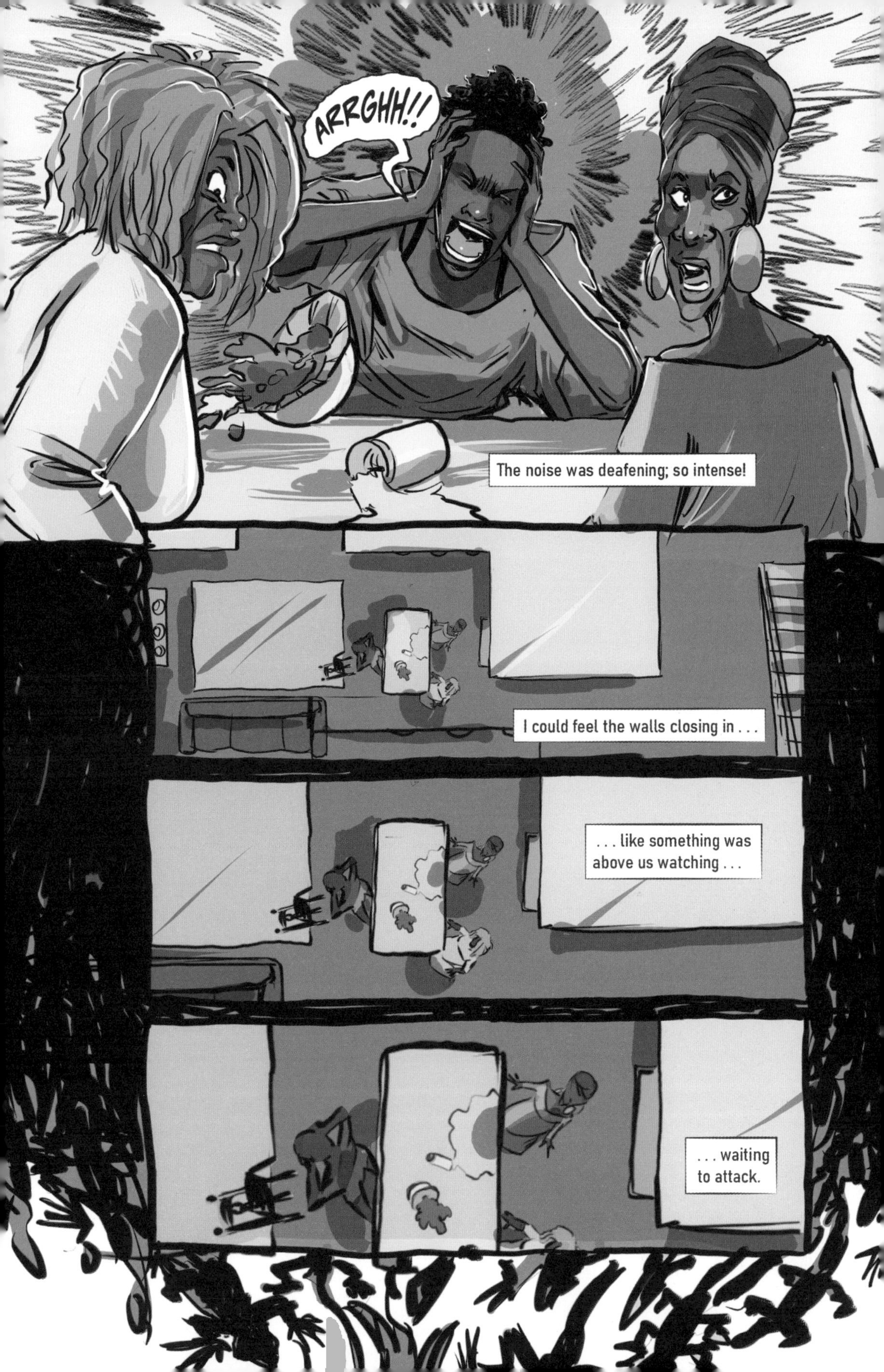
ARRGHH!!
The noise was deafening; so intense!
I could feel the walls closing in . . .
. . . like something was above us watching . . .
. . . waiting to attack.

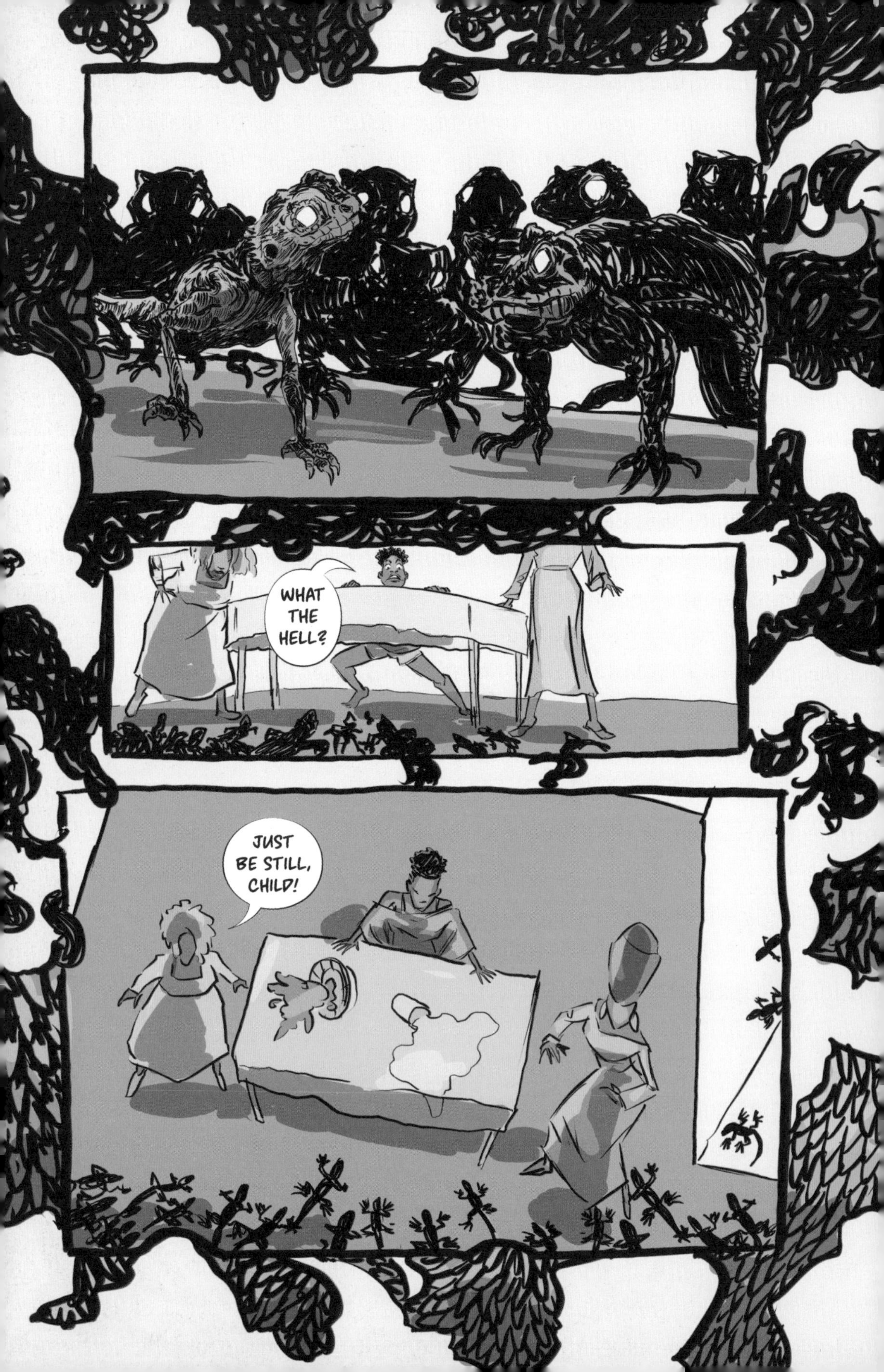
WHAT THE HELL?
JUST BE STILL, CHILD!

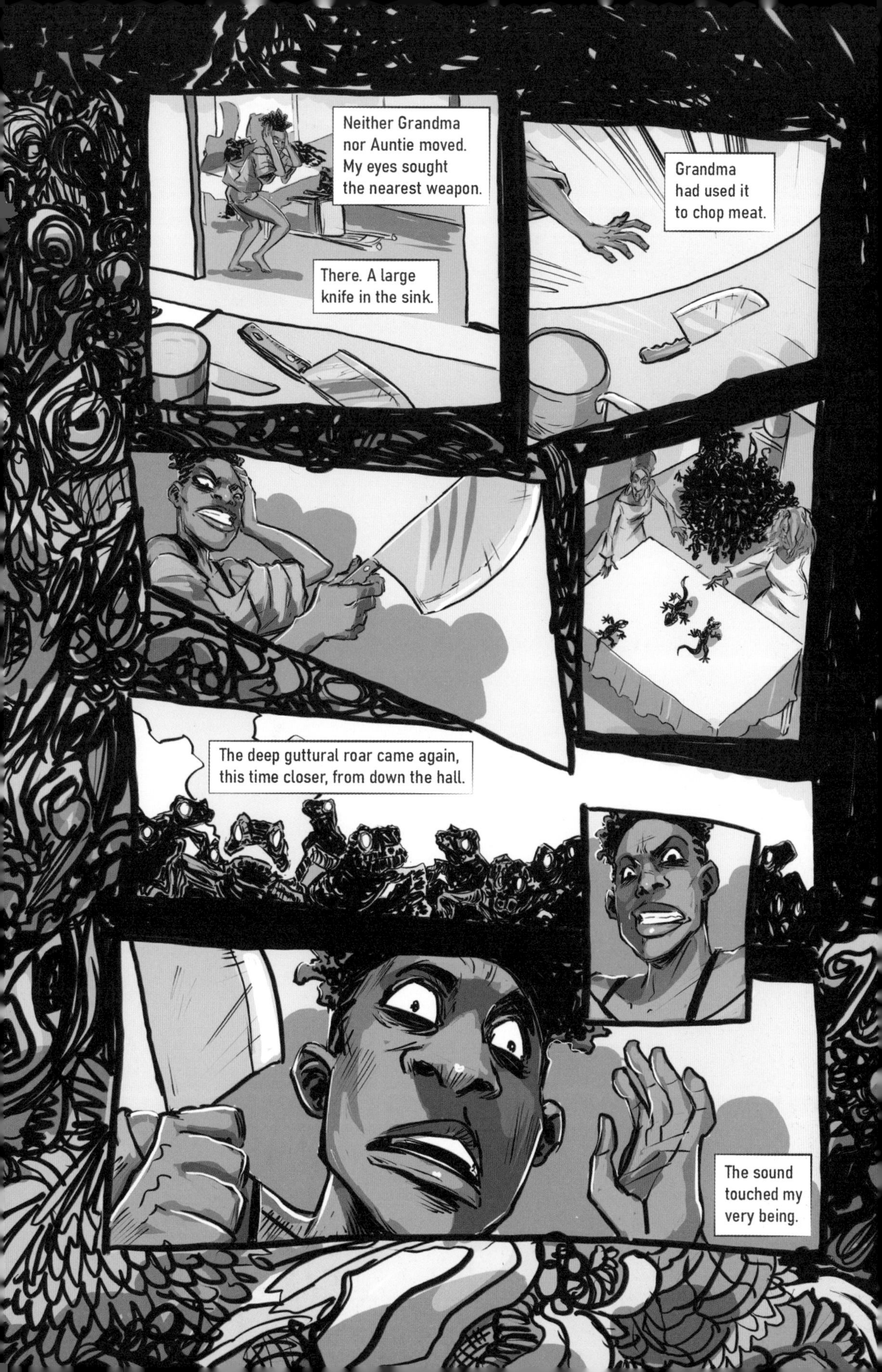
Neither Grandma nor Auntie moved. My eyes sought the nearest weapon.
There. A large knife in the sink.
Grandma had used it to chop meat.
The deep guttural roar came again, this time closer, from down the hall.
The sound touched my very being.

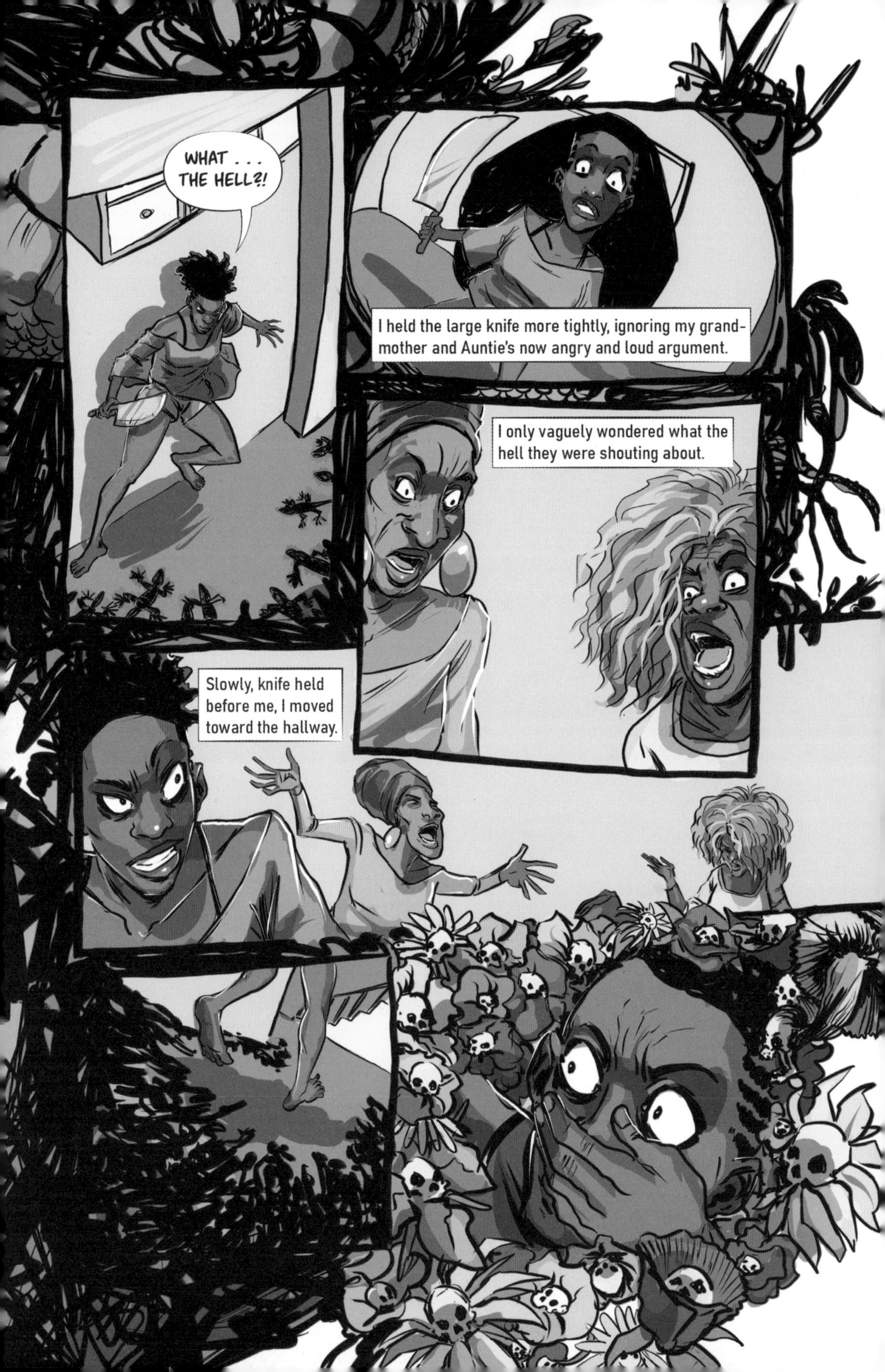
WHAT . . . THE HELL?!
I held the large knife more tightly, ignoring my grand-mother and Auntie's now angry and loud argument.
I only vaguely wondered what the hell they were shouting about.
Slowly, knife held before me, I moved toward the hallway.

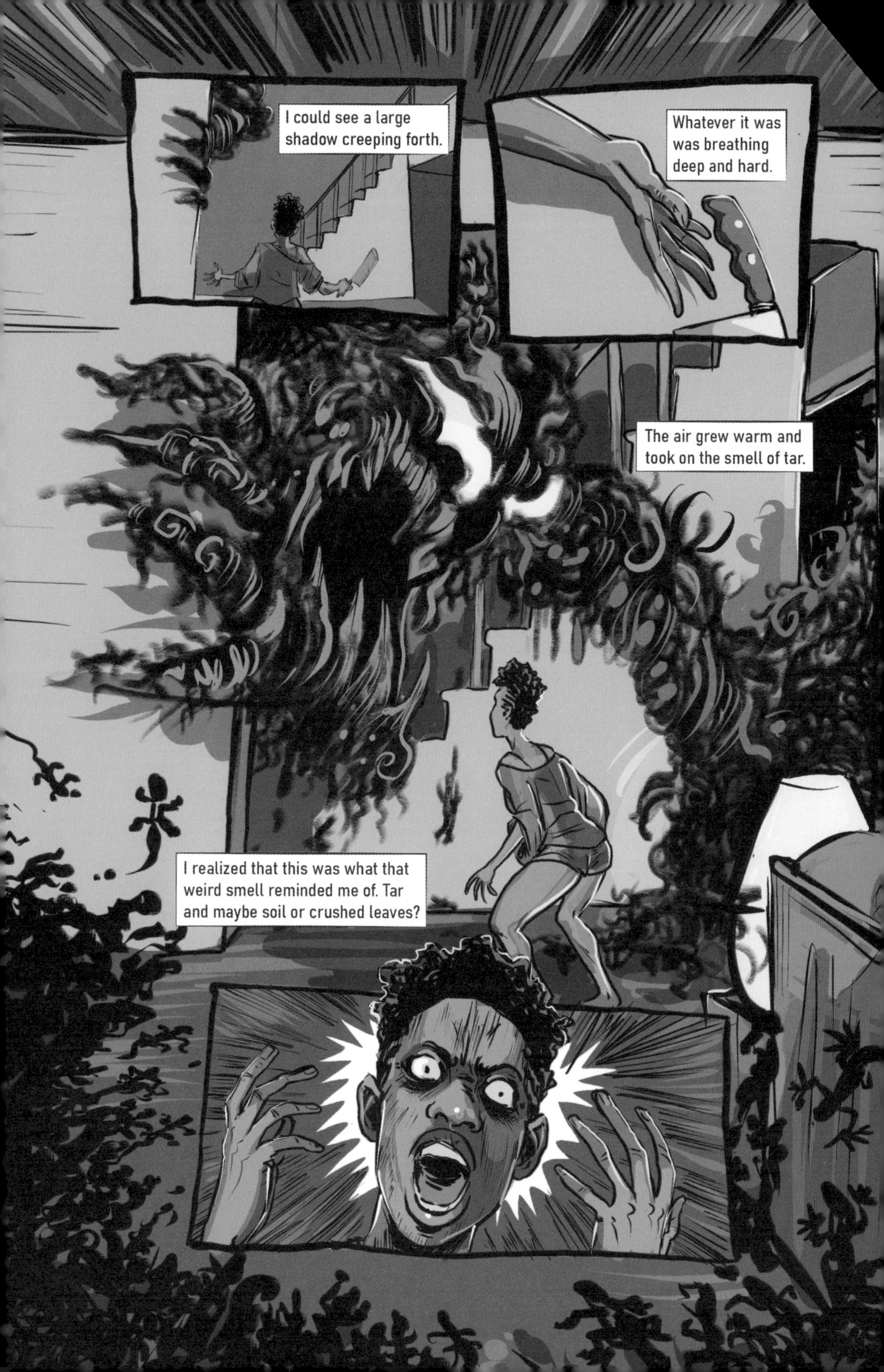
I could see a large shadow creeping forth.
Whatever it was was breathing deep and hard.
The air grew warm and took on the smell of tar.
I realized that this was what that weird smell reminded me of. Tar and maybe soil or crushed leaves?

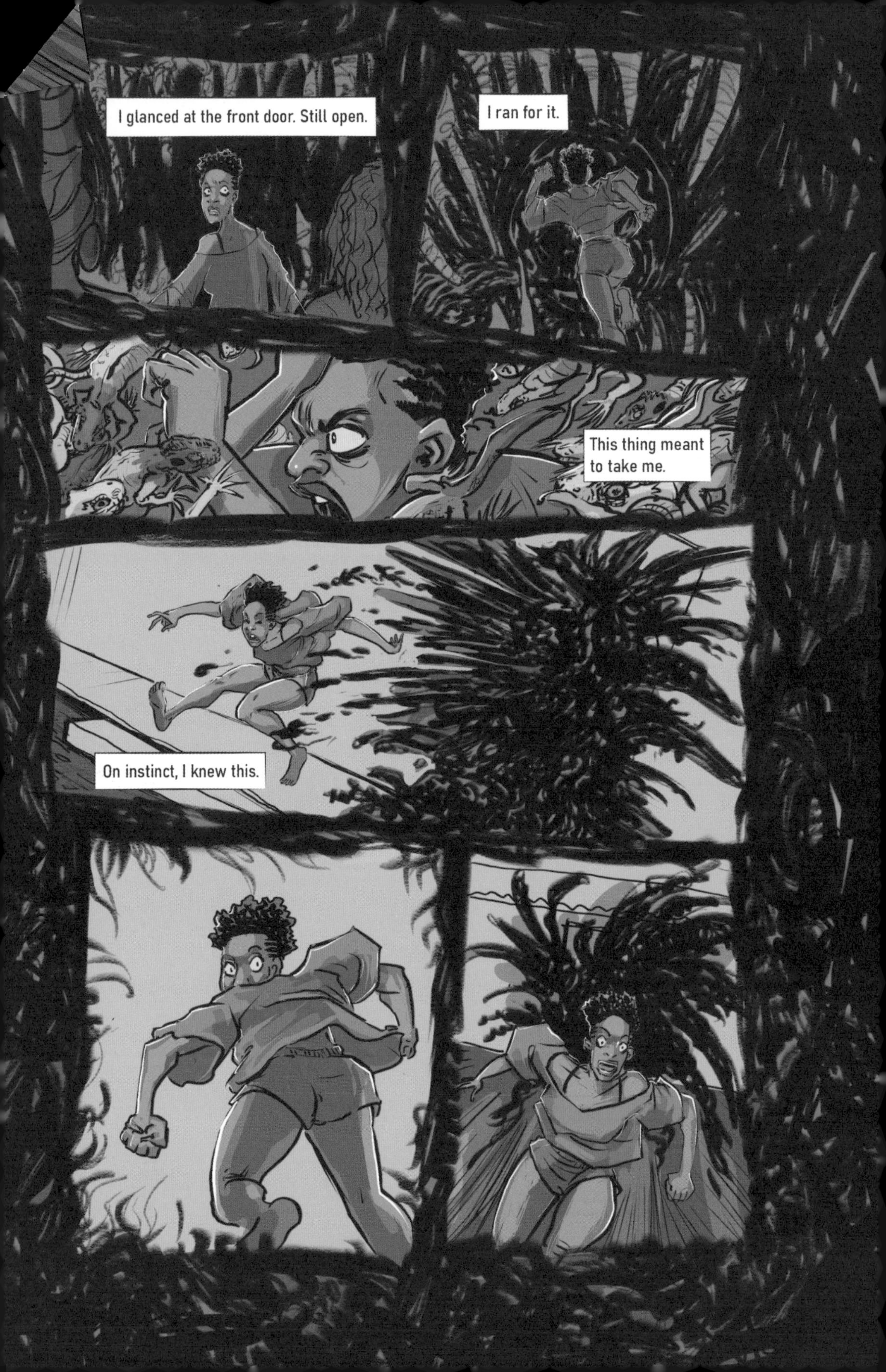
I glanced at the front door. Still open.
I ran for it.
This thing meant to take me.
On instinct, I knew this.

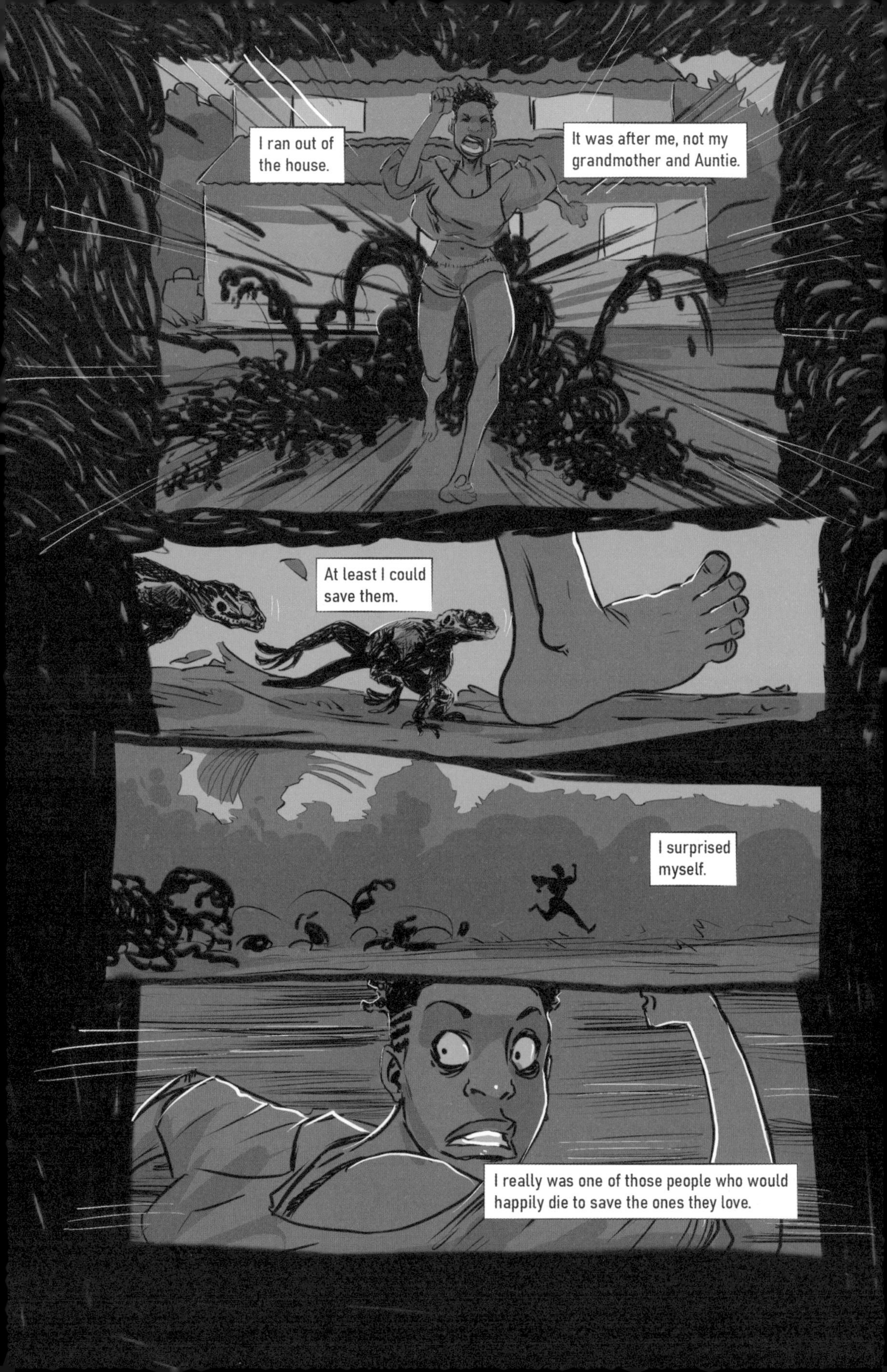
I ran out of the house.
It was after me, not my grandmother and Auntie.
At least I could save them.
I surprised myself.
I really was one of those people who would happily die to save the ones they love.

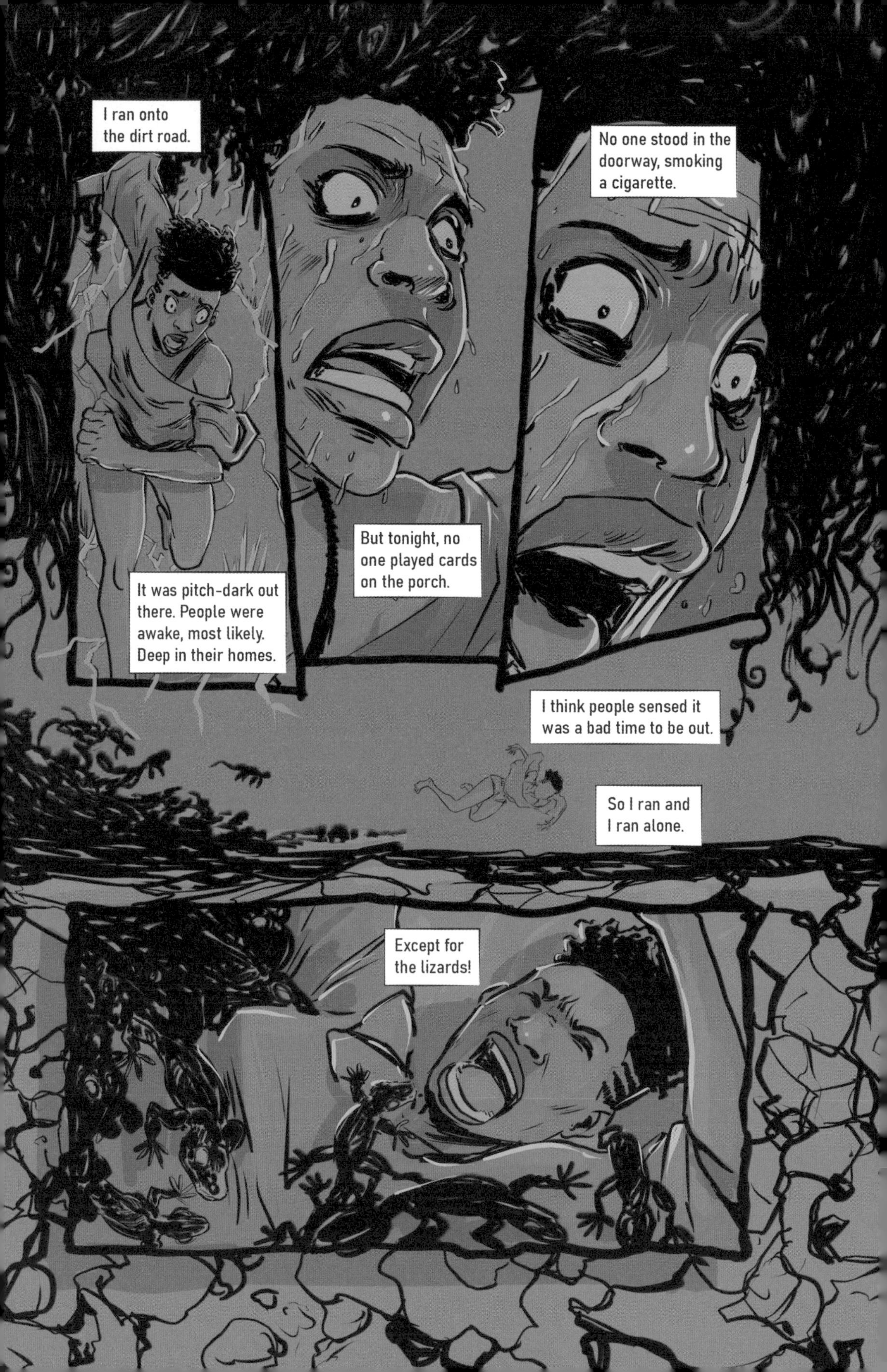
I ran onto the dirt road.
No one stood in the doorway, smoking a cigarette.
But tonight, no one played cards on the porch.
It was pitch-dark out there. People were awake, most likely. Deep in their homes.
I think people sensed it was a bad time to be out.
So I ran and I ran alone.
Except for the lizards!

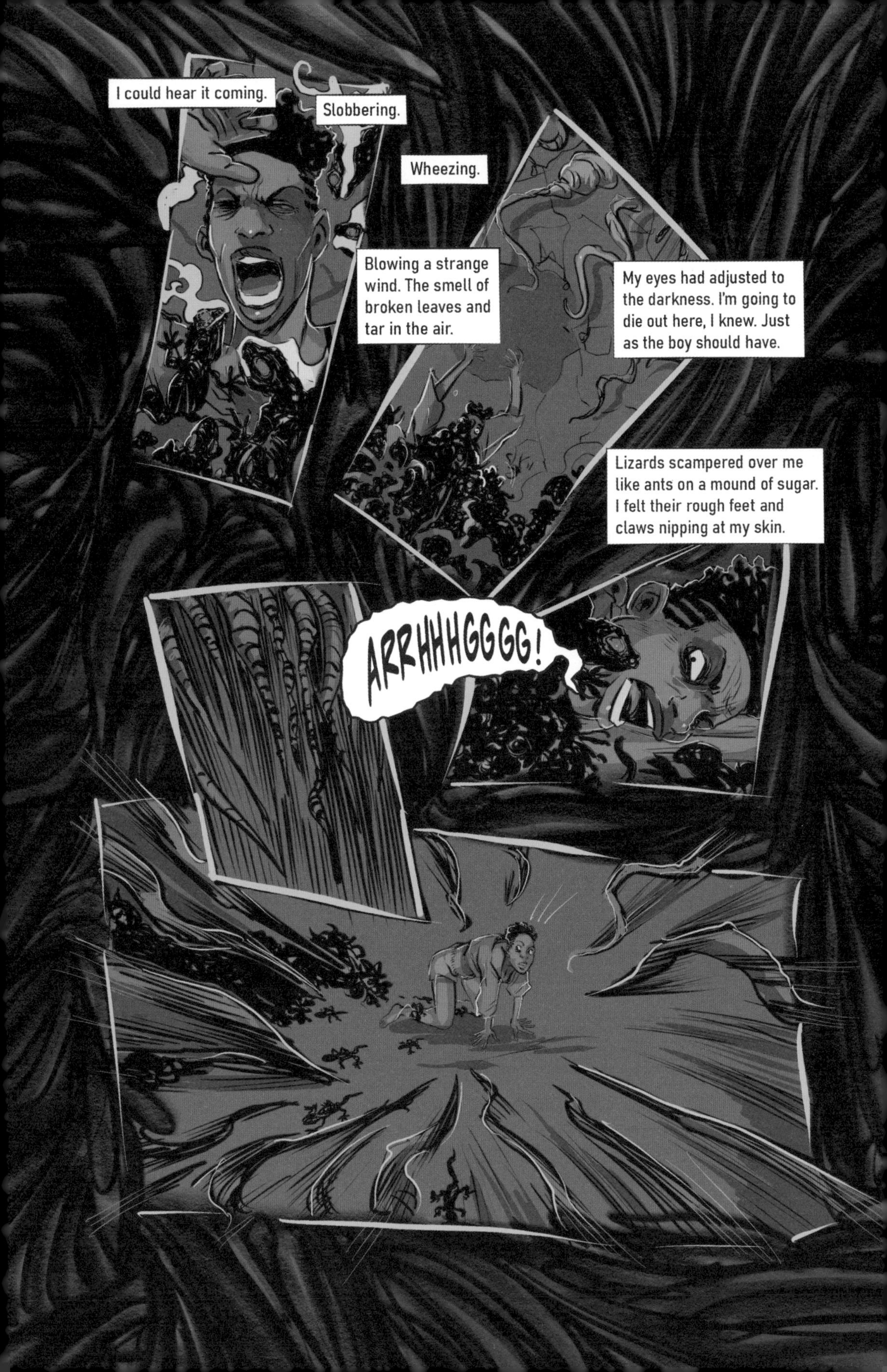
I could hear it coming.
Slobbering.
Wheezing.
Blowing a strange wind. The smell of broken leaves and tar in the air.
My eyes had adjusted to the darkness. I'm going to die out here, I knew. Just as the boy should have.
Lizards scampered over me like ants on a mound of sugar. I felt their rough feet and claws nipping at my skin.
ARRHHHGGGG!

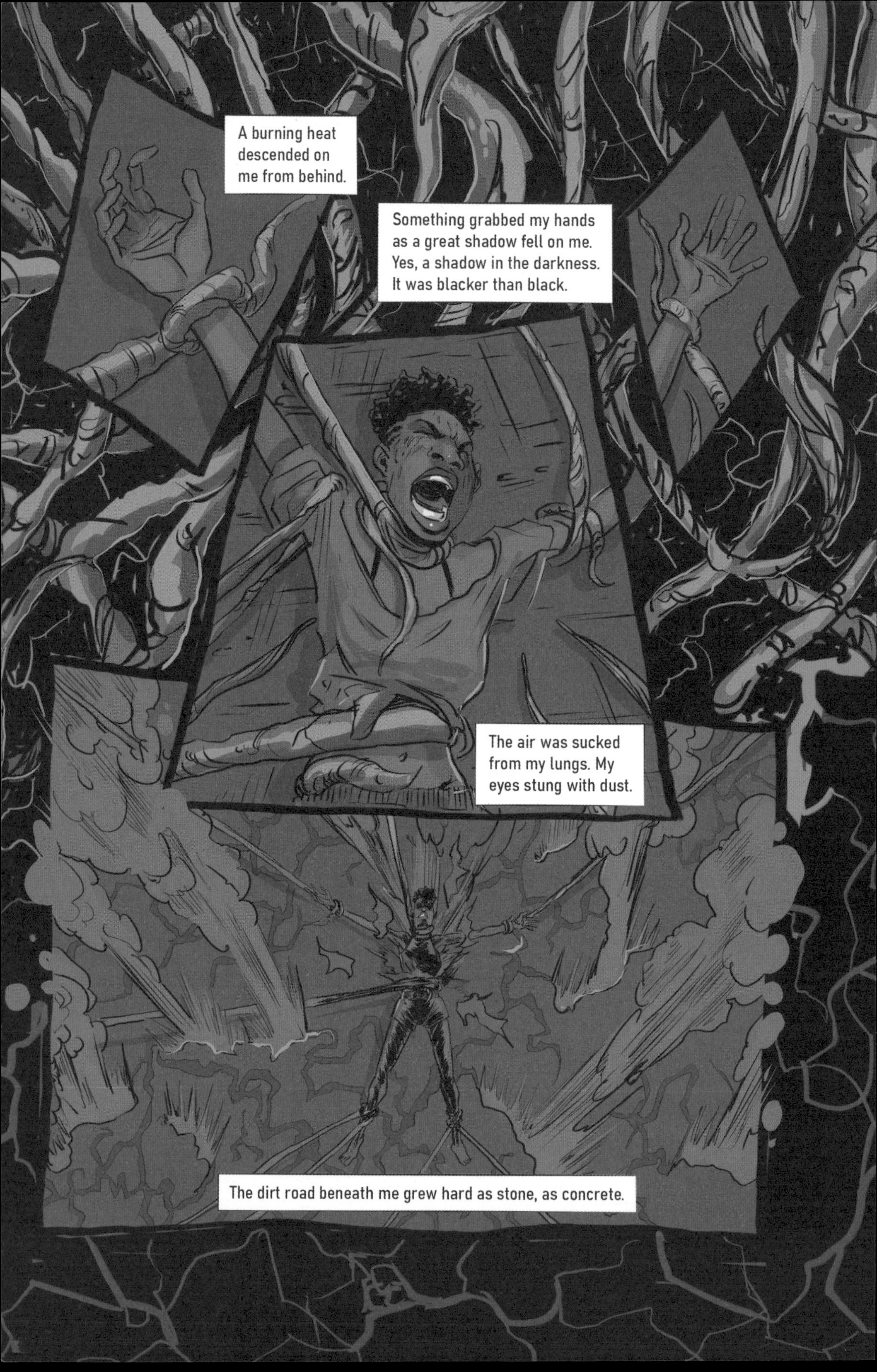
A burning heat descended on me from behind.
Something grabbed my hands as a great shadow fell on me. Yes, a shadow in the darkness. It was blacker than black.
The air was sucked from my lungs. My eyes stung with dust.
The dirt road beneath me grew hard as stone, as concrete.

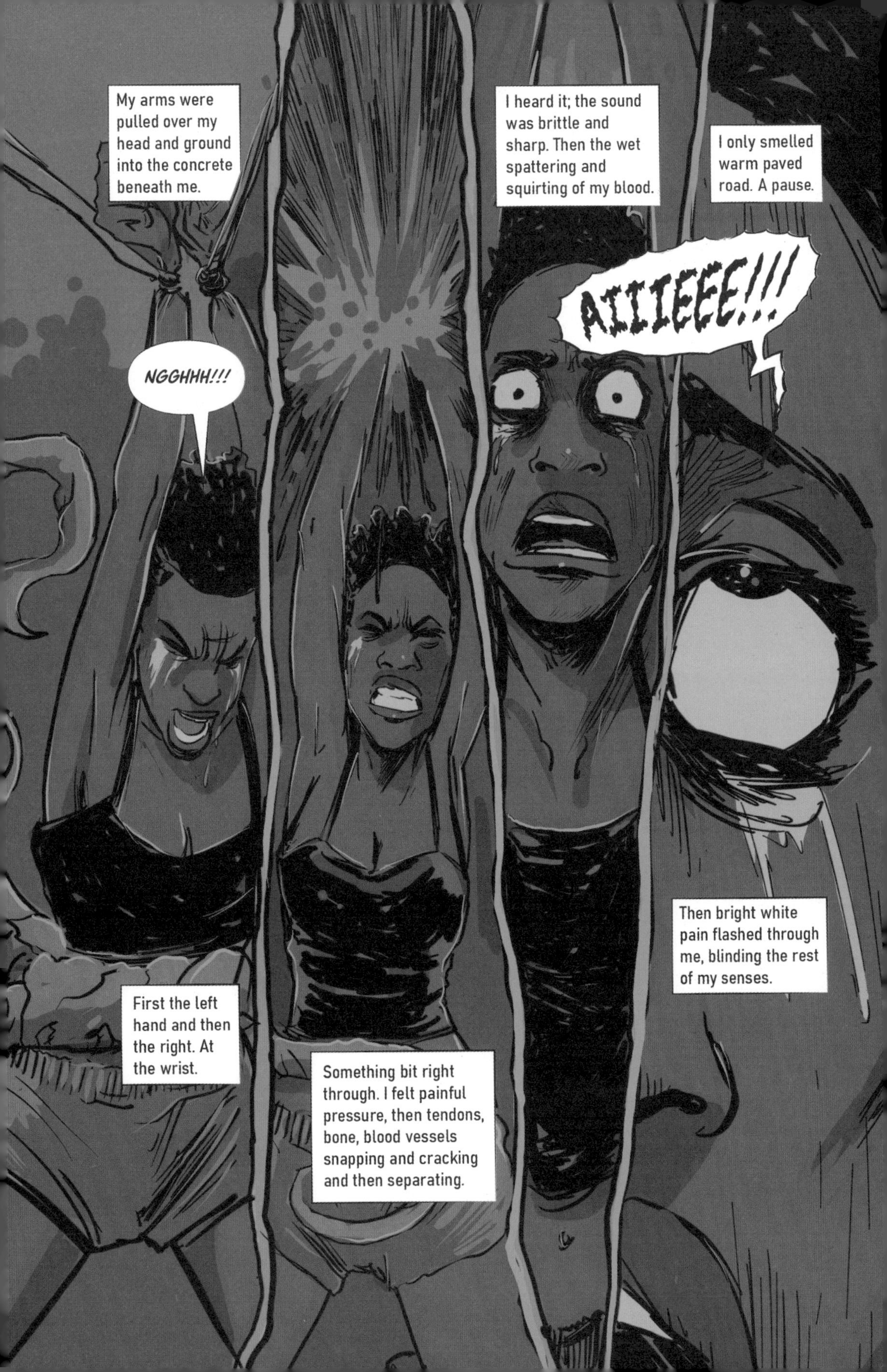
My arms were pulled over my head and ground into the concrete beneath me.
NGGHHH!!!
First the left hand and then the right. At the wrist.
Something bit right through. I felt painful pressure, then tendons, bone, blood vessels snapping and cracking and then separating.
I heard it; the sound was brittle and sharp. Then the wet spattering and squirting of my blood.
AIIIEEE!!!
I only smelled warm paved road. A pause.
Then bright white pain flashed through me, blinding the rest of my senses.

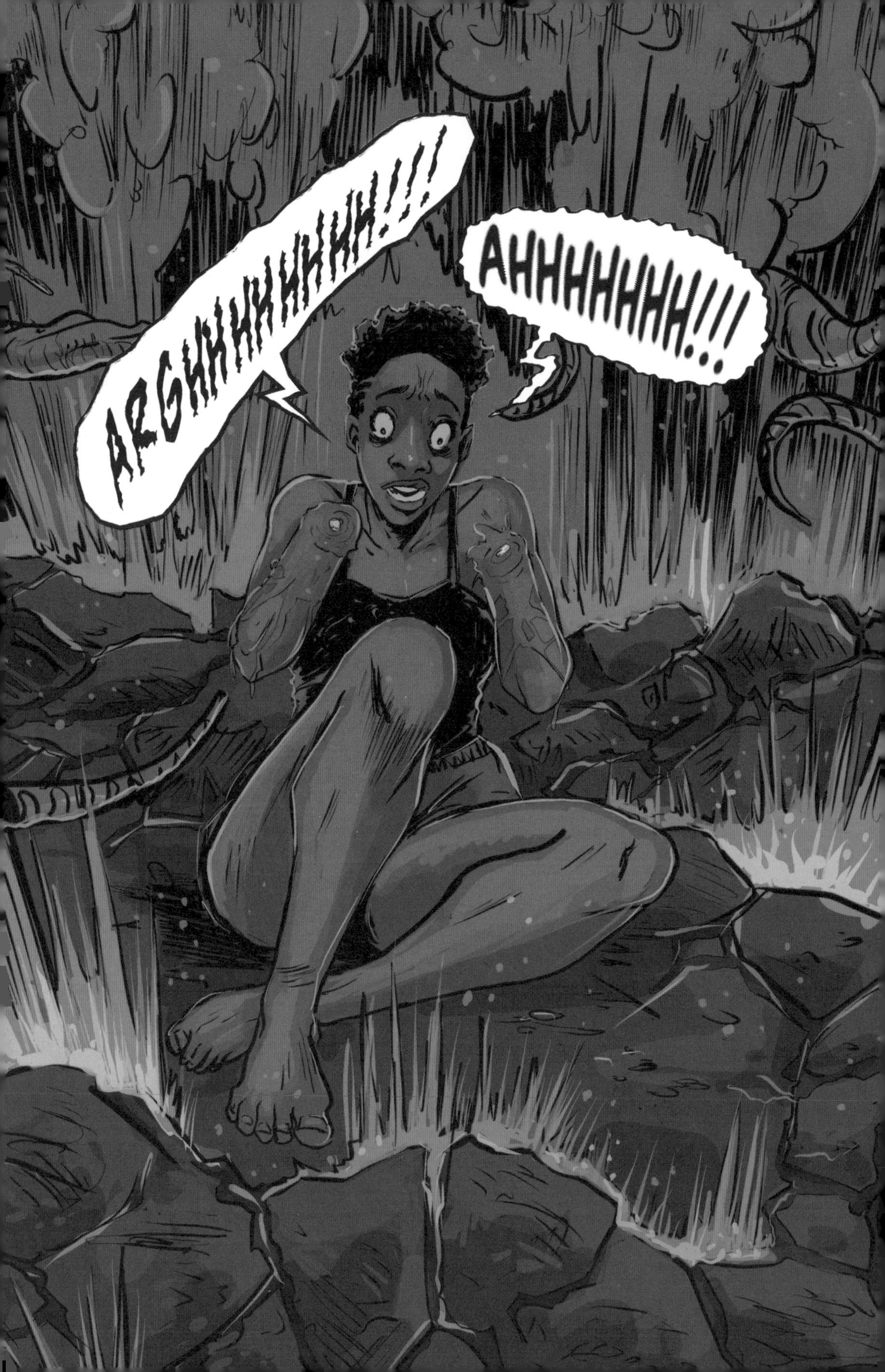
ARGHHHHHHH!!!
AHHHHHHH!!!

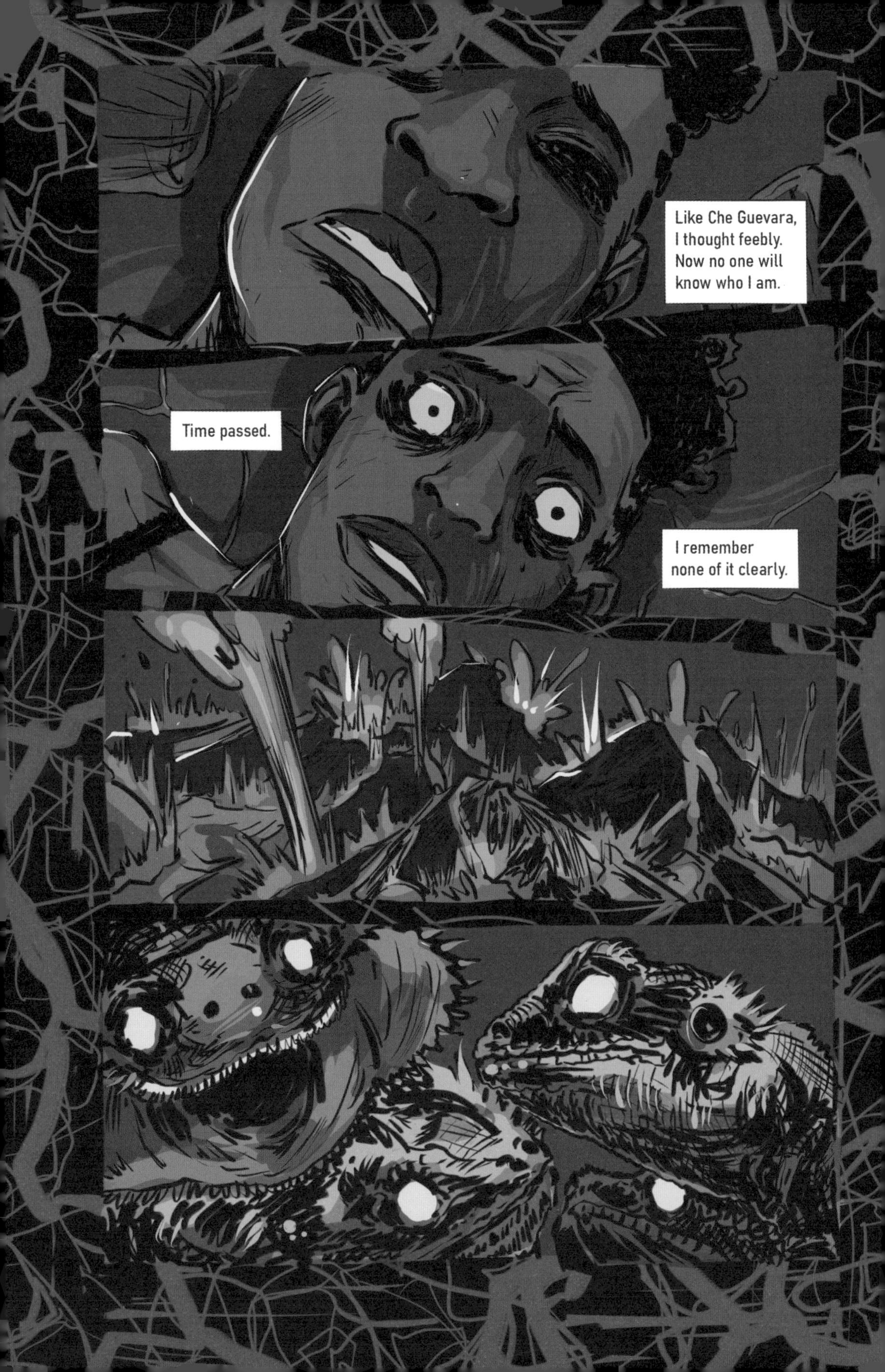
Like Che Guevara, I thought feebly. Now no one will know who I am.
Time passed.
I remember none of it clearly.

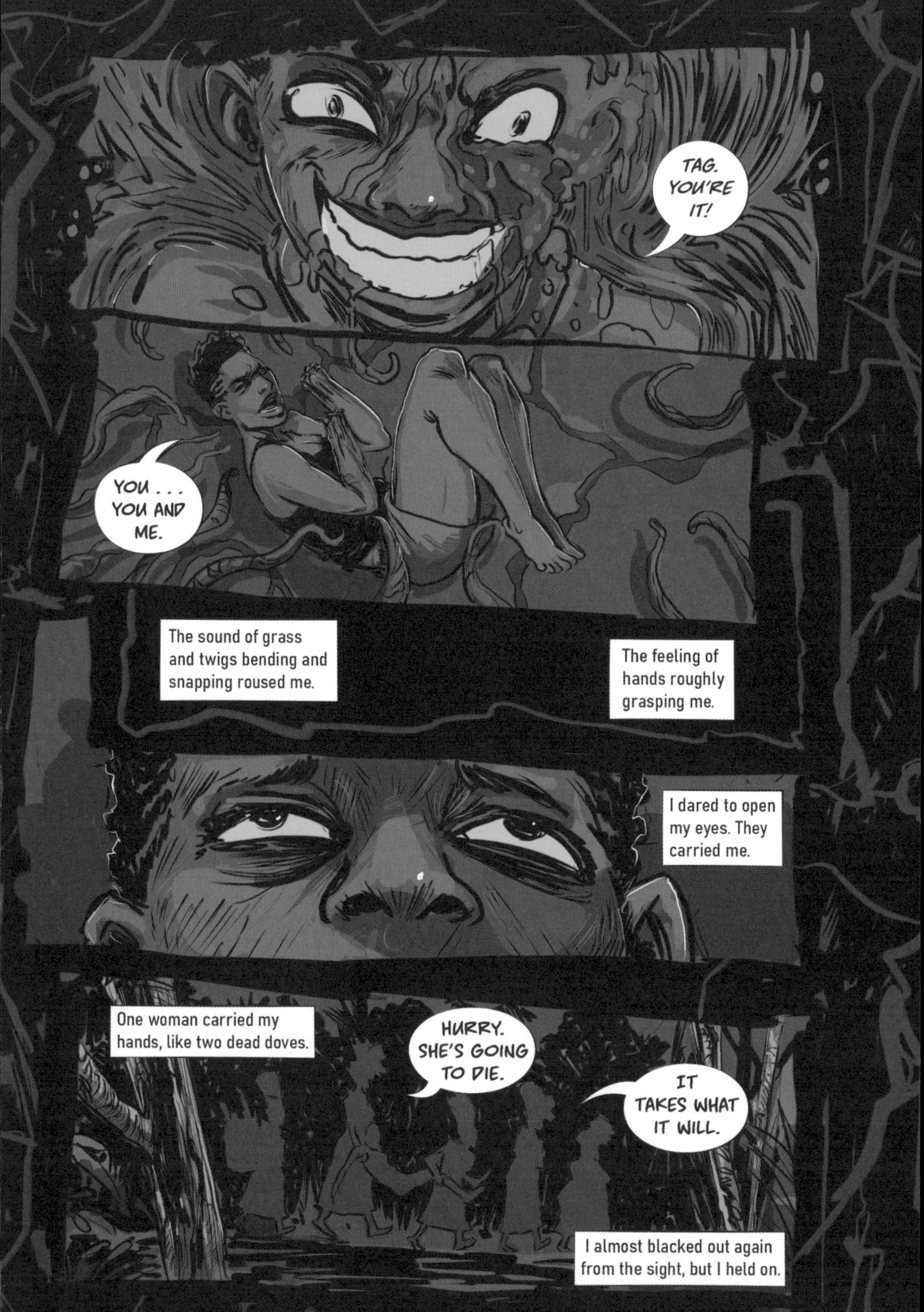
TAG. YOU'RE IT!
YOU . . . YOU AND ME.
The sound of grass and twigs bending and snapping roused me.
The feeling of hands roughly grasping me.
I dared to open my eyes. They carried me.
One woman carried my hands, like two dead doves.
HURRY. SHE'S GOING TO DIE.
IT TAKES WHAT IT WILL.
I almost blacked out again from the sight, but I held on.

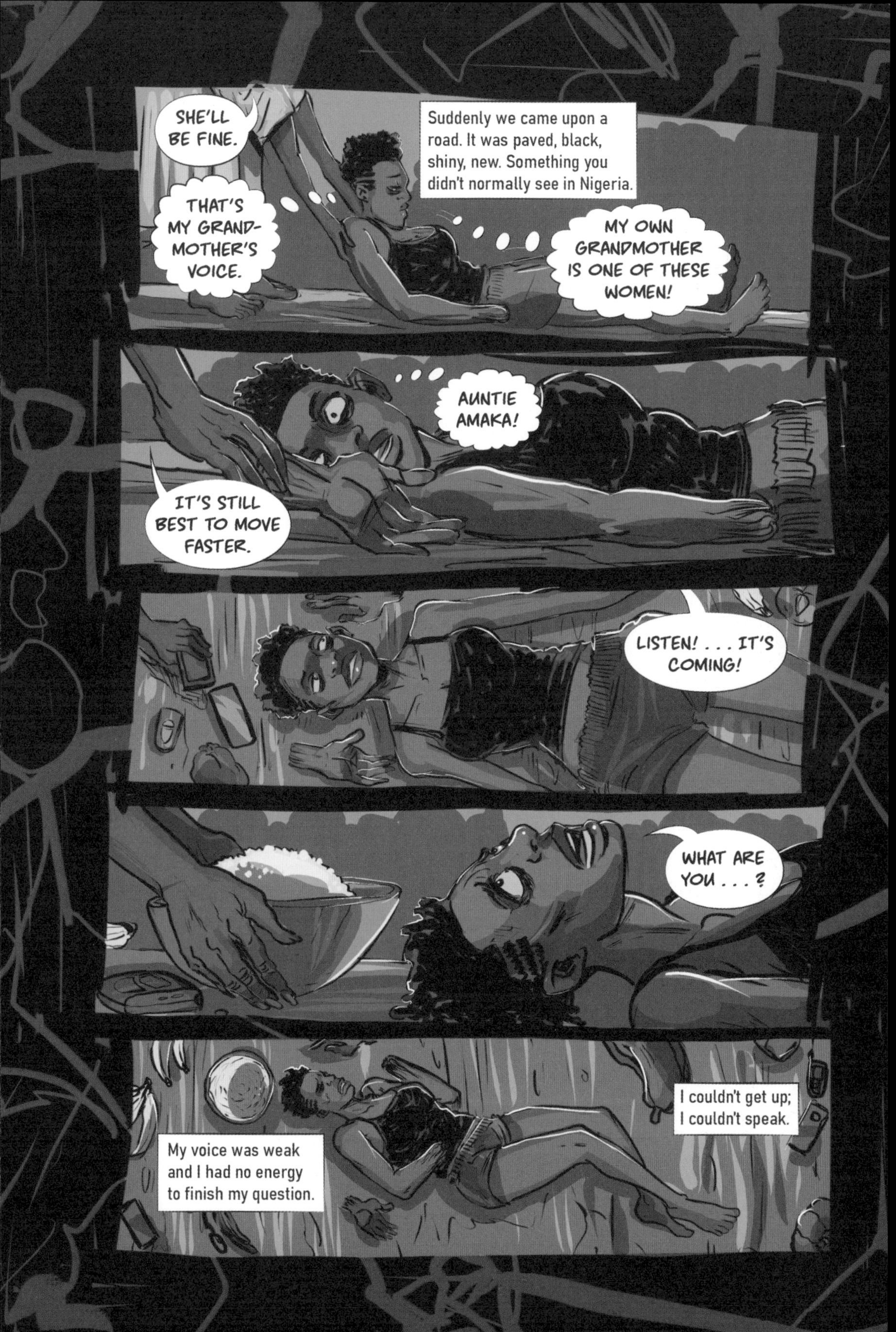
SHE'LL BE FINE.
Suddenly we came upon a road. It was paved, black, shiny, new. Something you didn't normally see in Nigeria.
THAT'S MY GRAND-MOTHER'S VOICE.
MY OWN GRANDMOTHER IS ONE OF THESE WOMEN!
AUNTIE AMAKA!
IT'S STILL BEST TO MOVE FASTER.
LISTEN! . . . IT'S COMING!
WHAT ARE YOU . . . ?
My voice was weak and I had no energy to finish my question.
I couldn't get up; I couldn't speak.

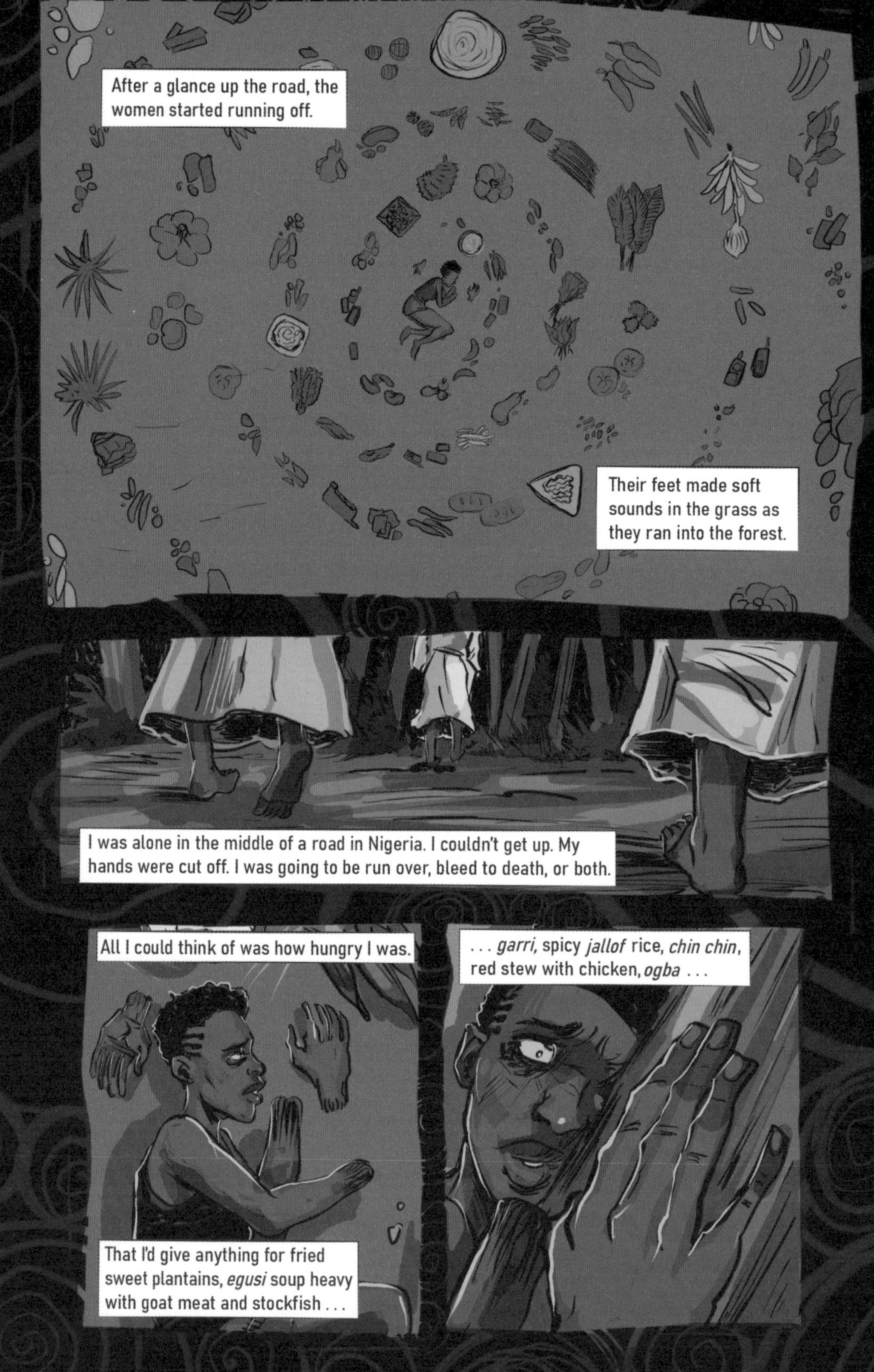
After a glance up the road, the women started running off.
Their feet made soft sounds in the grass as they ran into the forest.
I was alone in the middle of a road in Nigeria. I couldn't get up. My hands were cut off. I was going to be run over, bleed to death, or both.
All I could think of was how hungry I was.
That I'd give anything for fried sweet plantains, *egusi* soup heavy with goat meat and stockfish . . .
. . . *garri,* spicy *jallof* rice, *chin chin*, red stew with chicken, *ogba* . . .

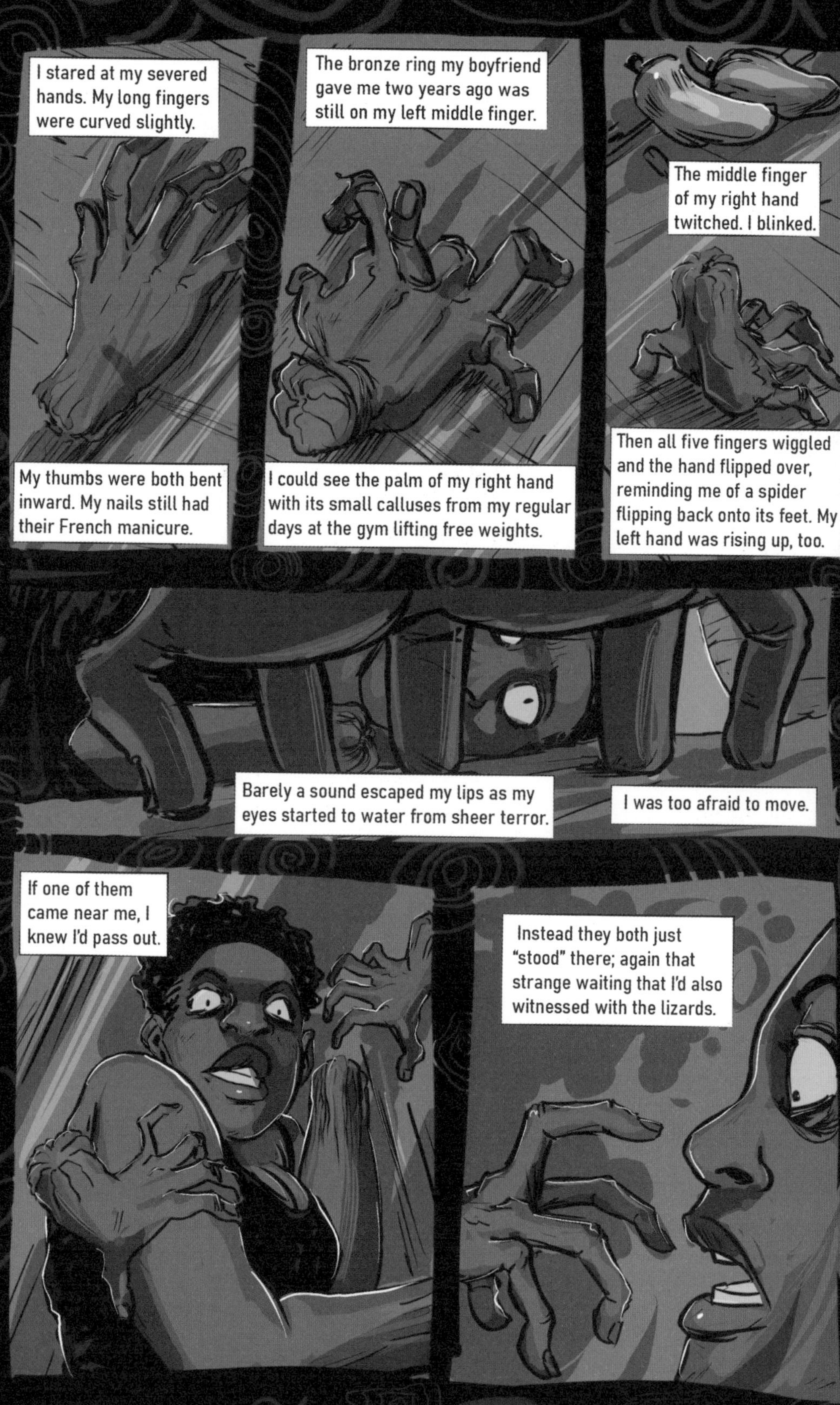
I stared at my severed hands. My long fingers were curved slightly.
My thumbs were both bent inward. My nails still had their French manicure.
The bronze ring my boyfriend gave me two years ago was still on my left middle finger.
I could see the palm of my right hand with its small calluses from my regular days at the gym lifting free weights.
The middle finger of my right hand twitched. I blinked.
Then all five fingers wiggled and the hand flipped over, reminding me of a spider flipping back onto its feet. My left hand was rising up, too.
Barely a sound escaped my lips as my eyes started to water from sheer terror.
I was too afraid to move.
If one of them came near me, I knew I'd pass out.
Instead they both just "stood" there; again that strange waiting that I'd also witnessed with the lizards.

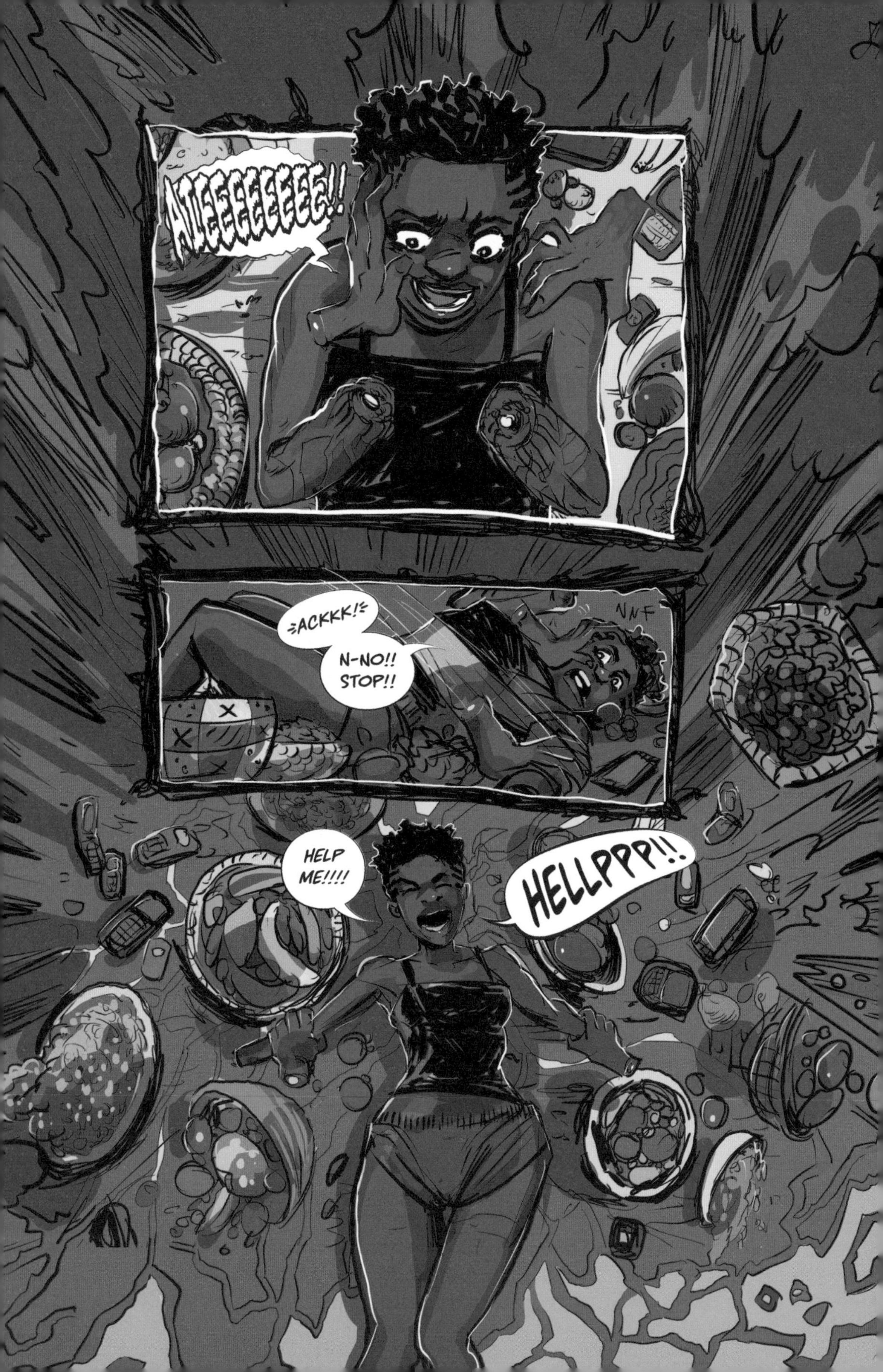
AIEEEEEEEEE!!
ACKKK!
N-NO!! STOP!!
NNF
HELP ME!!!!
HELLPPP!!

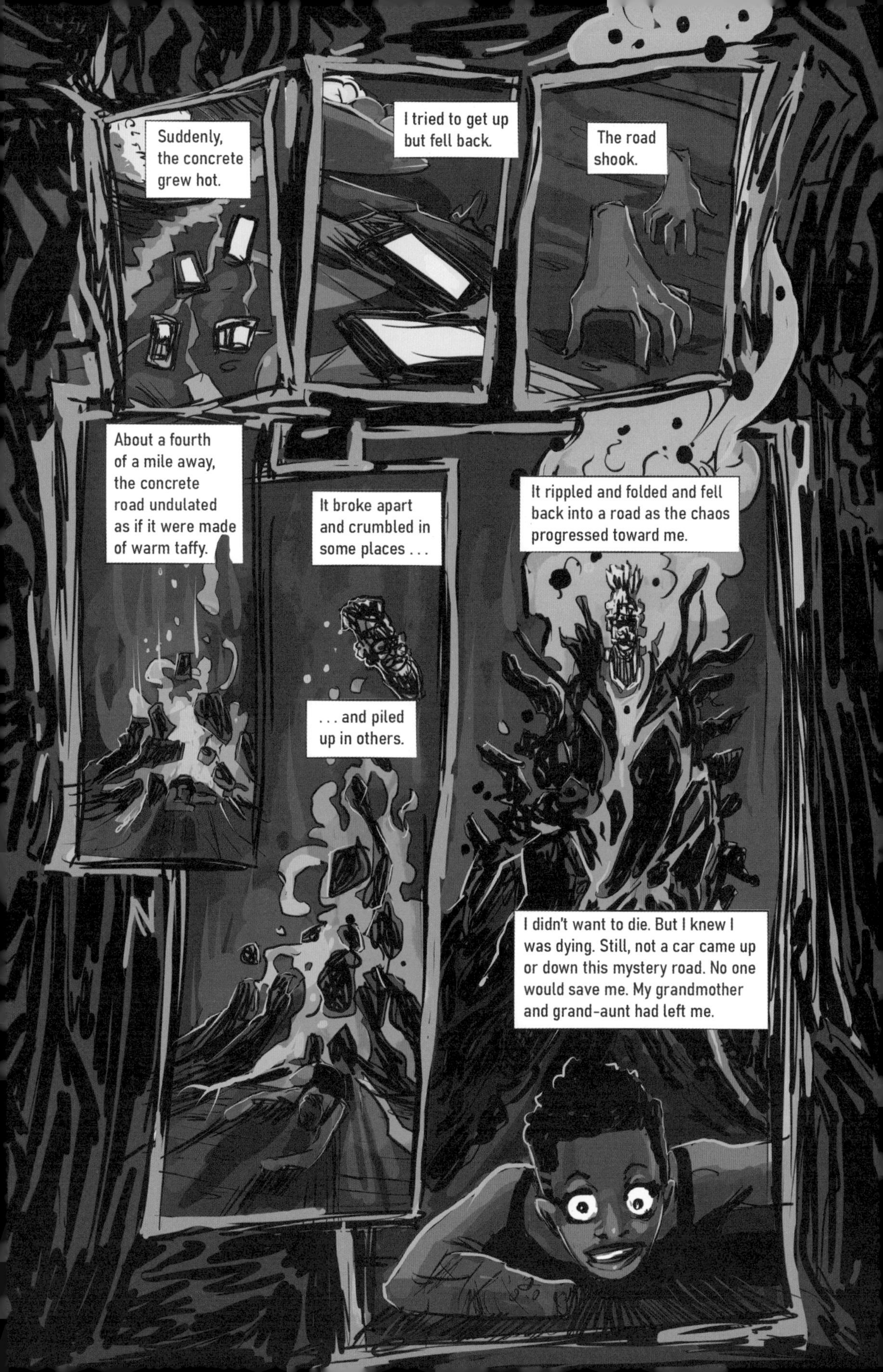
Suddenly, the concrete grew hot.
I tried to get up but fell back.
The road shook.
About a fourth of a mile away, the concrete road undulated as if it were made of warm taffy.
It broke apart and crumbled in some places . . .
. . . and piled up in others.
It rippled and folded and fell back into a road as the chaos progressed toward me.
I didn't want to die. But I knew I was dying. Still, not a car came up or down this mystery road. No one would save me. My grandmother and grand-aunt had left me.

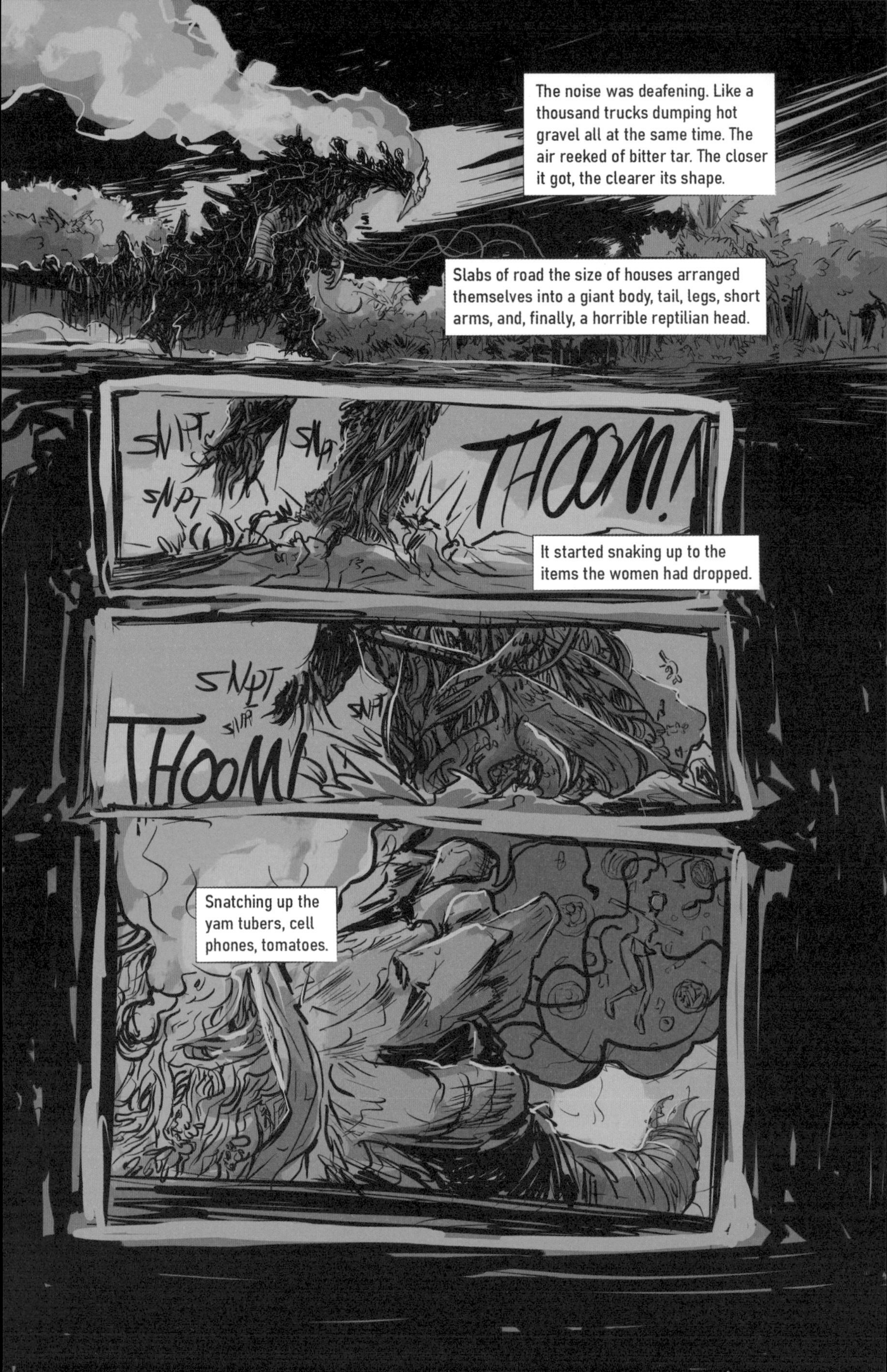
The noise was deafening. Like a thousand trucks dumping hot gravel all at the same time. The air reeked of bitter tar. The closer it got, the clearer its shape.
Slabs of road the size of houses arranged themselves into a giant body, tail, legs, short arms, and, finally, a horrible reptilian head.
SNPT
SNPT
SNPT
THOOM!
It started snaking up to the items the women had dropped.
SNPT
SNPT
THOOM
Snatching up the yam tubers, cell phones, tomatoes.

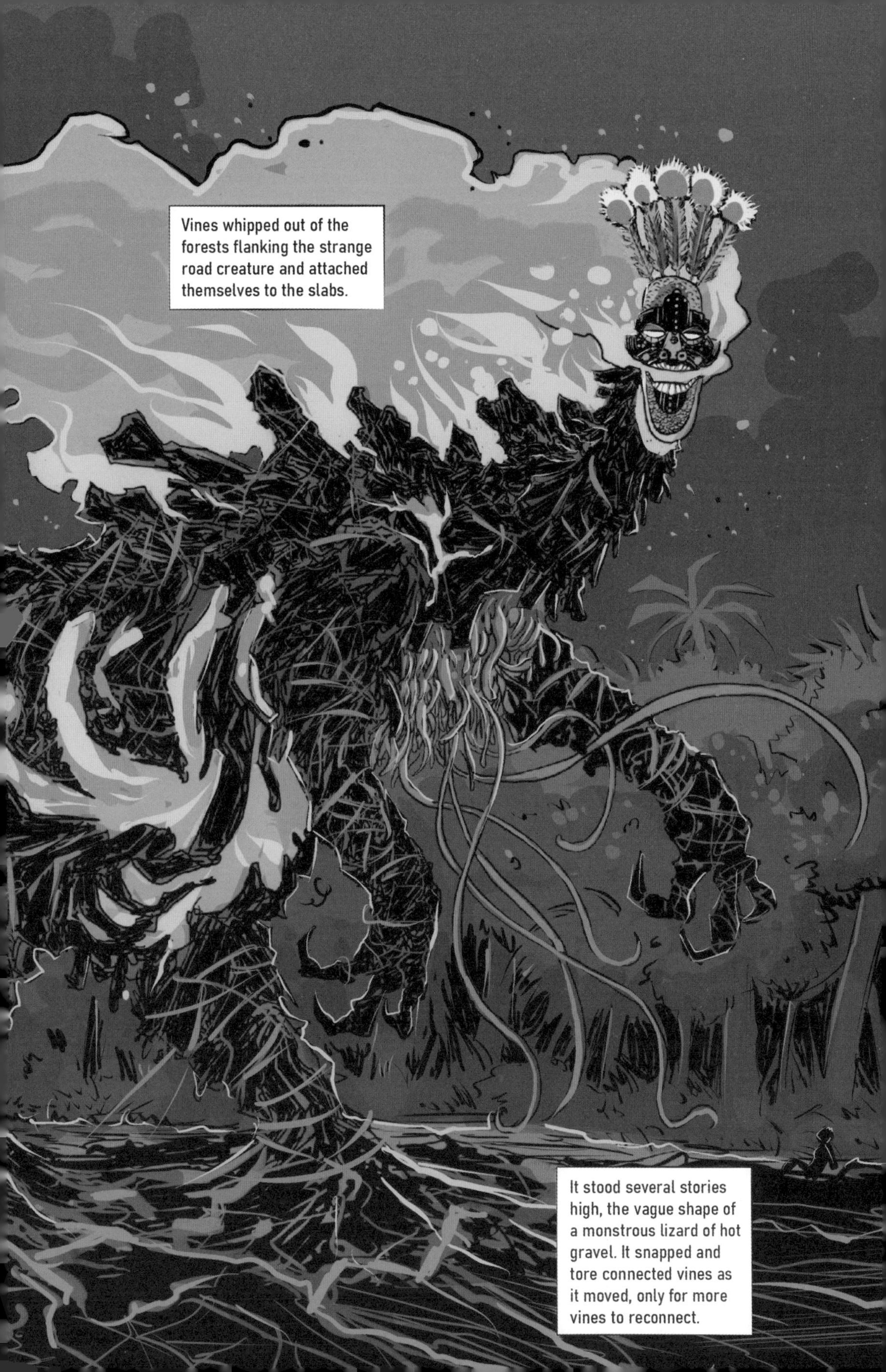
Vines whipped out of the forests flanking the strange road creature and attached themselves to the slabs.
It stood several stories high, the vague shape of a monstrous lizard of hot gravel. It snapped and tore connected vines as it moved, only for more vines to reconnect.

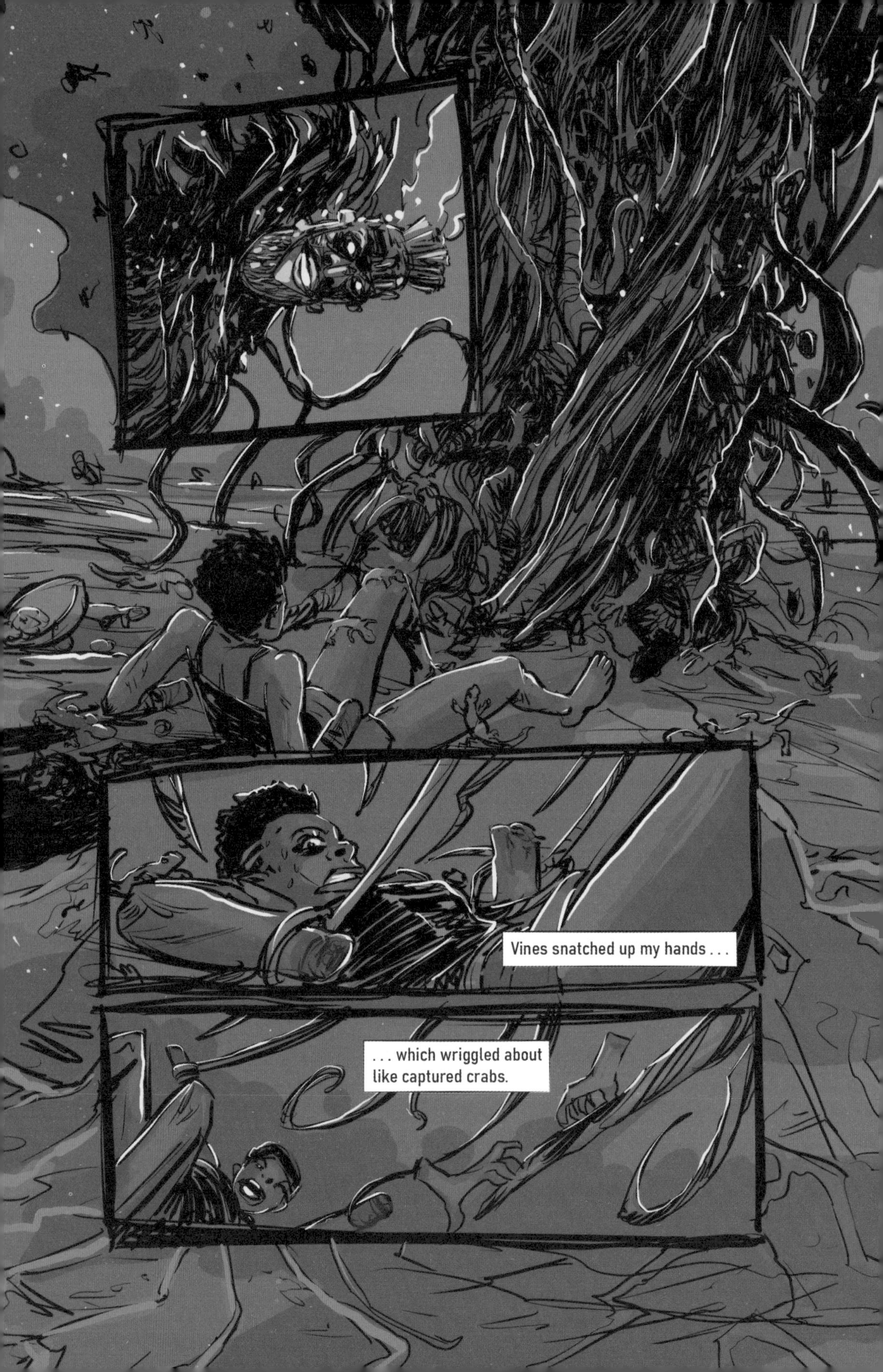
Vines snatched up my hands . . .
. . . which wriggled about like captured crabs.

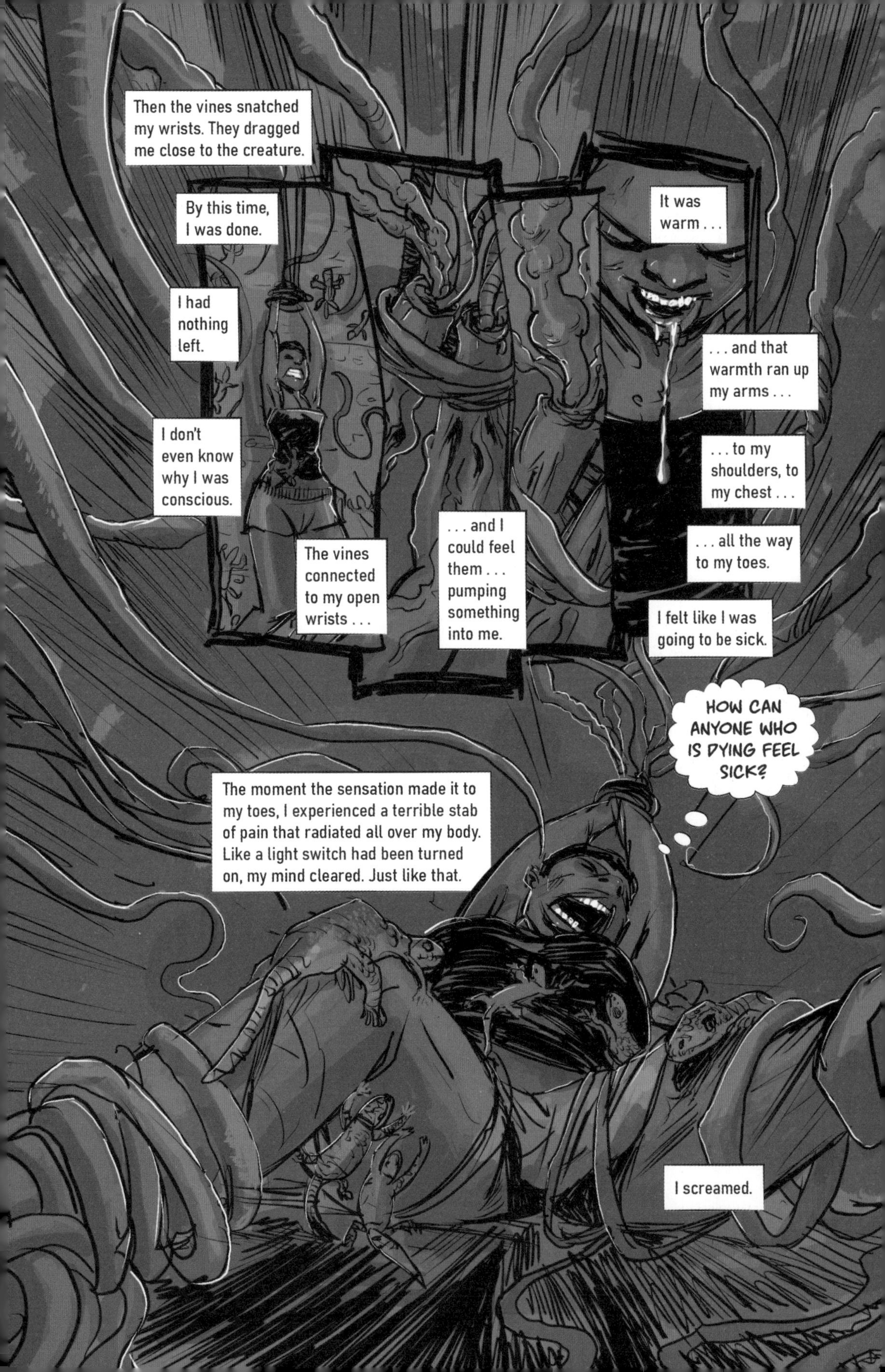
Then the vines snatched my wrists. They dragged me close to the creature.
By this time, I was done.
I had nothing left.
I don't even know why I was conscious.
The vines connected to my open wrists . . .
. . . and I could feel them . . . pumping something into me.
It was warm . . .
. . . and that warmth ran up my arms . . .
. . . to my shoulders, to my chest . . .
. . . all the way to my toes.
I felt like I was going to be sick.
HOW CAN ANYONE WHO IS DYING FEEL SICK?
The moment the sensation made it to my toes, I experienced a terrible stab of pain that radiated all over my body. Like a light switch had been turned on, my mind cleared. Just like that.
I screamed.

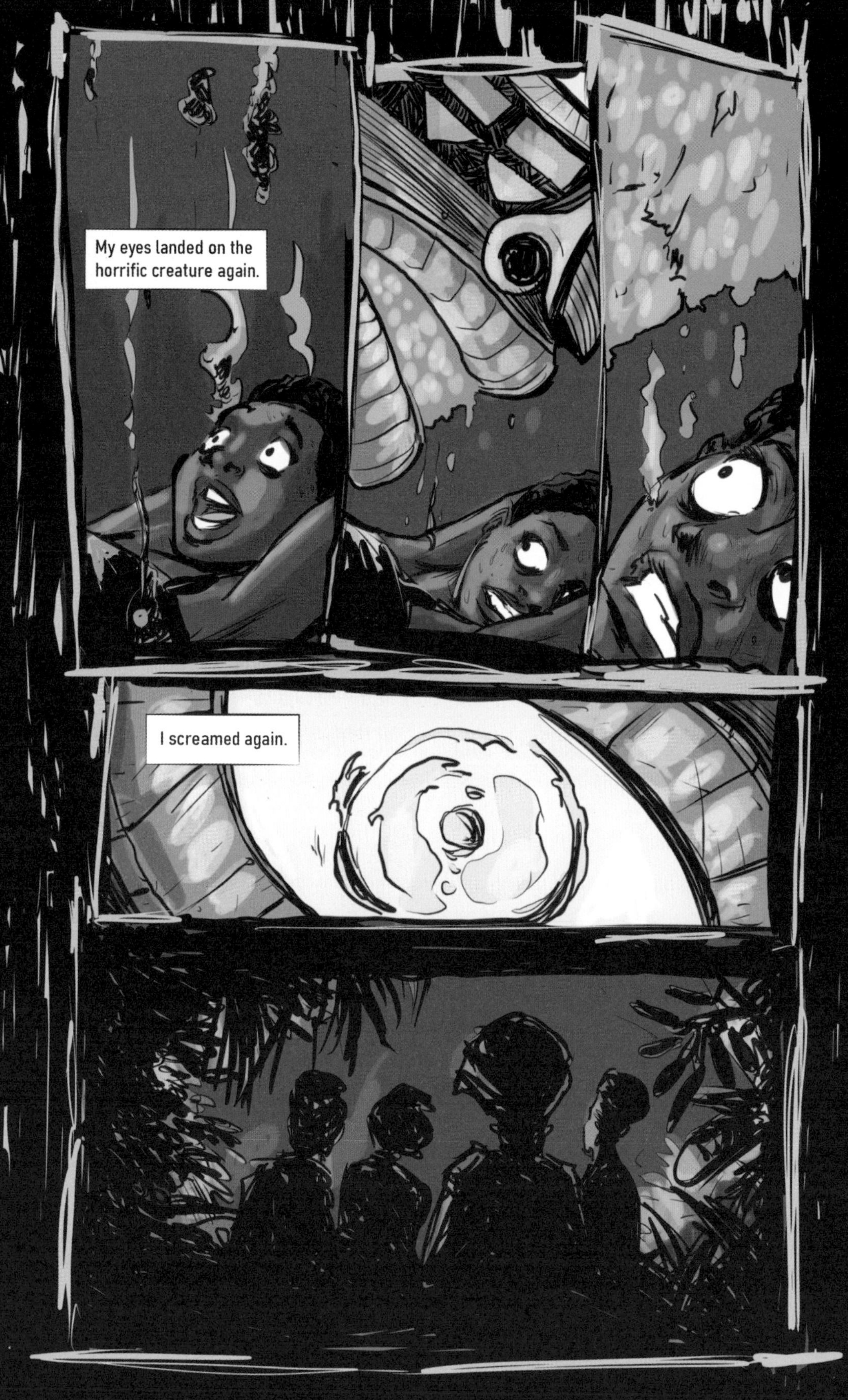
My eyes landed on the horrific creature again.
I screamed again.

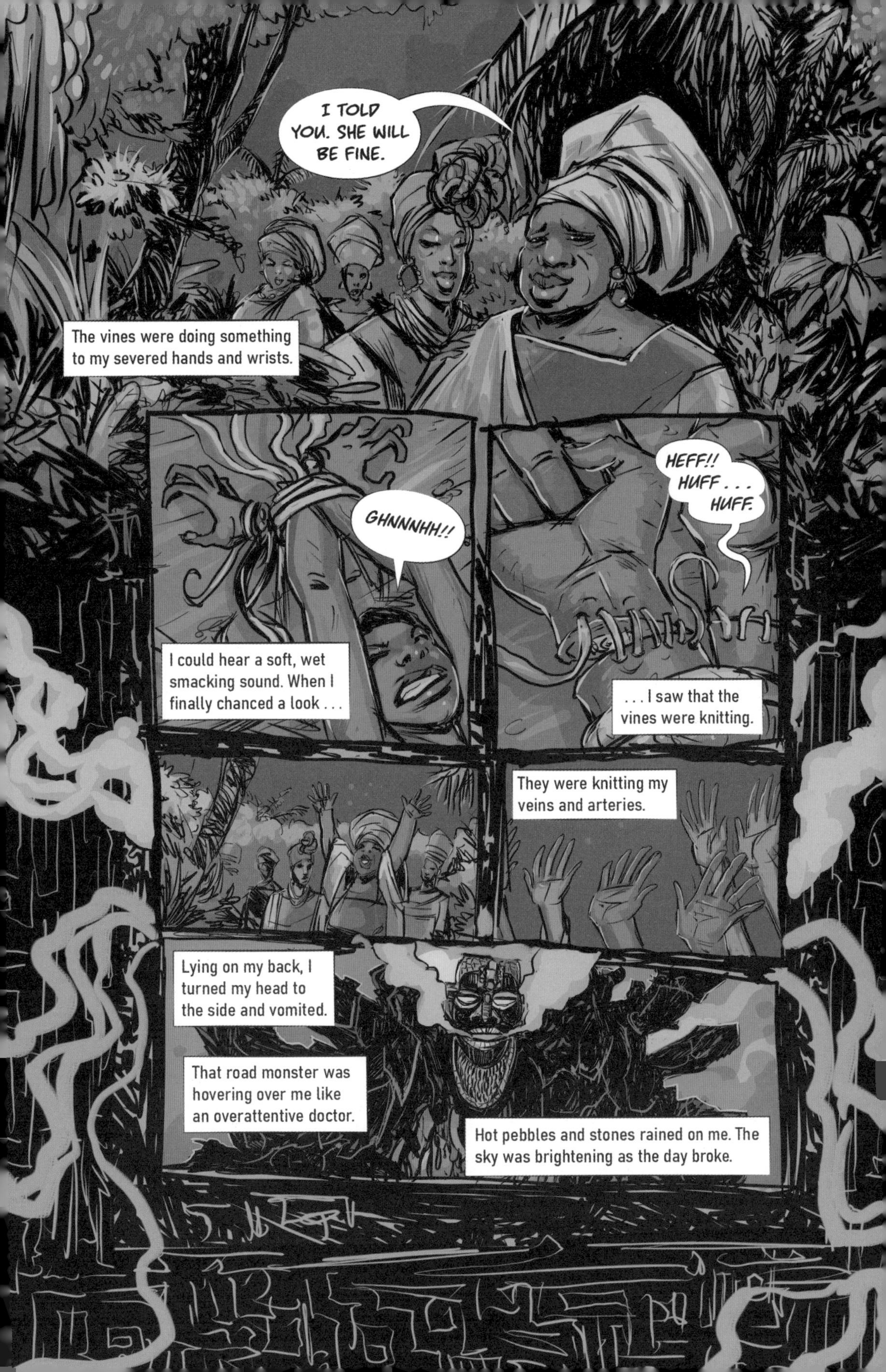
I TOLD YOU. SHE WILL BE FINE.
The vines were doing something to my severed hands and wrists.
GHNNNHH!!
I could hear a soft, wet smacking sound. When I finally chanced a look . . .
HEFF!! HUFF . . . HUFF.
. . . I saw that the vines were knitting.
They were knitting my veins and arteries.
Lying on my back, I turned my head to the side and vomited.
That road monster was hovering over me like an overattentive doctor.
Hot pebbles and stones rained on me. The sky was brightening as the day broke.

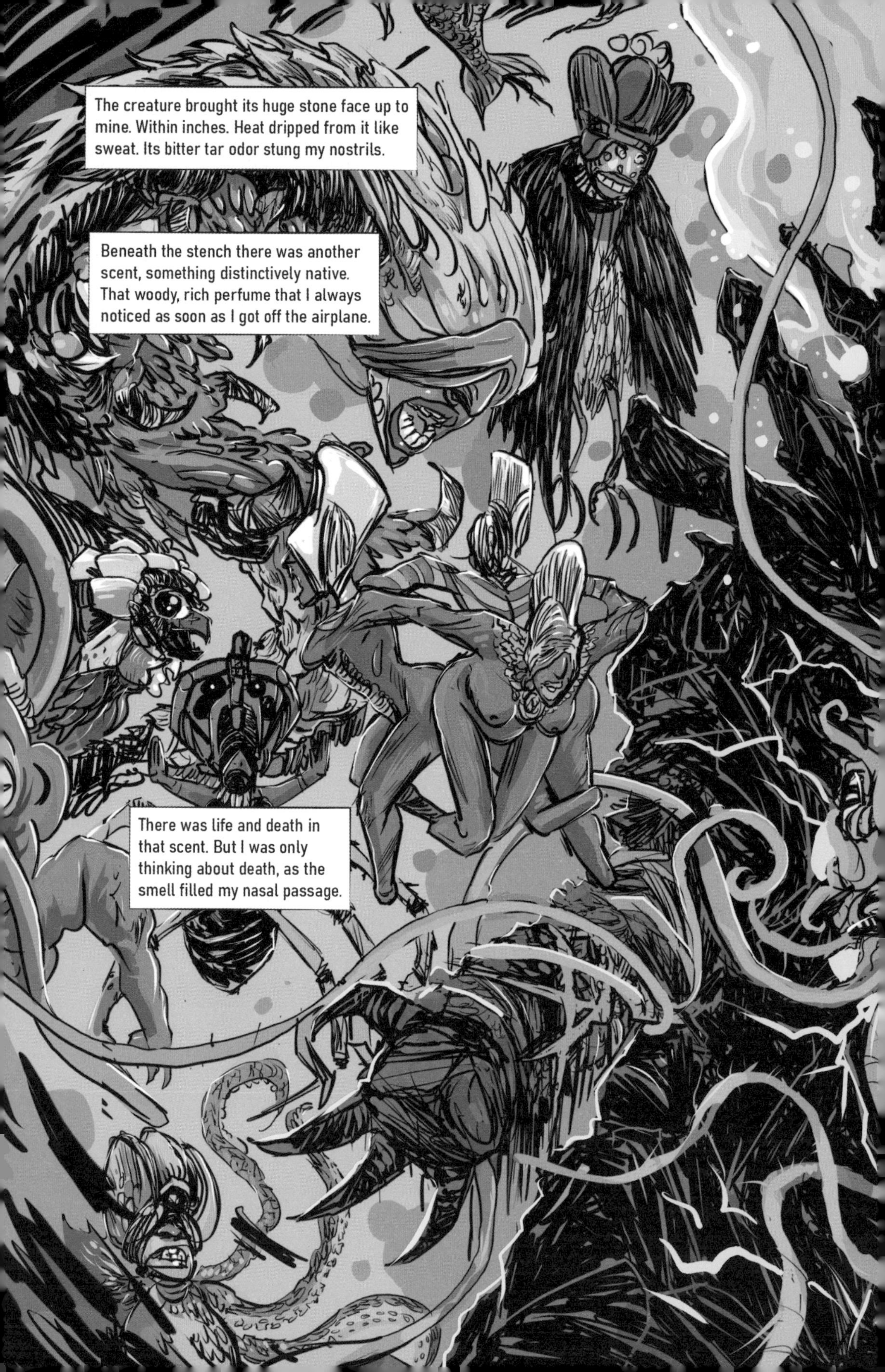
The creature brought its huge stone face up to mine. Within inches. Heat dripped from it like sweat. Its bitter tar odor stung my nostrils.
Beneath the stench there was another scent, something distinctively native. That woody, rich perfume that I always noticed as soon as I got off the airplane.
There was life and death in that scent. But I was only thinking about death, as the smell filled my nasal passage.

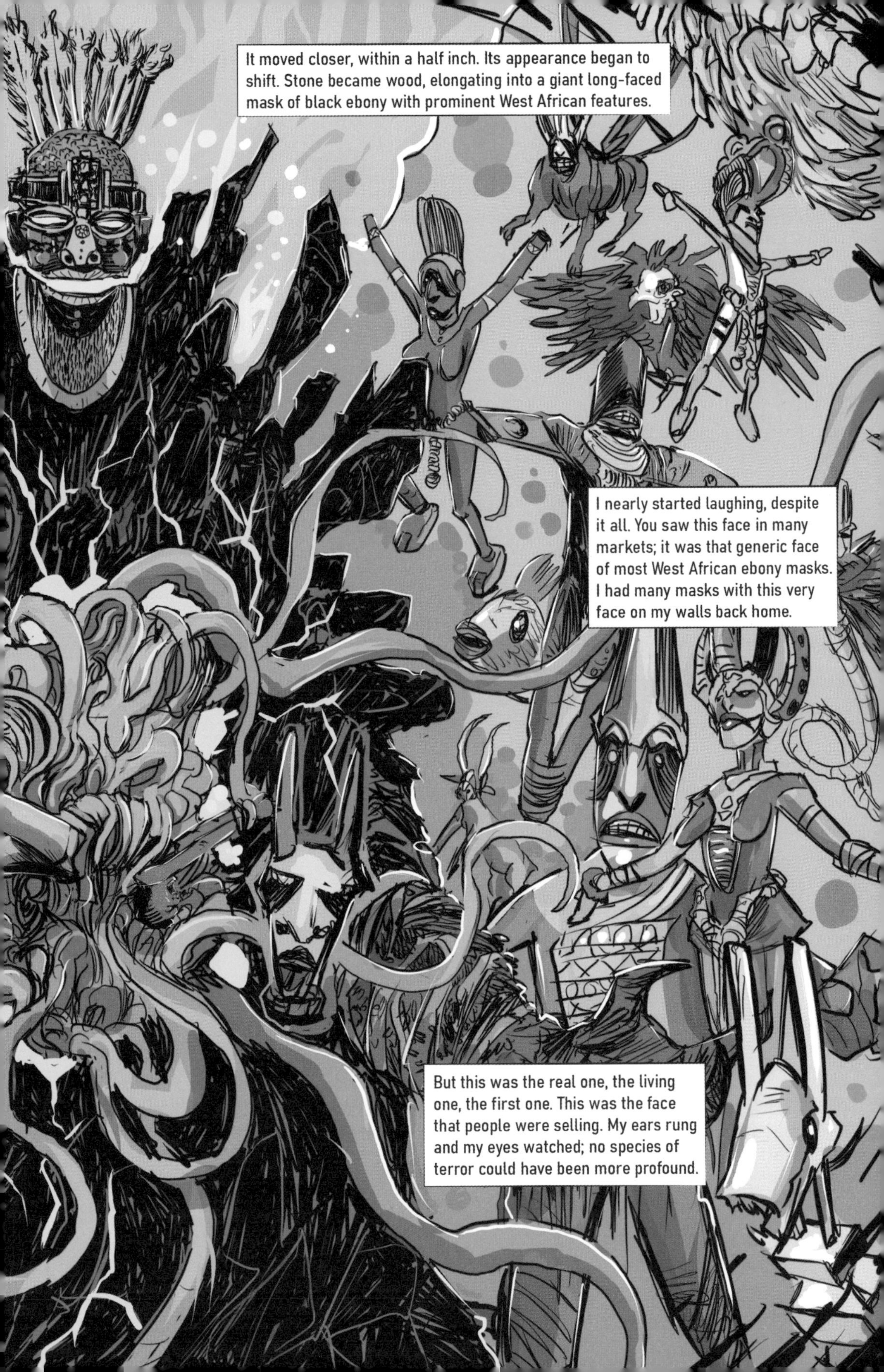
It moved closer, within a half inch. Its appearance began to shift. Stone became wood, elongating into a giant long-faced mask of black ebony with prominent West African features.
I nearly started laughing, despite it all. You saw this face in many markets; it was that generic face of most West African ebony masks. I had many masks with this very face on my walls back home.
But this was the real one, the living one, the first one. This was the face that people were selling. My ears rung and my eyes watched; no species of terror could have been more profound.

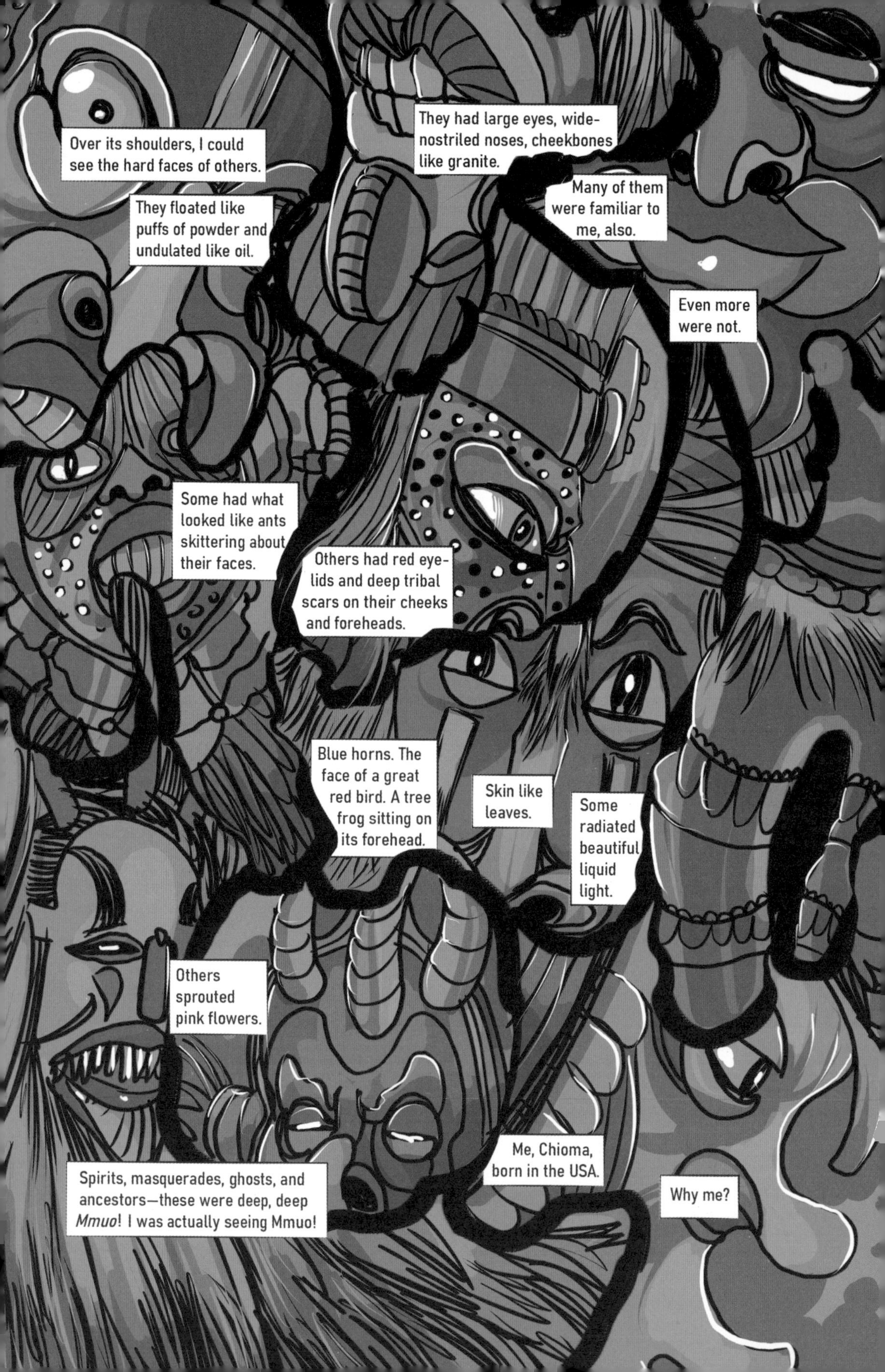
Over its shoulders, I could see the hard faces of others.
They floated like puffs of powder and undulated like oil.
They had large eyes, wide-nostriled noses, cheekbones like granite.
Many of them were familiar to me, also.
Even more were not.
Some had what looked like ants skittering about their faces.
Others had red eye-lids and deep tribal scars on their cheeks and foreheads.
Blue horns. The face of a great red bird. A tree frog sitting on its forehead.
Skin like leaves.
Some radiated beautiful liquid light.
Others sprouted pink flowers.
Spirits, masquerades, ghosts, and ancestors—these were deep, deep *Mmuo*! I was actually seeing Mmuo!
Me, Chioma, born in the USA.
Why me?

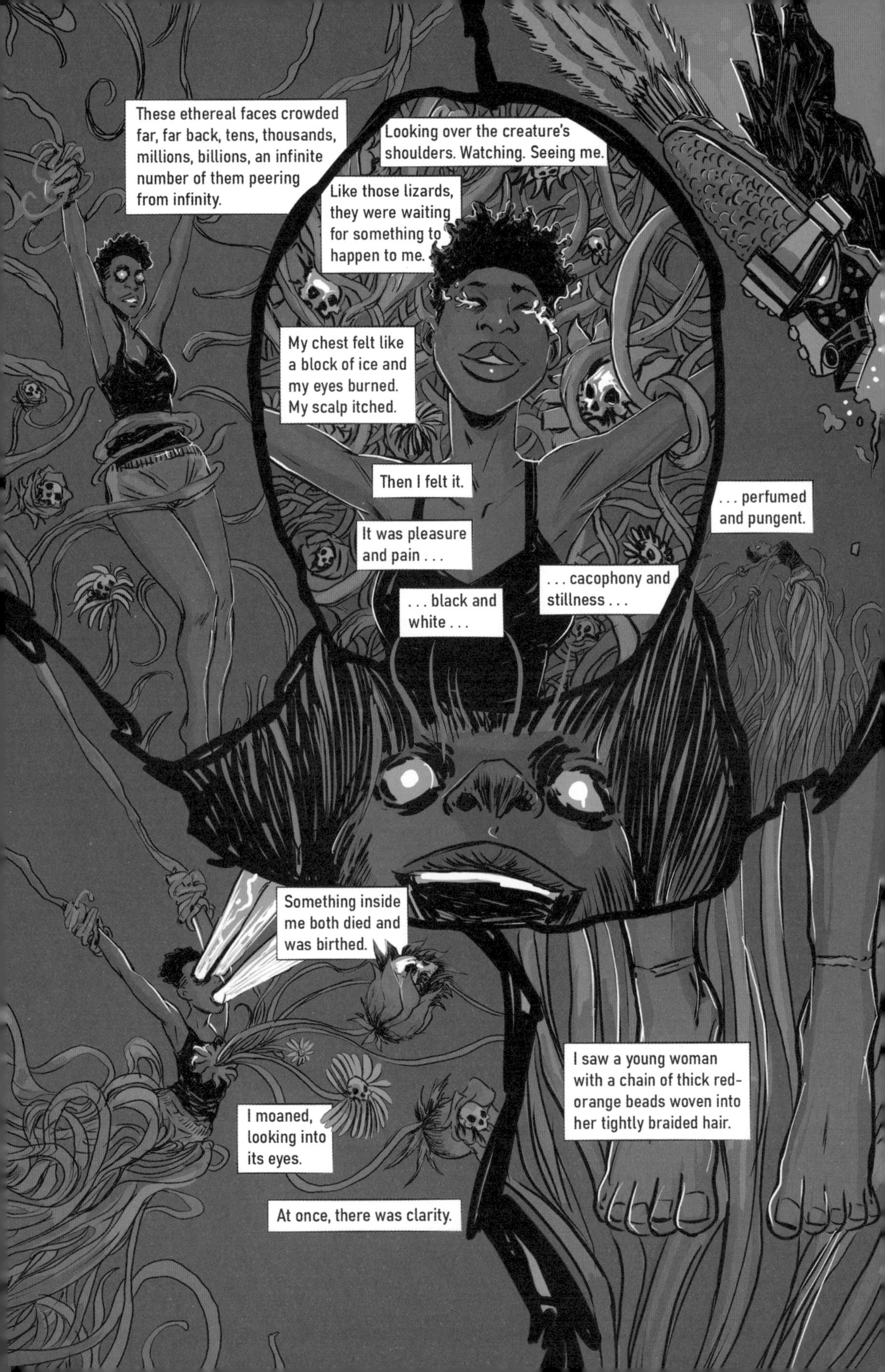
These ethereal faces crowded far, far back, tens, thousands, millions, billions, an infinite number of them peering from infinity.
Looking over the creature's shoulders. Watching. Seeing me.
Like those lizards, they were waiting for something to happen to me.
My chest felt like a block of ice and my eyes burned. My scalp itched.
Then I felt it.
It was pleasure and pain . . .
. . . black and white . . .
. . . cacophony and stillness . . .
. . . perfumed and pungent.
Something inside me both died and was birthed.
I saw a young woman with a chain of thick red-orange beads woven into her tightly braided hair.
I moaned, looking into its eyes.
At once, there was clarity.

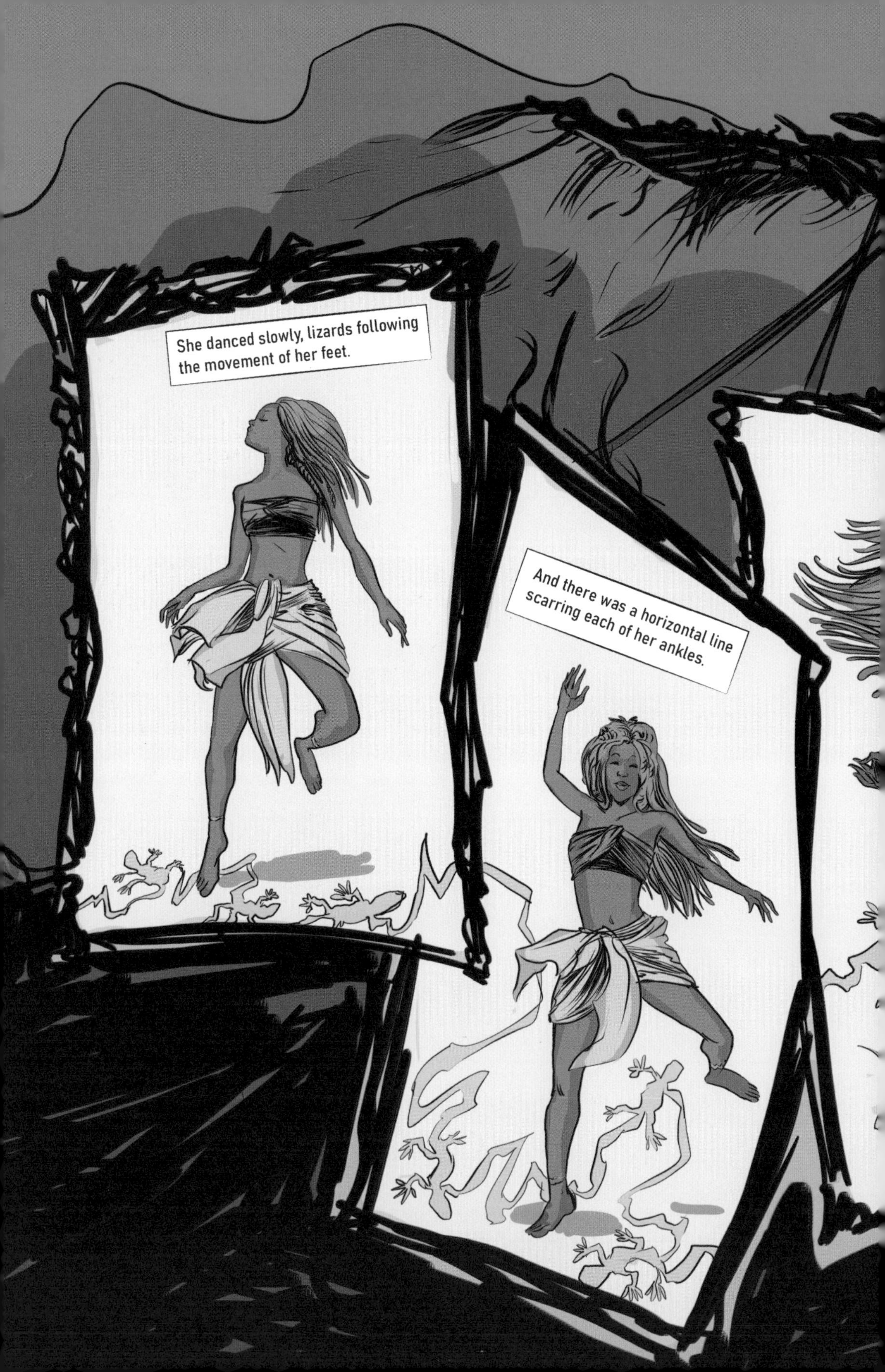
She danced slowly, lizards following the movement of her feet.
And there was a horizontal line scarring each of her ankles.

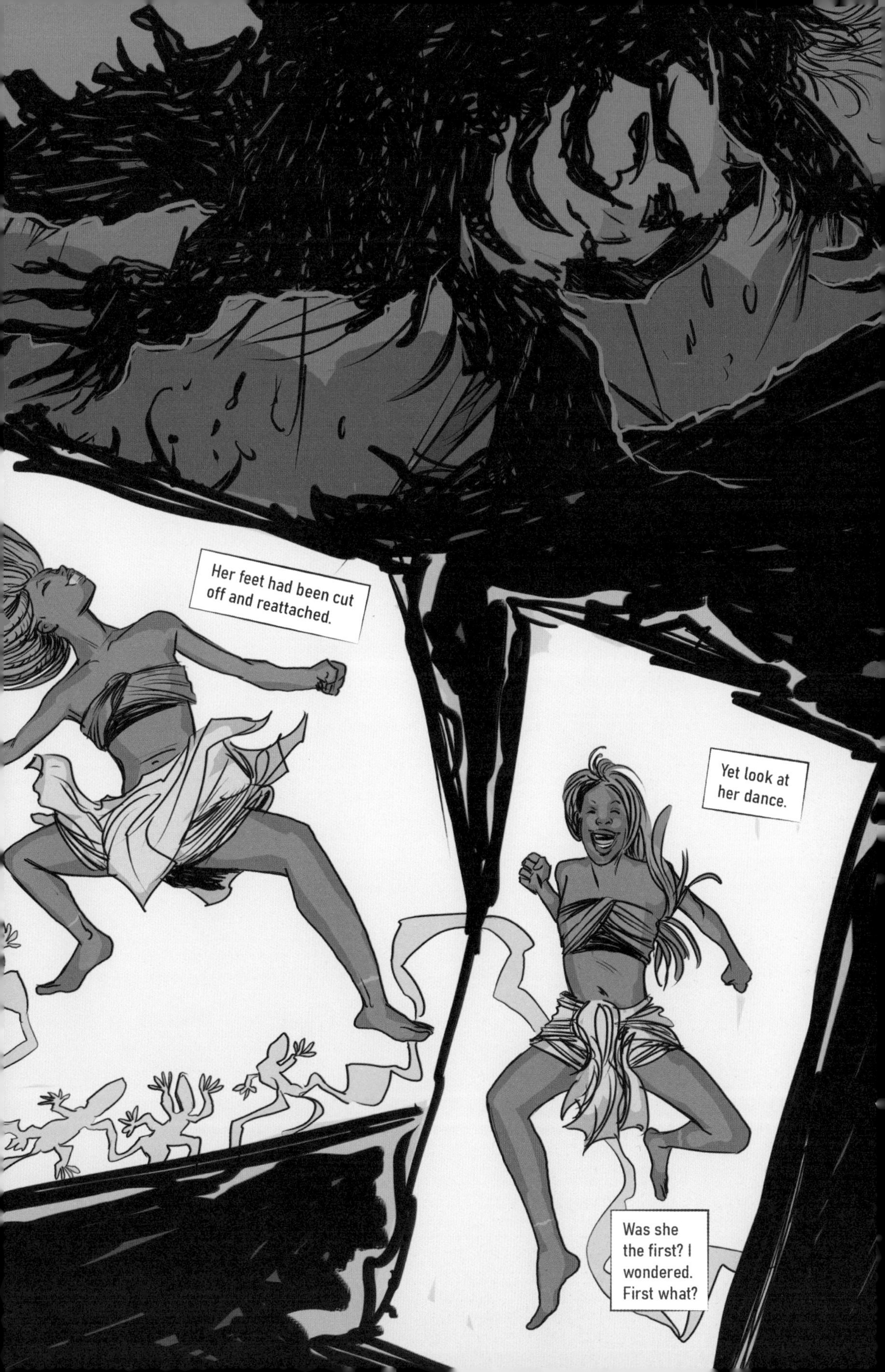
Her feet had been cut off and reattached.
Yet look at her dance.
Was she the first? I wondered. First what?

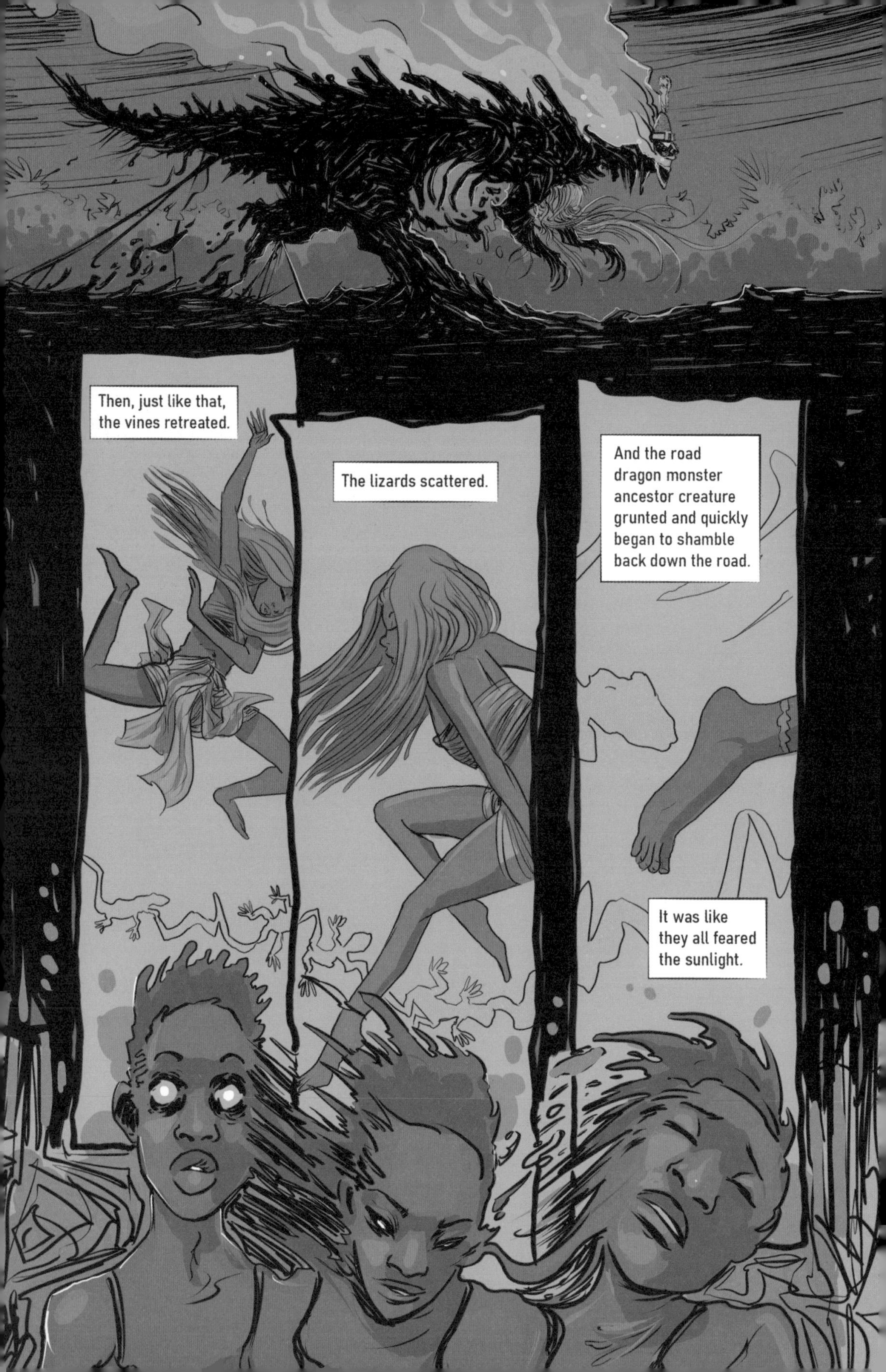
Then, just like that, the vines retreated.
The lizards scattered.
And the road dragon monster ancestor creature grunted and quickly began to shamble back down the road.
It was like they all feared the sunlight.

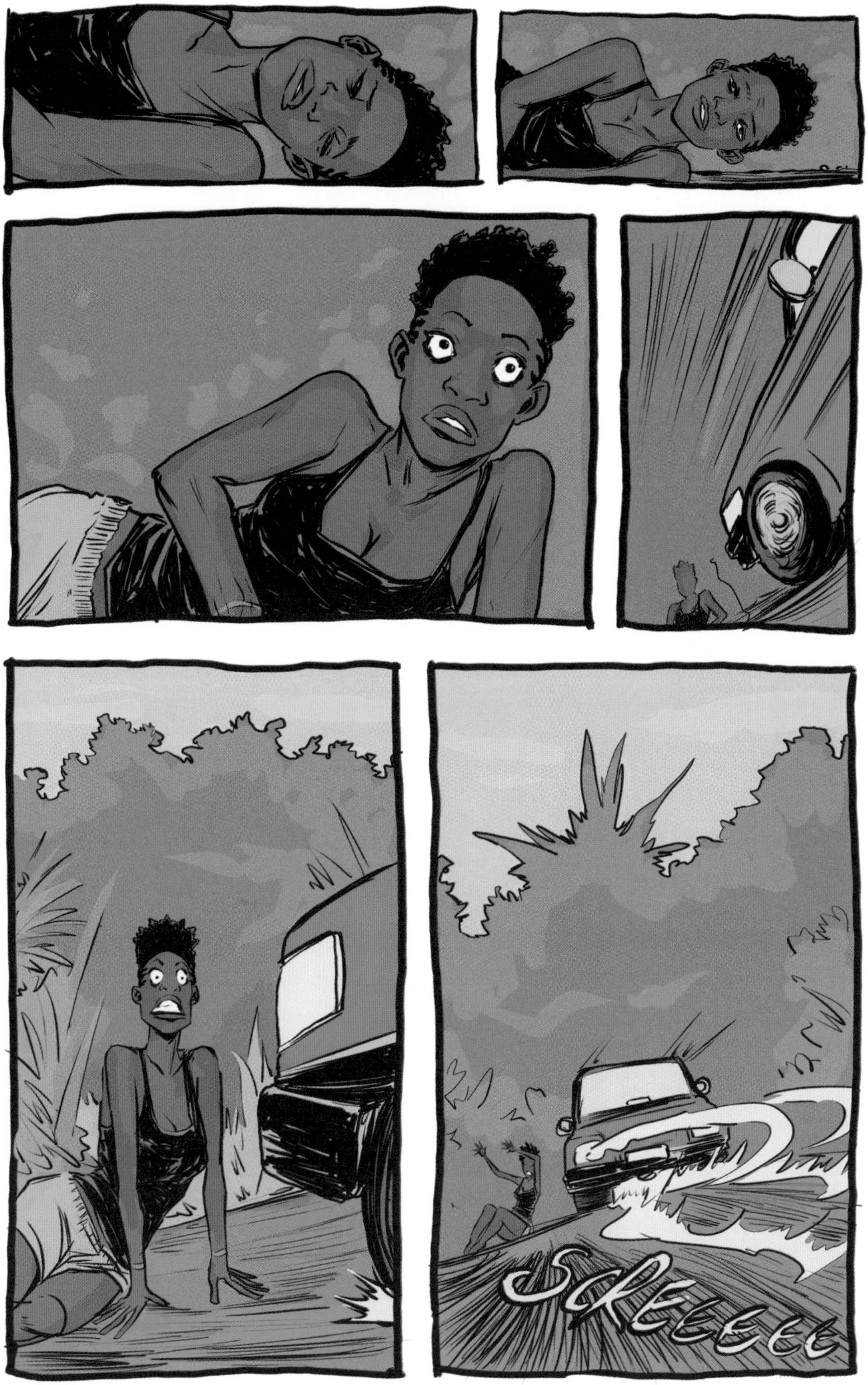
SCREEEEEE

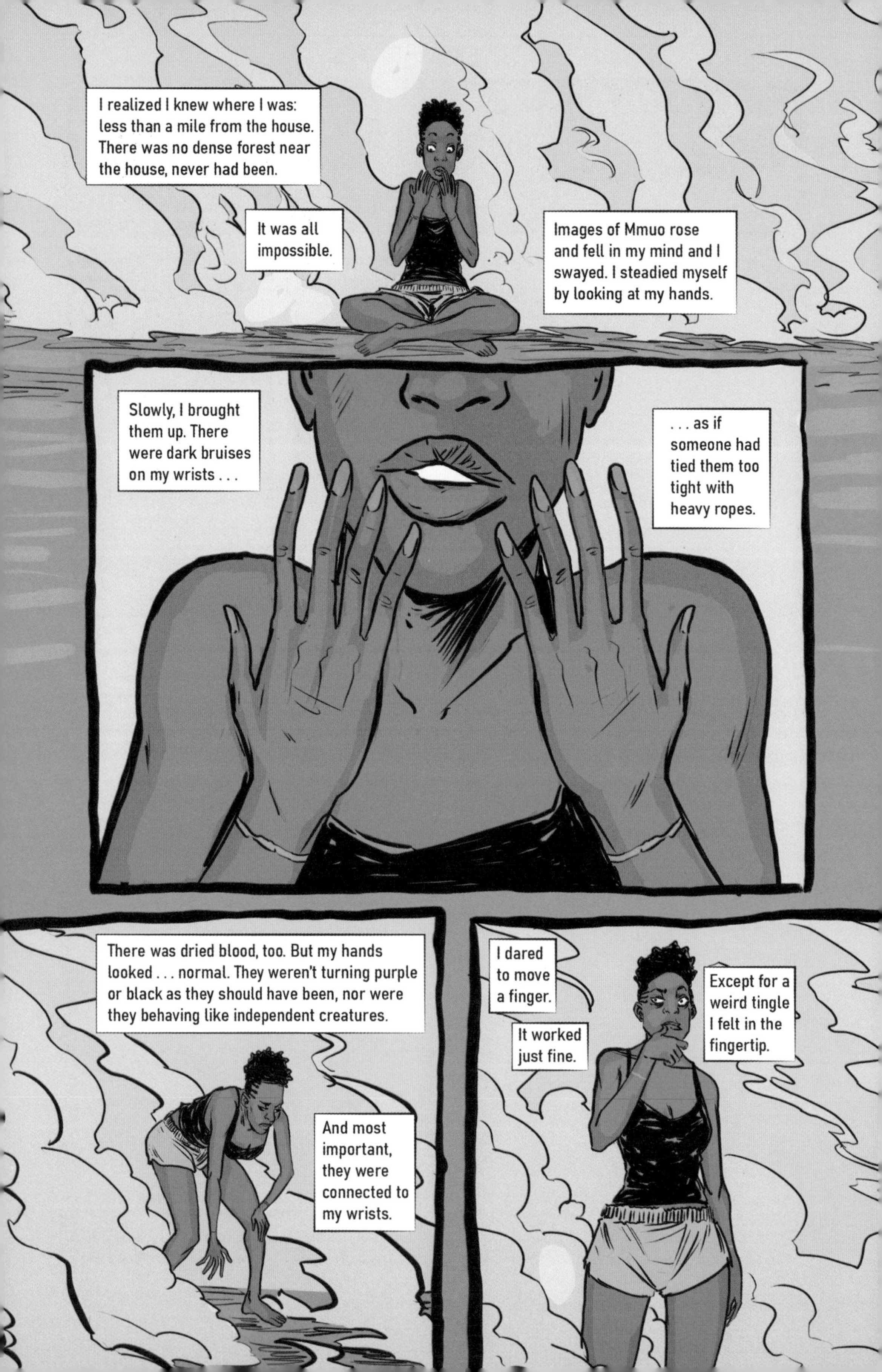
I realized I knew where I was: less than a mile from the house. There was no dense forest near the house, never had been.
It was all impossible.
Images of Mmuo rose and fell in my mind and I swayed. I steadied myself by looking at my hands.
Slowly, I brought them up. There were dark bruises on my wrists . . .
. . . as if someone had tied them too tight with heavy ropes.
There was dried blood, too. But my hands looked . . . normal. They weren't turning purple or black as they should have been, nor were they behaving like independent creatures.
And most important, they were connected to my wrists.
I dared to move a finger.
It worked just fine.
Except for a weird tingle I felt in the fingertip.

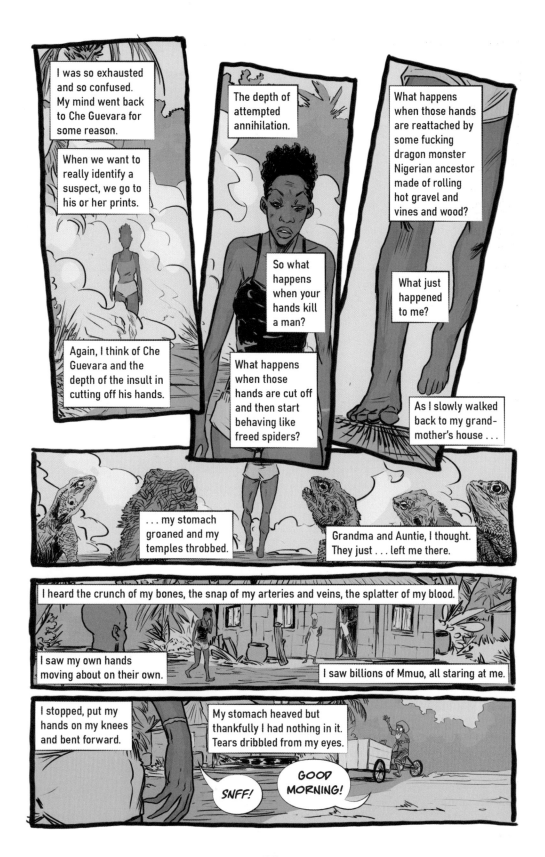

I was so exhausted and so confused. My mind went back to Che Guevara for some reason.

When we want to really identify a suspect, we go to his or her prints.

Again, I think of Che Guevara and the depth of the insult in cutting off his hands.

The depth of attempted annihilation.

So what happens when your hands kill a man?

What happens when those hands are cut off and then start behaving like freed spiders?

What happens when those hands are reattached by some fucking dragon monster Nigerian ancestor made of rolling hot gravel and vines and wood?

What just happened to me?

As I slowly walked back to my grand-mother's house . . .

. . . my stomach groaned and my temples throbbed.

Grandma and Auntie, I thought. They just . . . left me there.

I heard the crunch of my bones, the snap of my arteries and veins, the splatter of my blood.

I saw my own hands moving about on their own.

I saw billions of Mmuo, all staring at me.

I stopped, put my hands on my knees and bent forward.

My stomach heaved but thankfully I had nothing in it. Tears dribbled from my eyes.

SNFF!

GOOD MORNING!

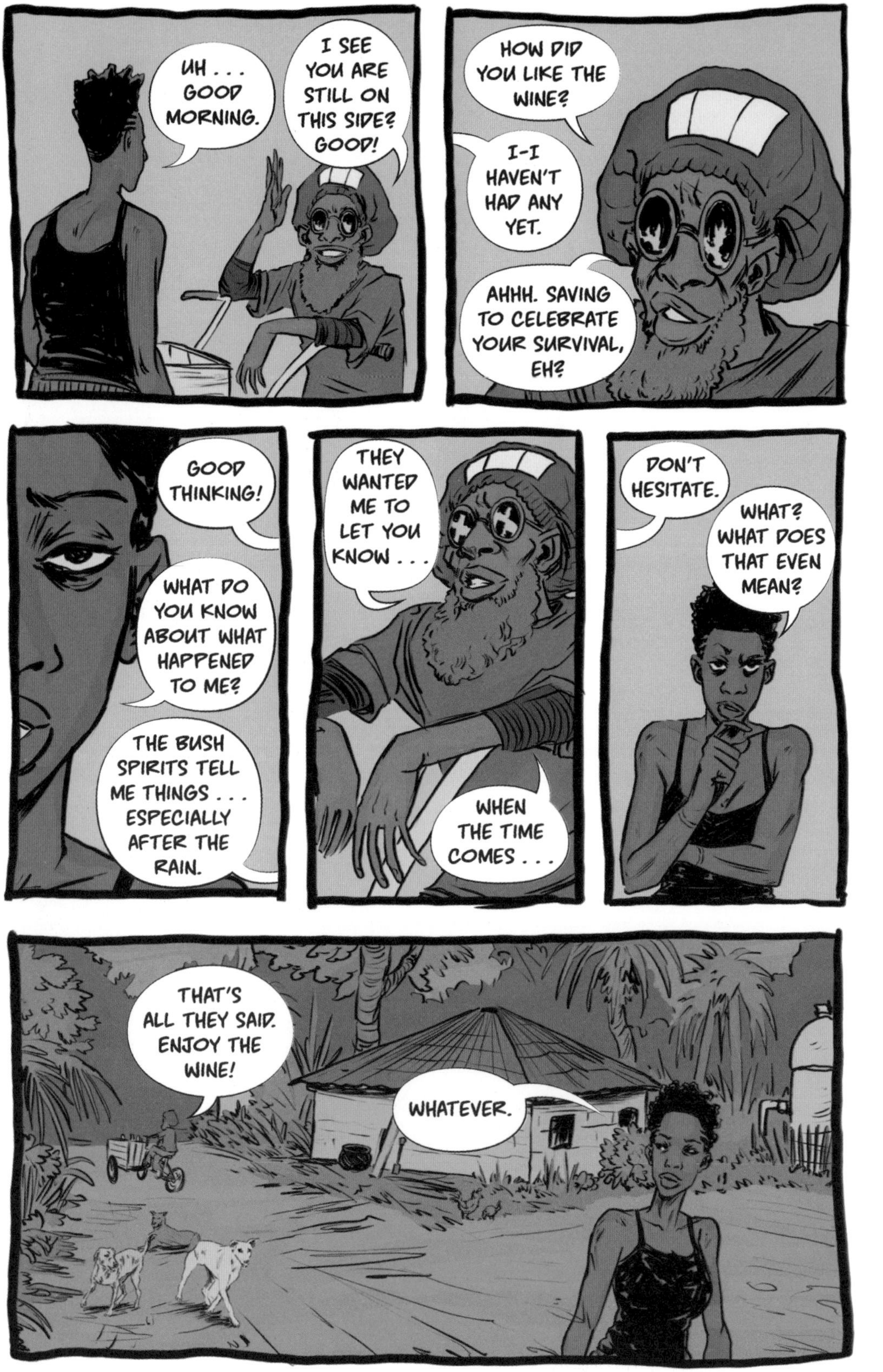
UH . . . GOOD MORNING.
I SEE YOU ARE STILL ON THIS SIDE? GOOD!
HOW DID YOU LIKE THE WINE?
I-I HAVEN'T HAD ANY YET.
AHHH. SAVING TO CELEBRATE YOUR SURVIVAL, EH?
GOOD THINKING!
WHAT DO YOU KNOW ABOUT WHAT HAPPENED TO ME?
THE BUSH SPIRITS TELL ME THINGS . . . ESPECIALLY AFTER THE RAIN.
THEY WANTED ME TO LET YOU KNOW . . .
WHEN THE TIME COMES . . .
DON'T HESITATE.
WHAT? WHAT DOES THAT EVEN MEAN?
THAT'S ALL THEY SAID. ENJOY THE WINE!
WHATEVER.

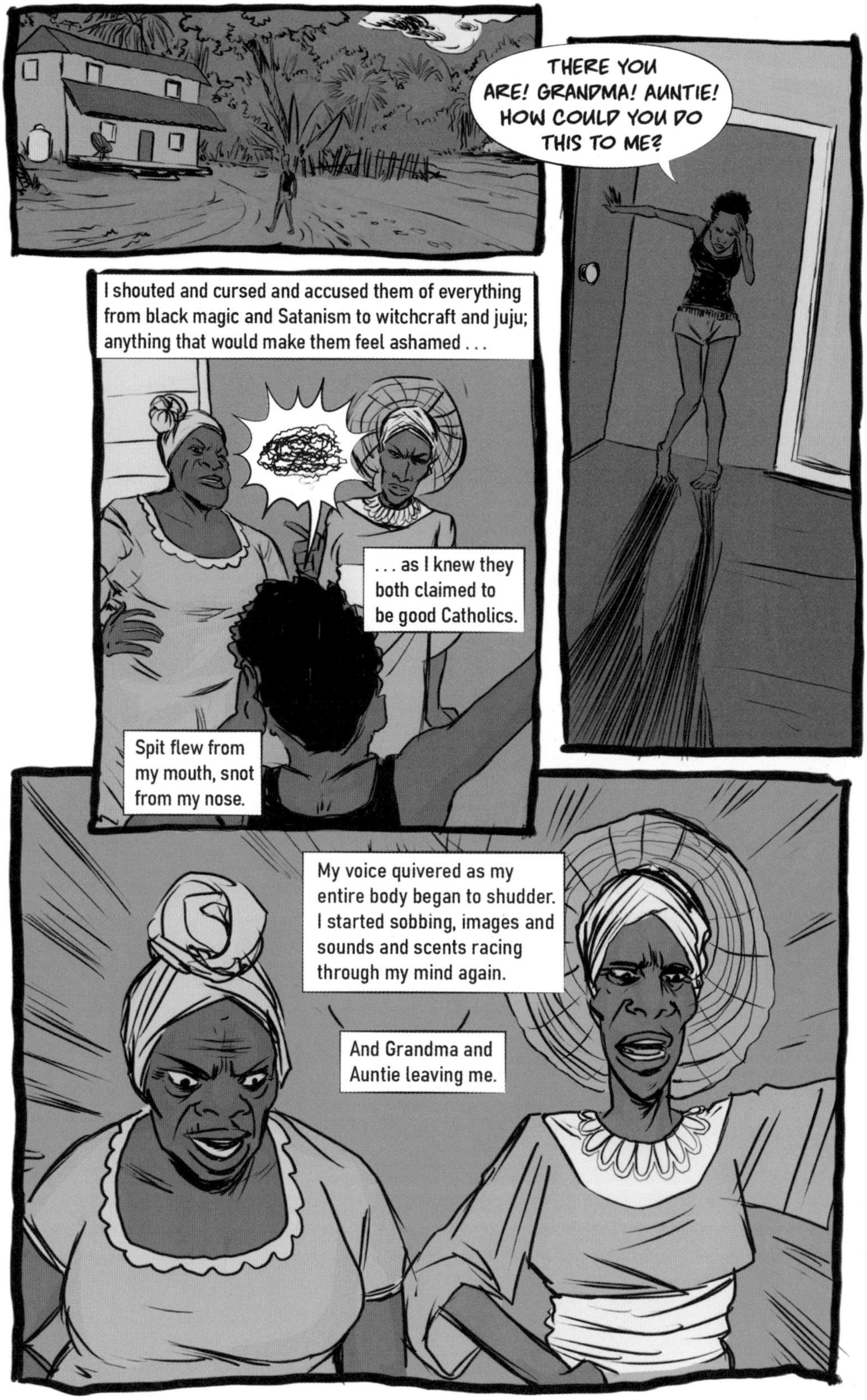
THERE YOU ARE! GRANDMA! AUNTIE! HOW COULD YOU DO THIS TO ME?
I shouted and cursed and accused them of everything from black magic and Satanism to witchcraft and juju; anything that would make them feel ashamed . . .
. . . as I knew they both claimed to be good Catholics.
Spit flew from my mouth, snot from my nose.
My voice quivered as my entire body began to shudder. I started sobbing, images and sounds and scents racing through my mind again.
And Grandma and Auntie leaving me.

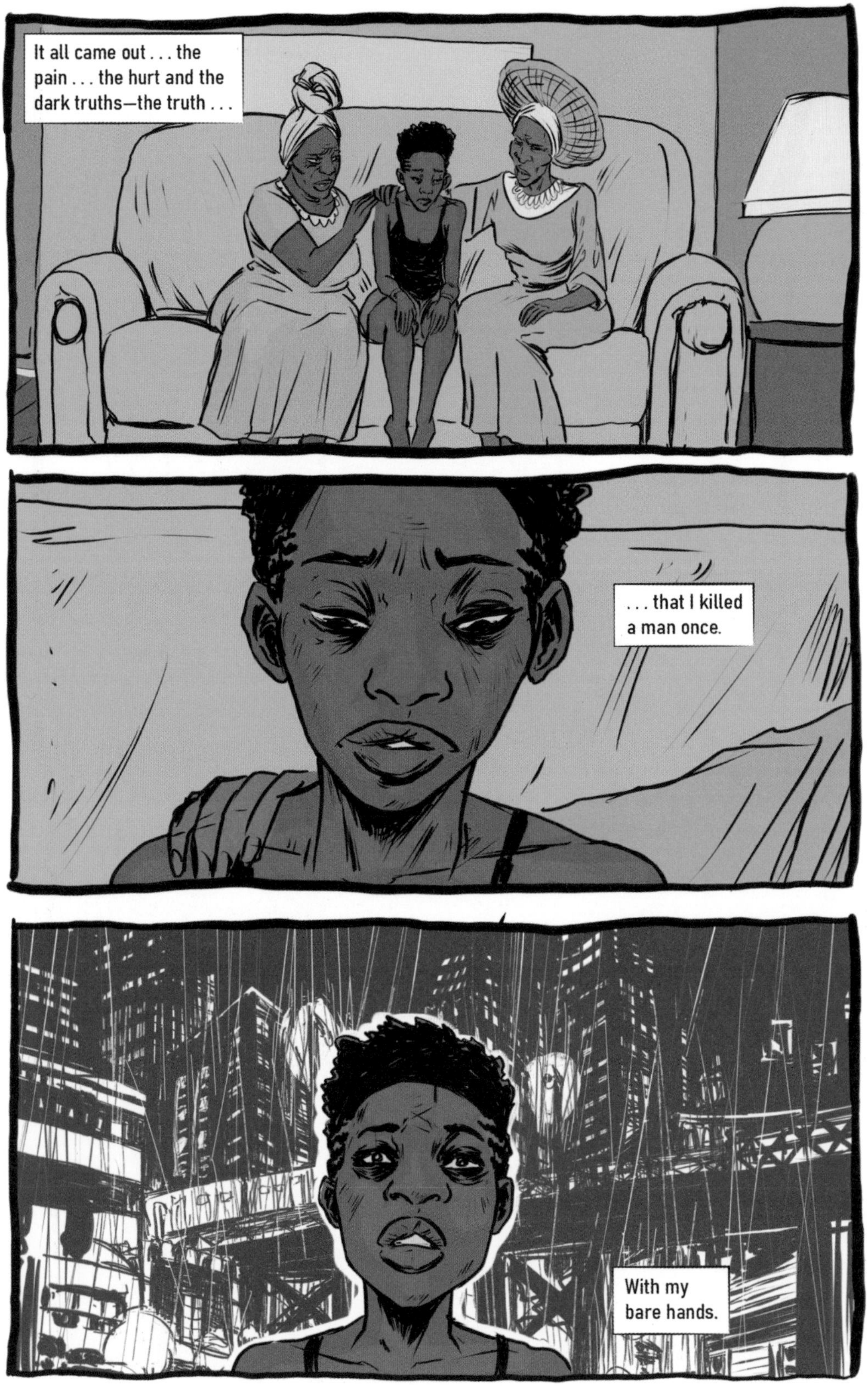
It all came out . . . the pain . . . the hurt and the dark truths—the truth . . .
. . . that I killed a man once.
With my bare hands.

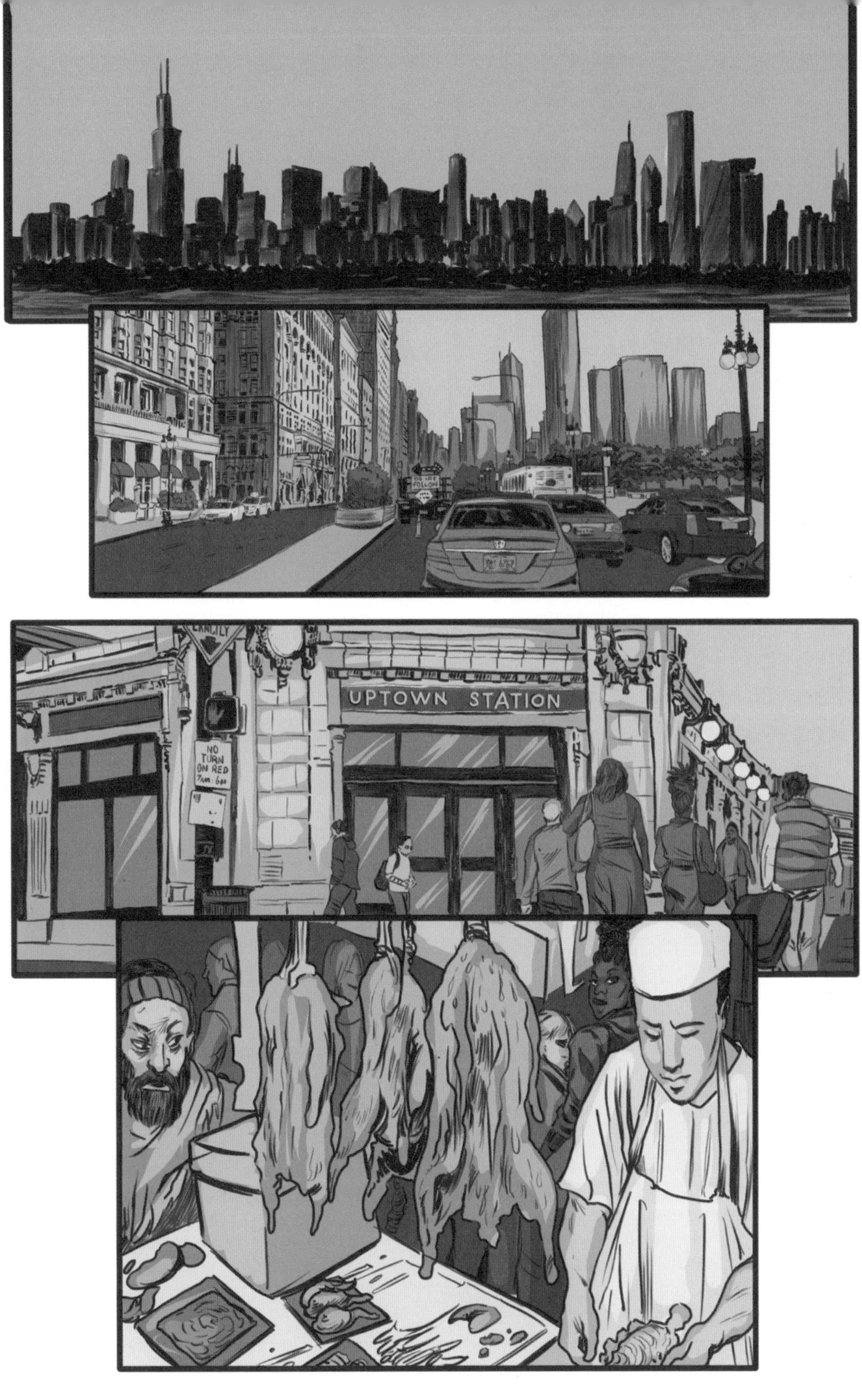
UPTOWN STATION
NO TURN ON RED

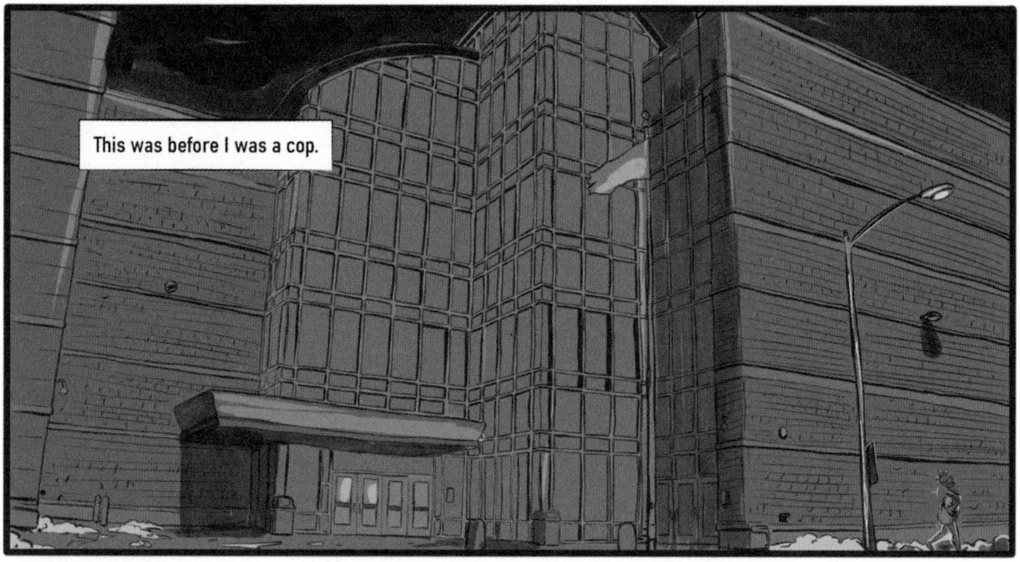
This was before I was a cop.

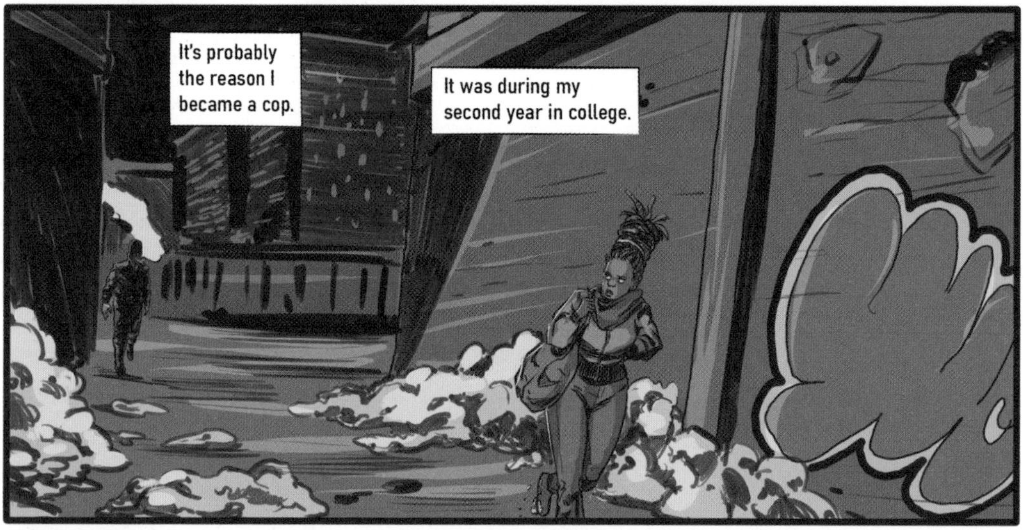
It's probably the reason I became a cop.
It was during my second year in college.

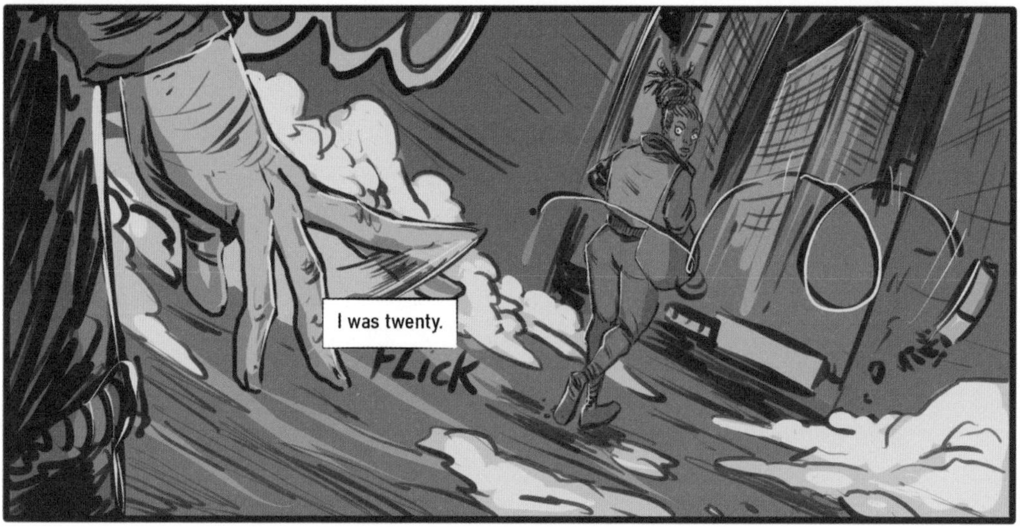
I was twenty.
FLICK

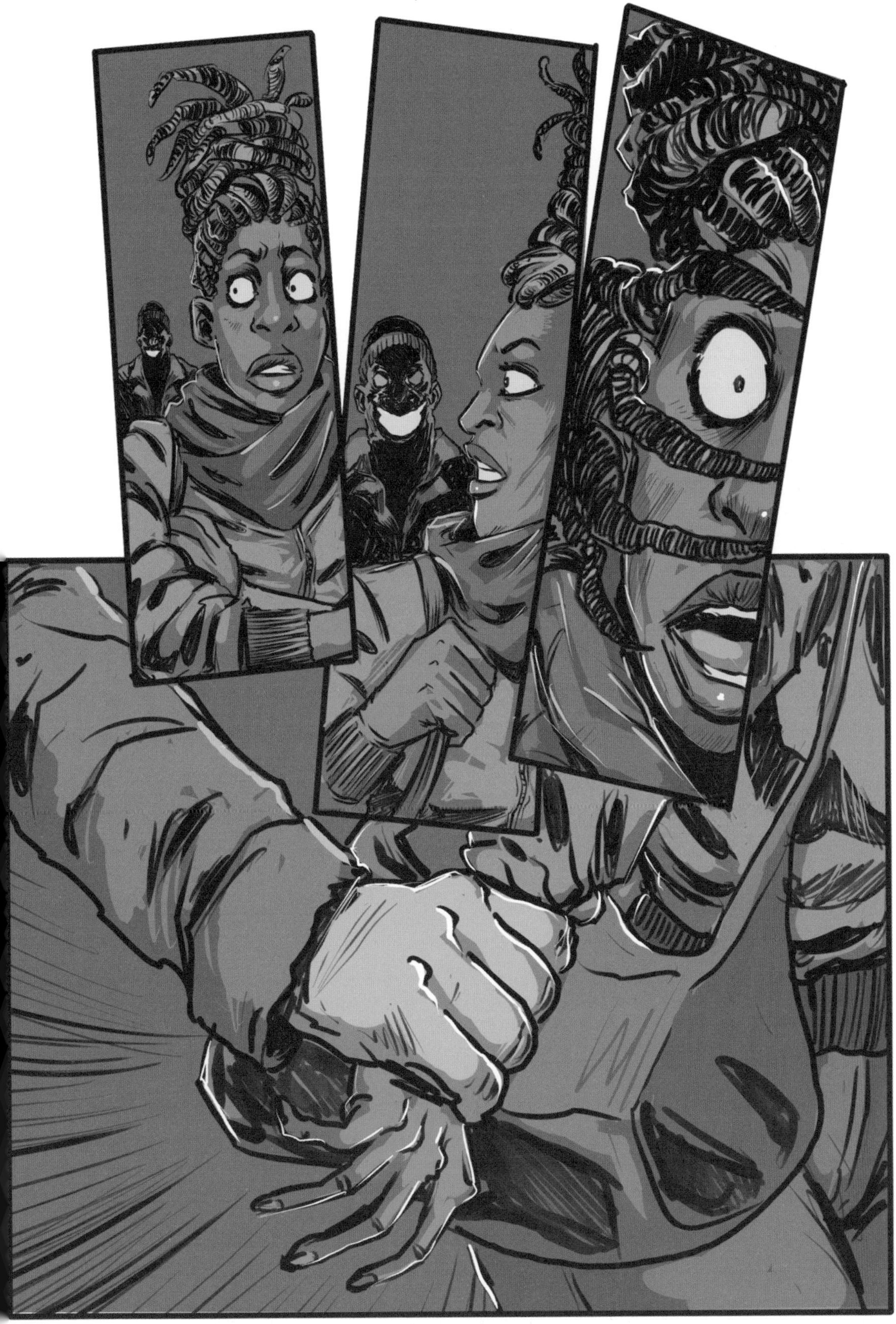

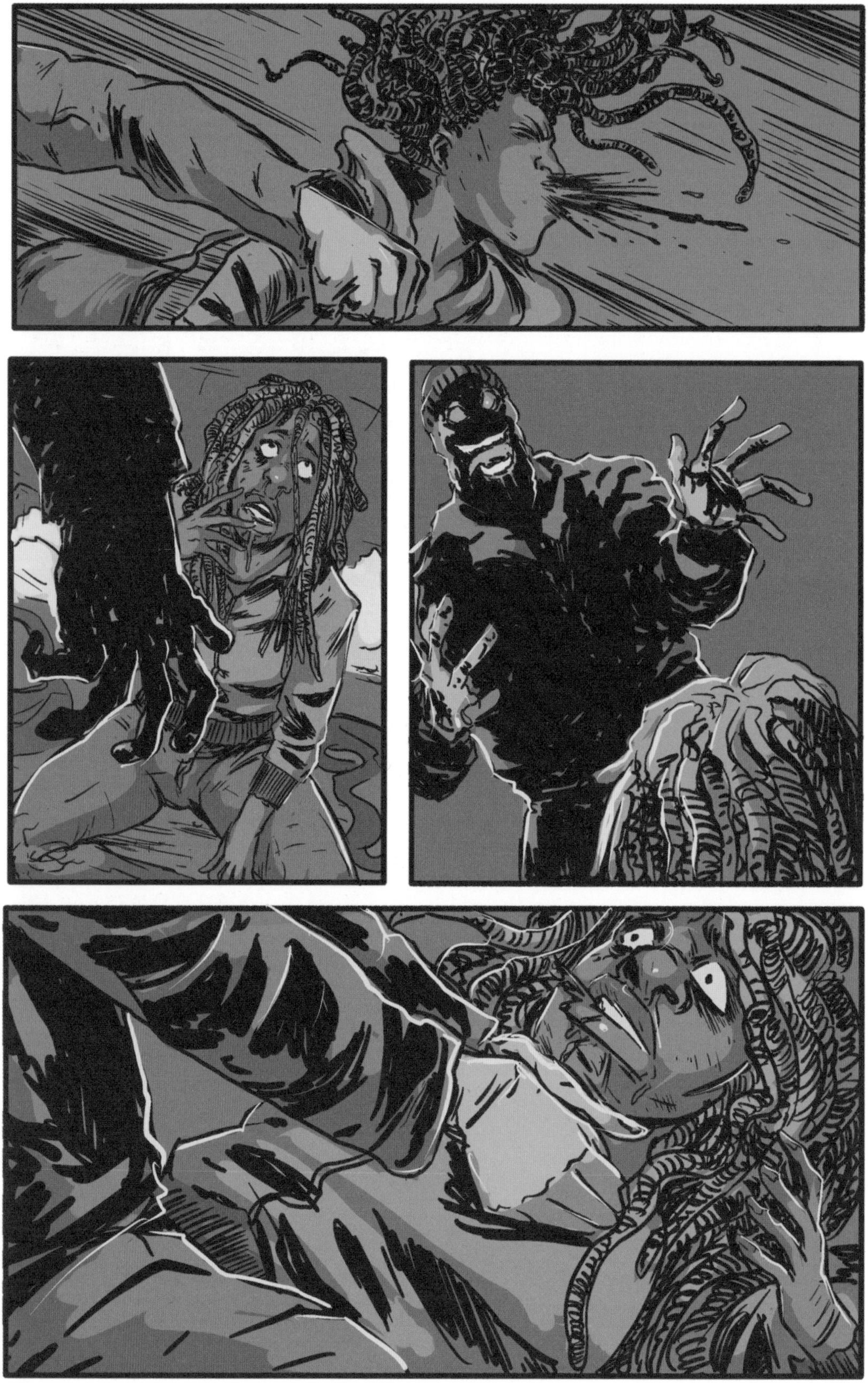

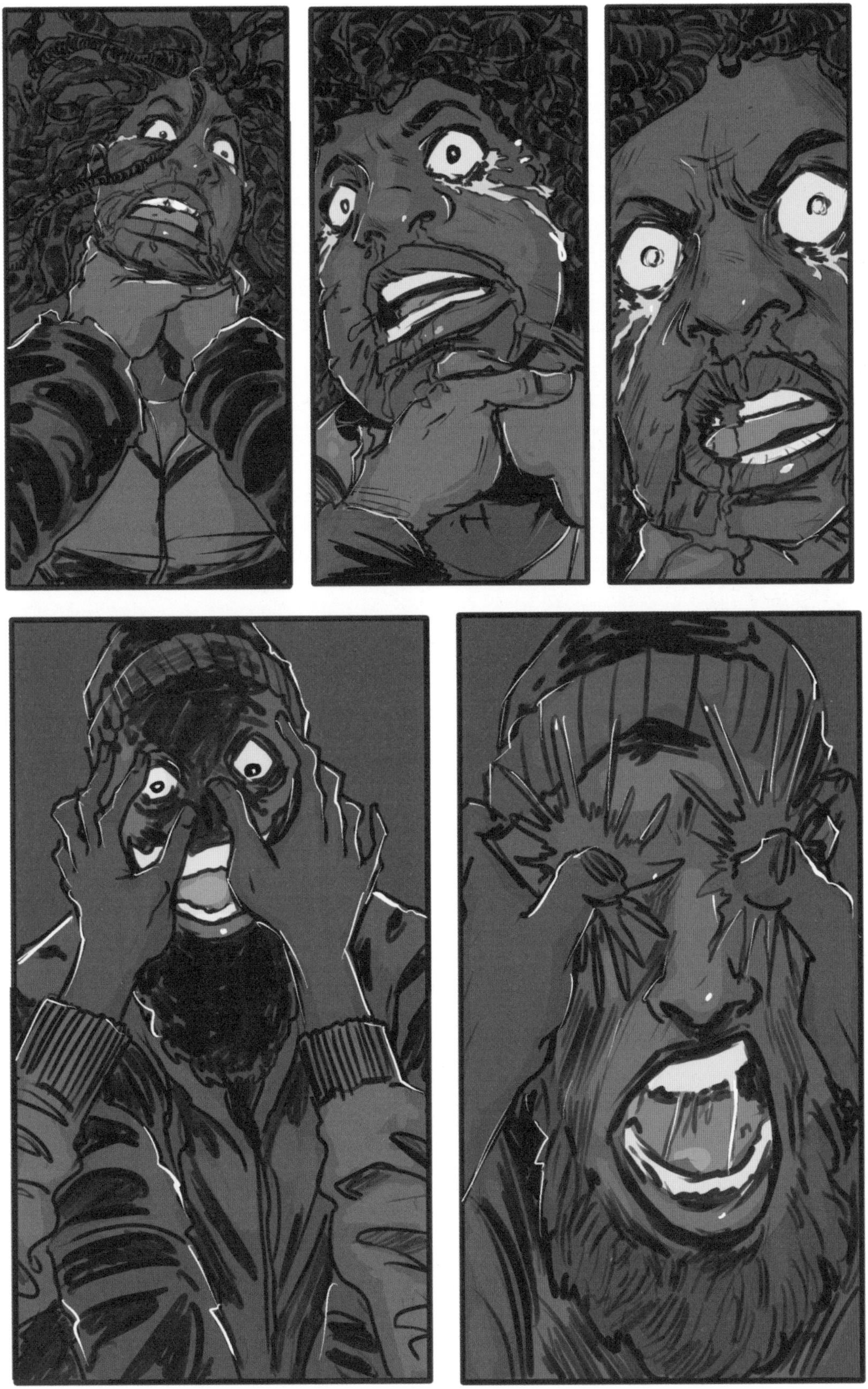

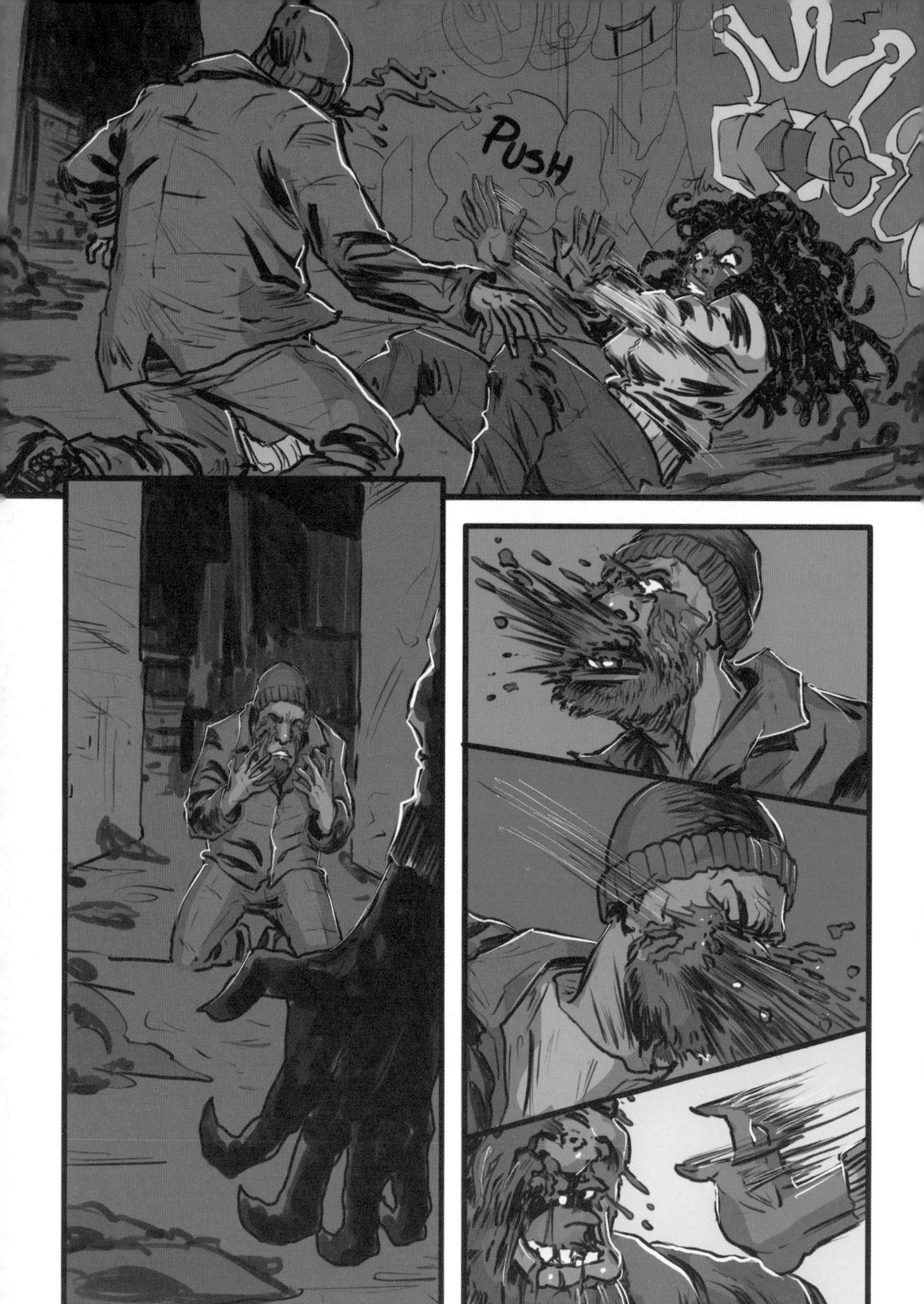
PUSH

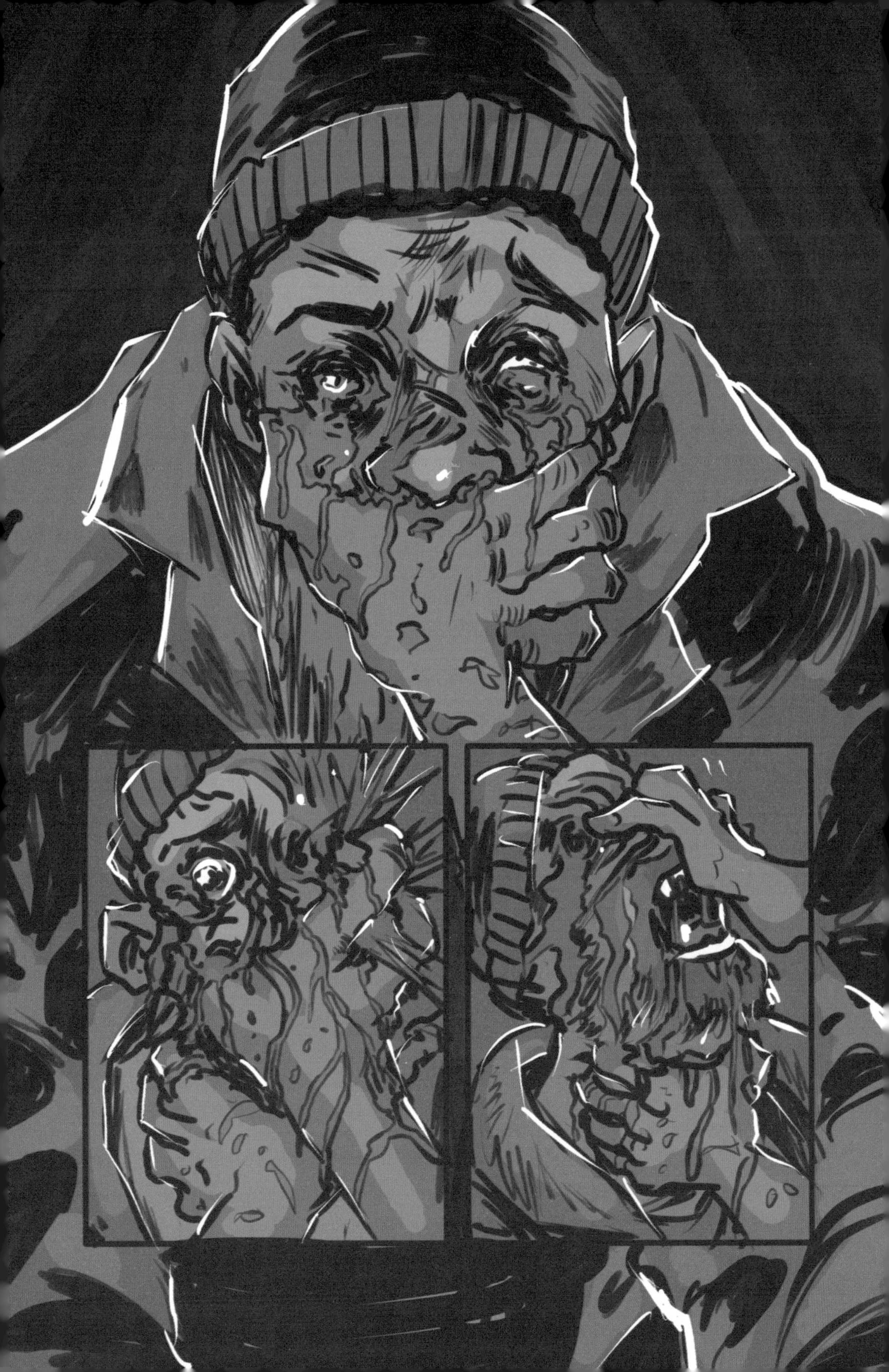

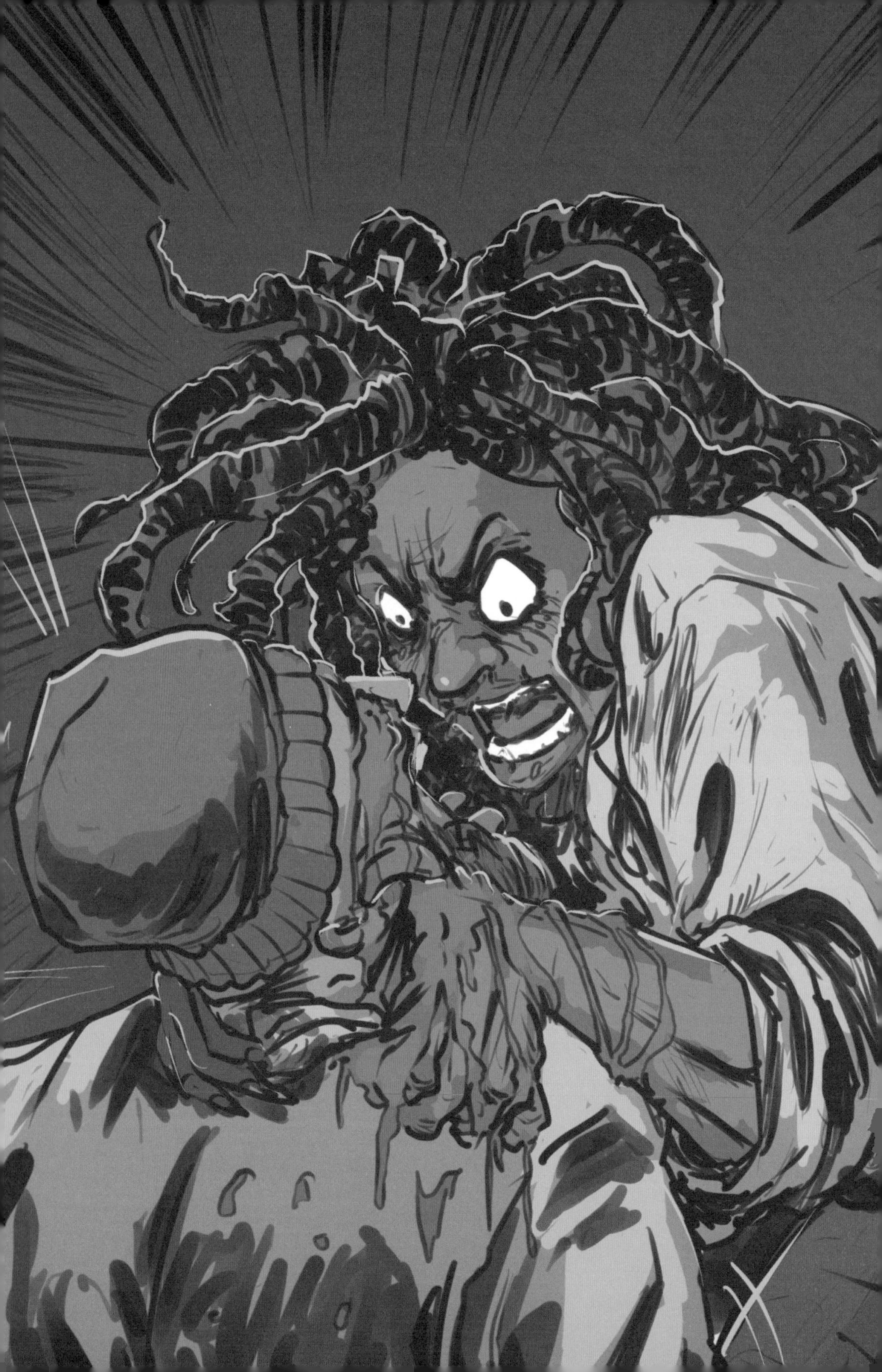

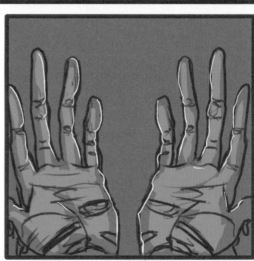

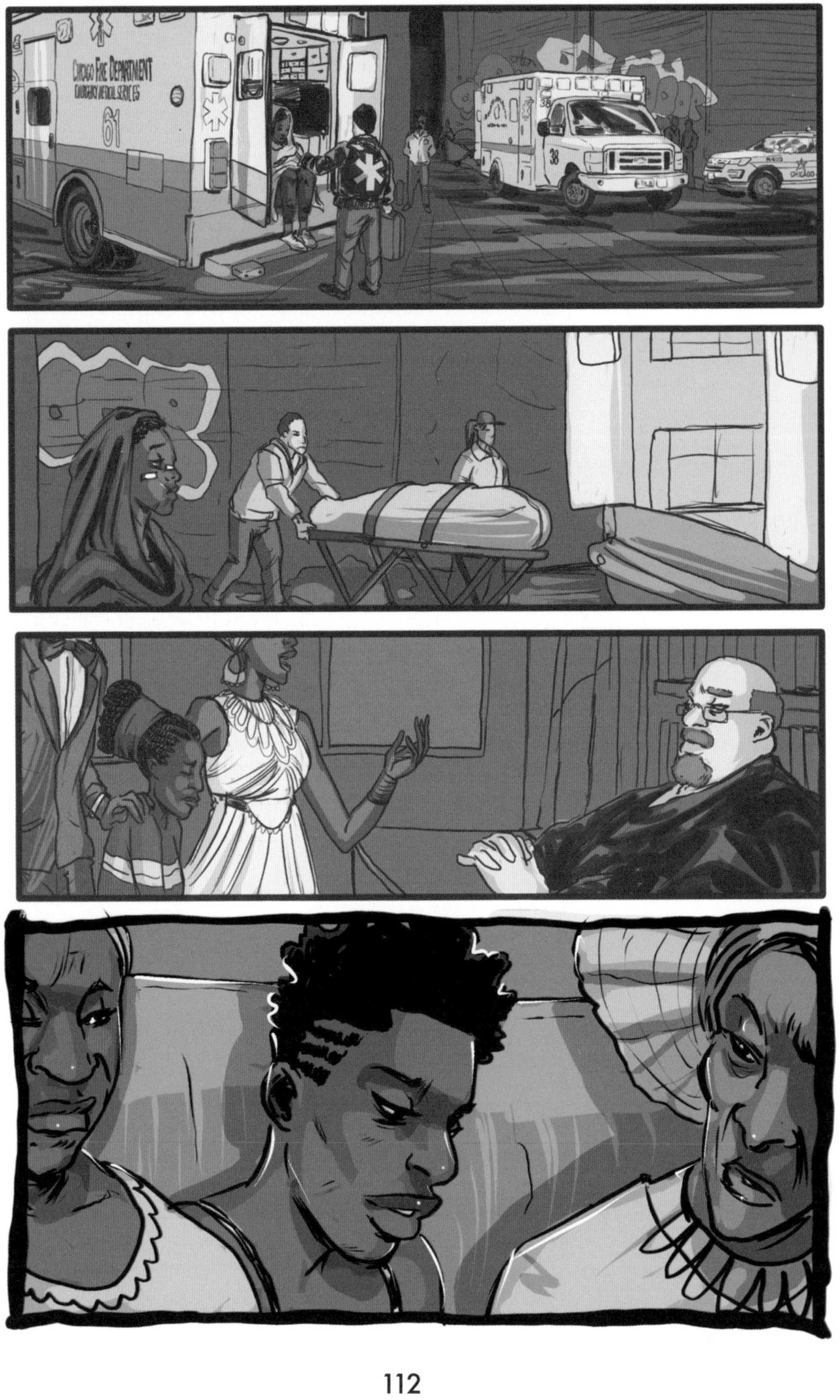
Chicago Fire Department
61
38

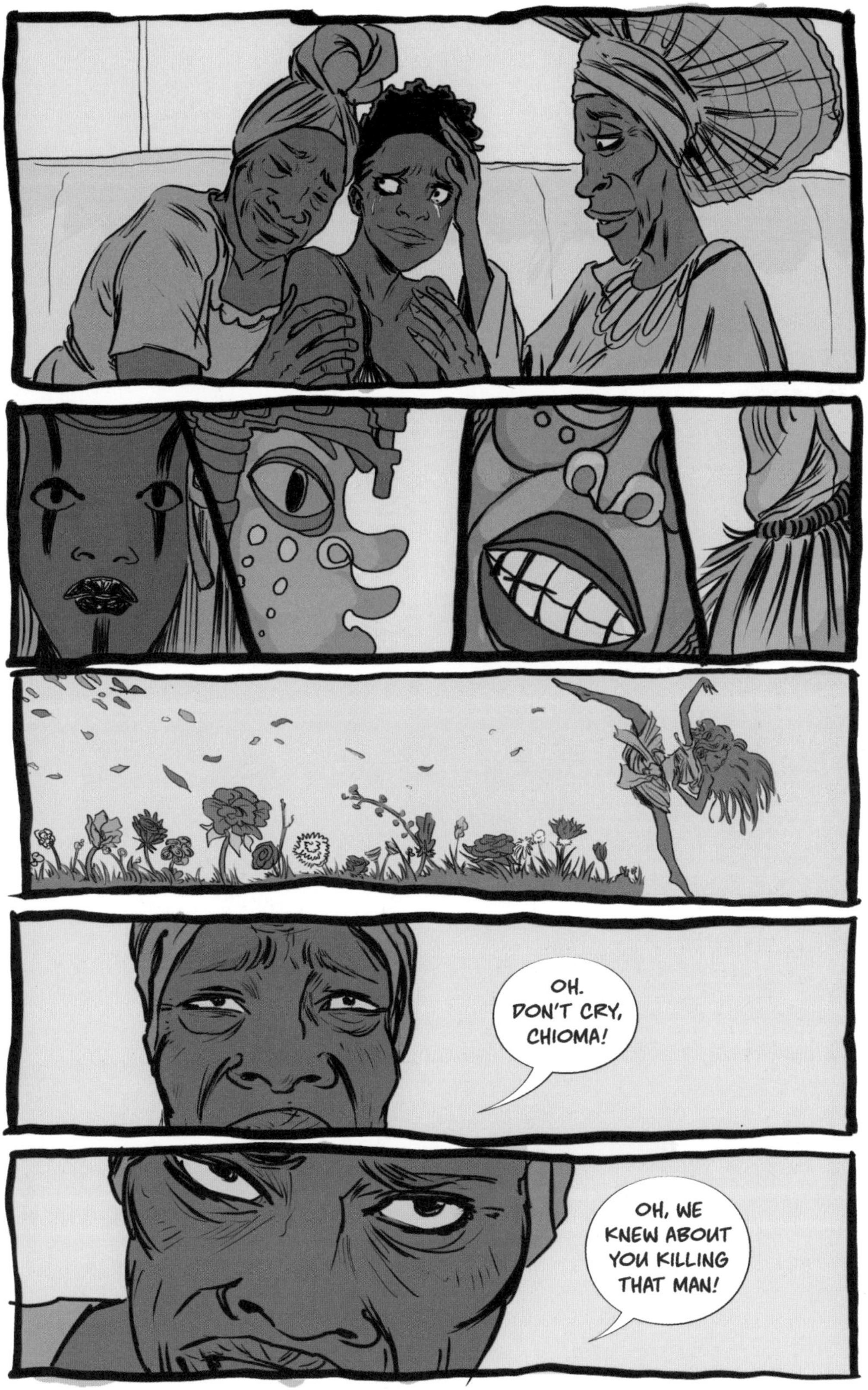
OH.
DON'T CRY,
CHIOMA!
OH, WE
KNEW ABOUT
YOU KILLING
THAT MAN!

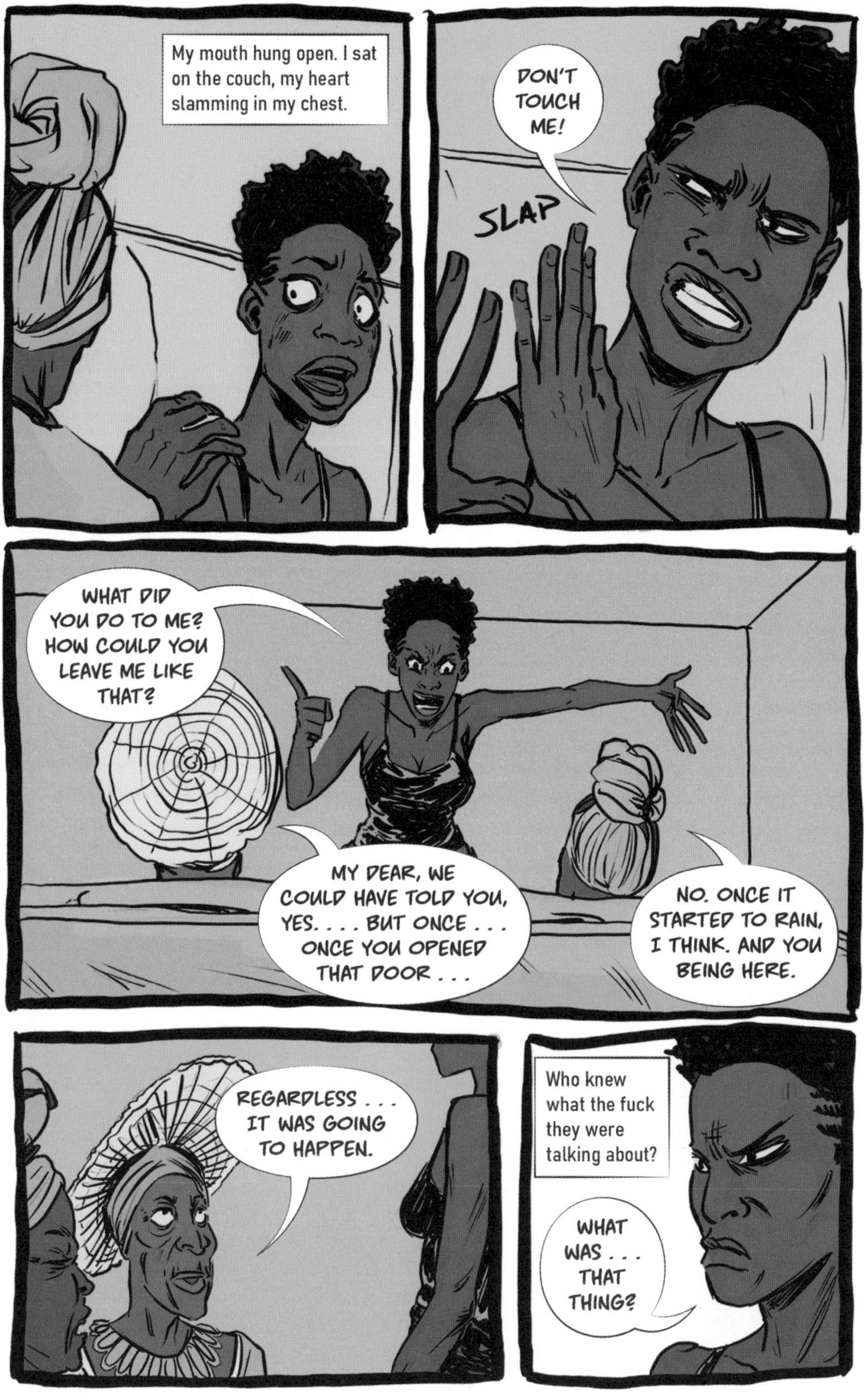
My mouth hung open. I sat on the couch, my heart slamming in my chest.
DON'T TOUCH ME!
SLAP
WHAT DID YOU DO TO ME? HOW COULD YOU LEAVE ME LIKE THAT?
MY DEAR, WE COULD HAVE TOLD YOU, YES. . . . BUT ONCE . . . ONCE YOU OPENED THAT DOOR . . .
NO. ONCE IT STARTED TO RAIN, I THINK. AND YOU BEING HERE.
REGARDLESS . . . IT WAS GOING TO HAPPEN.
Who knew what the fuck they were talking about?
WHAT WAS . . . THAT THING?

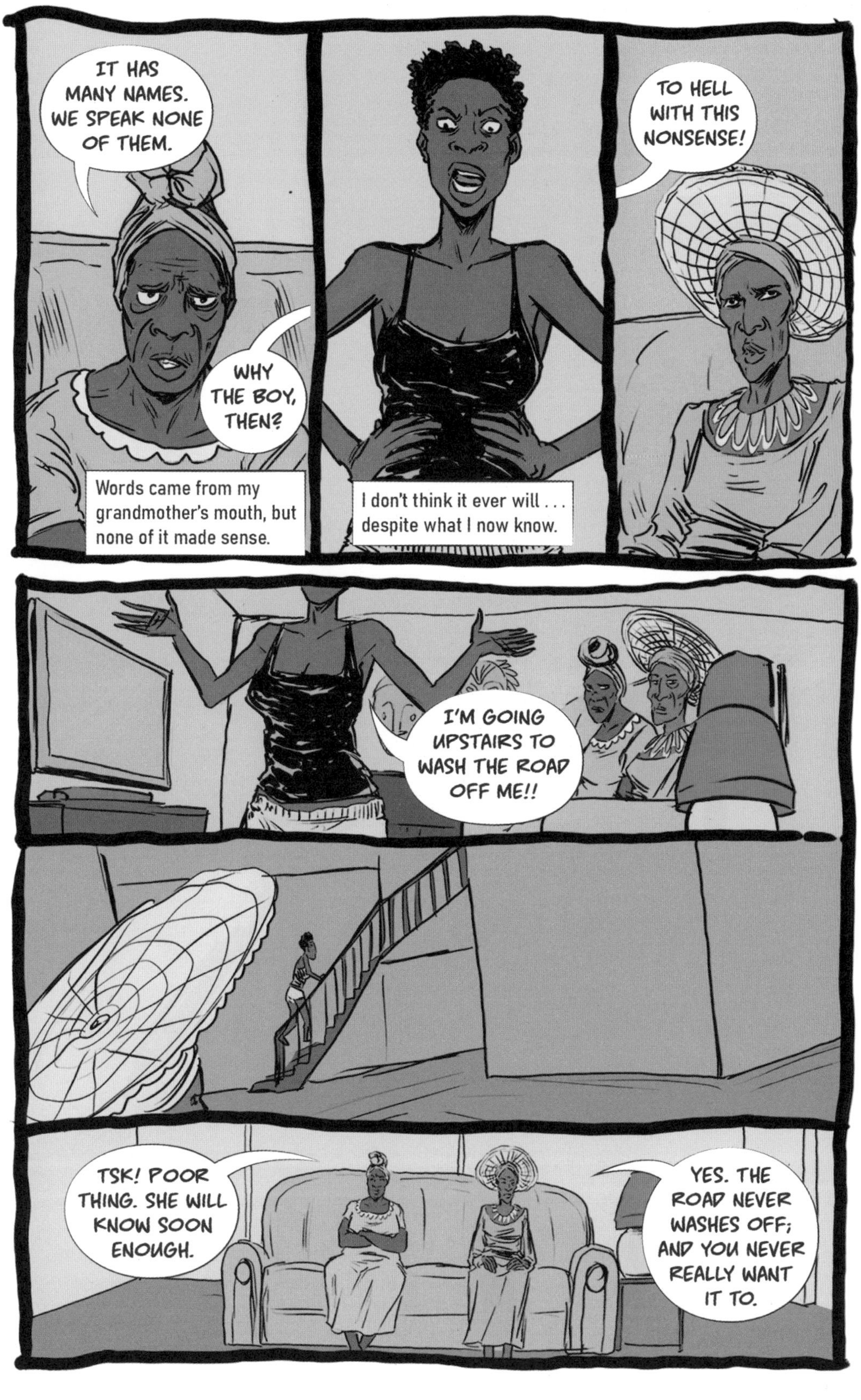
IT HAS MANY NAMES. WE SPEAK NONE OF THEM.
WHY THE BOY, THEN?
Words came from my grandmother's mouth, but none of it made sense.
I don't think it ever will . . . despite what I now know.
TO HELL WITH THIS NONSENSE!
I'M GOING UPSTAIRS TO WASH THE ROAD OFF ME!!
TSK! POOR THING. SHE WILL KNOW SOON ENOUGH.
YES. THE ROAD NEVER WASHES OFF; AND YOU NEVER REALLY WANT IT TO.

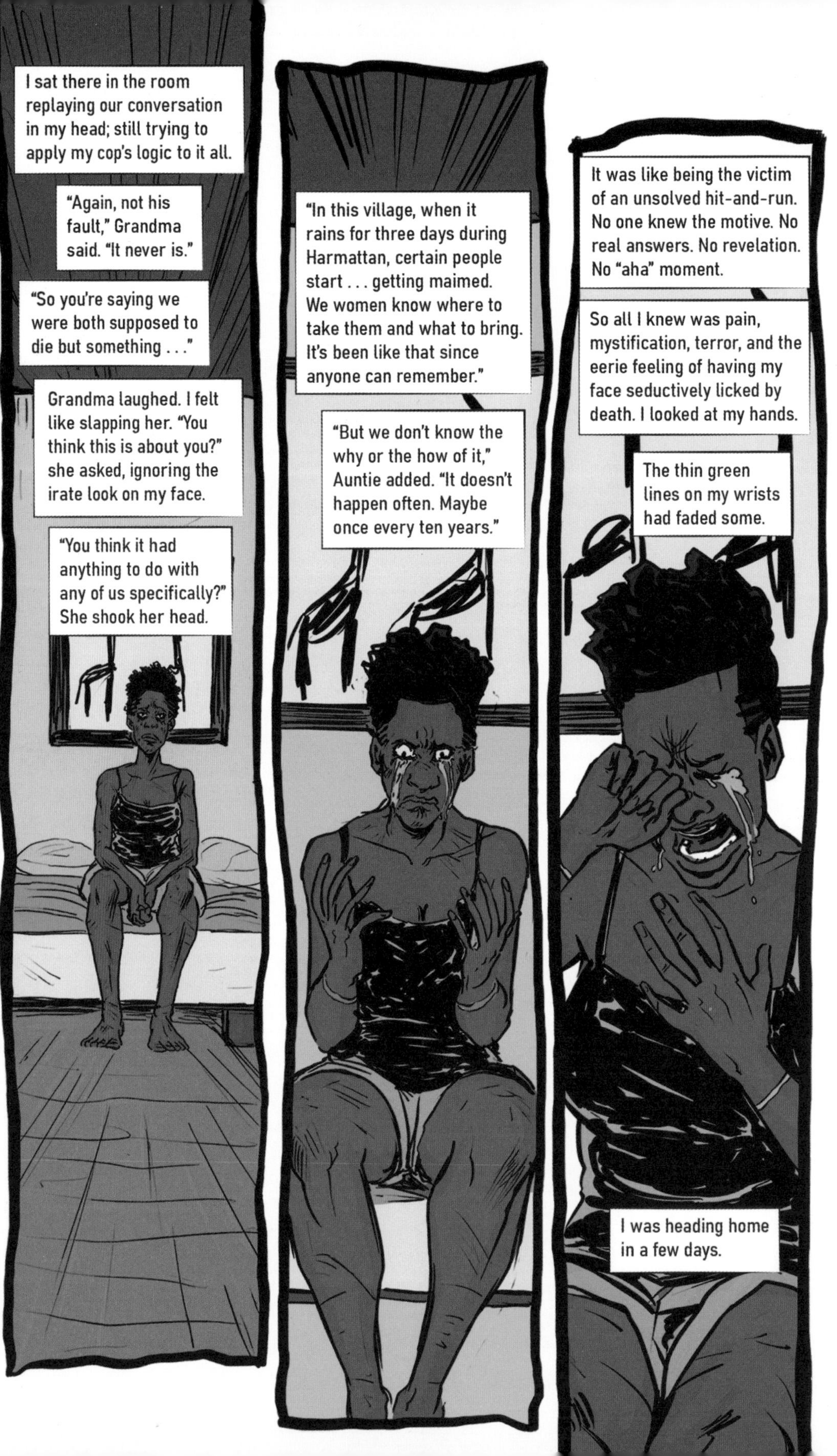
I sat there in the room replaying our conversation in my head; still trying to apply my cop's logic to it all.
"Again, not his fault," Grandma said. "It never is."
"So you're saying we were both supposed to die but something . . ."
Grandma laughed. I felt like slapping her. "You think this is about you?" she asked, ignoring the irate look on my face.
"You think it had anything to do with any of us specifically?" She shook her head.
"In this village, when it rains for three days during Harmattan, certain people start . . . getting maimed. We women know where to take them and what to bring. It's been like that since anyone can remember."
"But we don't know the why or the how of it," Auntie added. "It doesn't happen often. Maybe once every ten years."
It was like being the victim of an unsolved hit-and-run. No one knew the motive. No real answers. No revelation. No "aha" moment.
So all I knew was pain, mystification, terror, and the eerie feeling of having my face seductively licked by death. I looked at my hands.
The thin green lines on my wrists had faded some.
I was heading home in a few days.

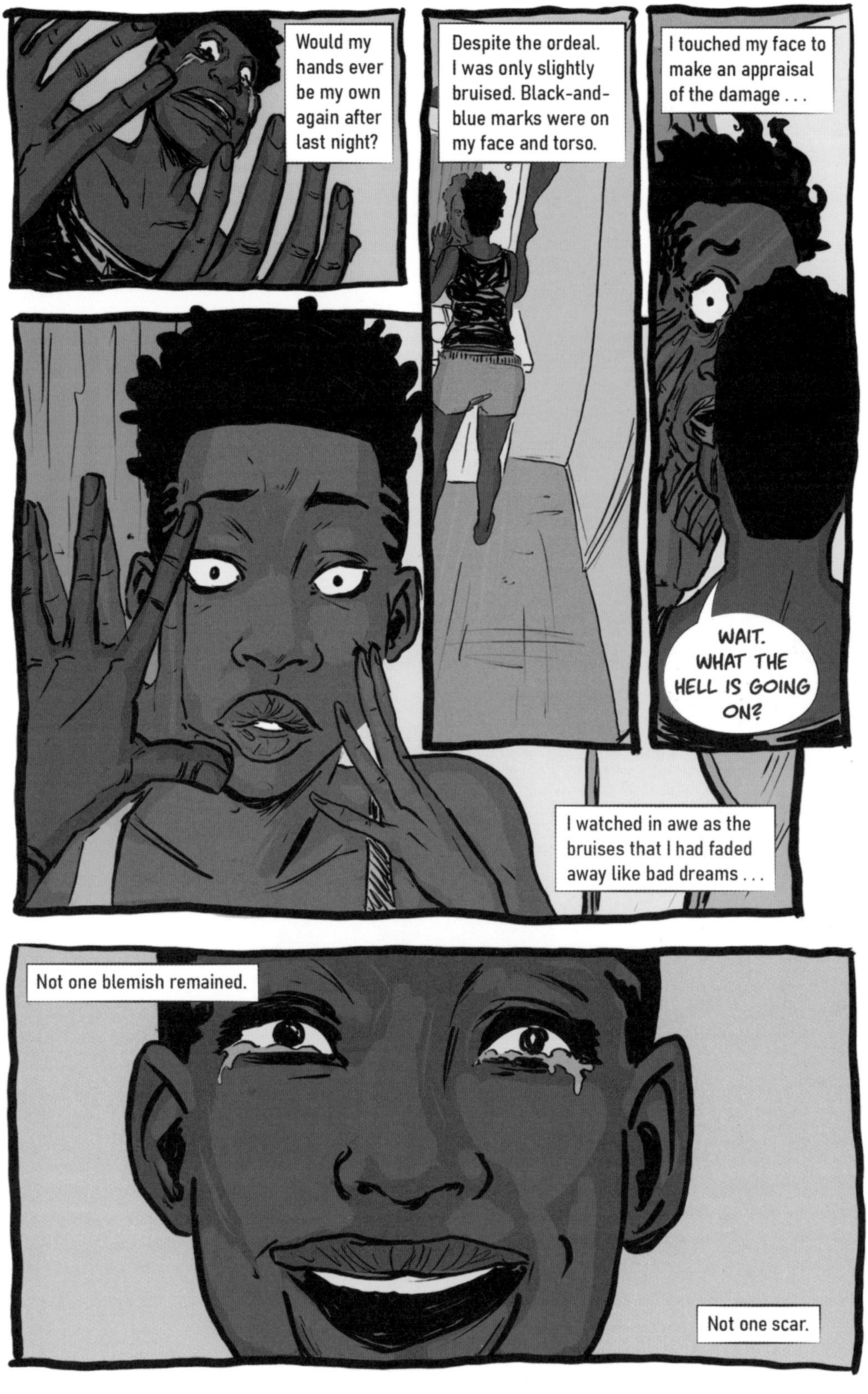
Would my hands ever be my own again after last night?
Despite the ordeal. I was only slightly bruised. Black-and-blue marks were on my face and torso.
I touched my face to make an appraisal of the damage . . .
WAIT. WHAT THE HELL IS GOING ON?
I watched in awe as the bruises that I had faded away like bad dreams . . .
Not one blemish remained.
Not one scar.

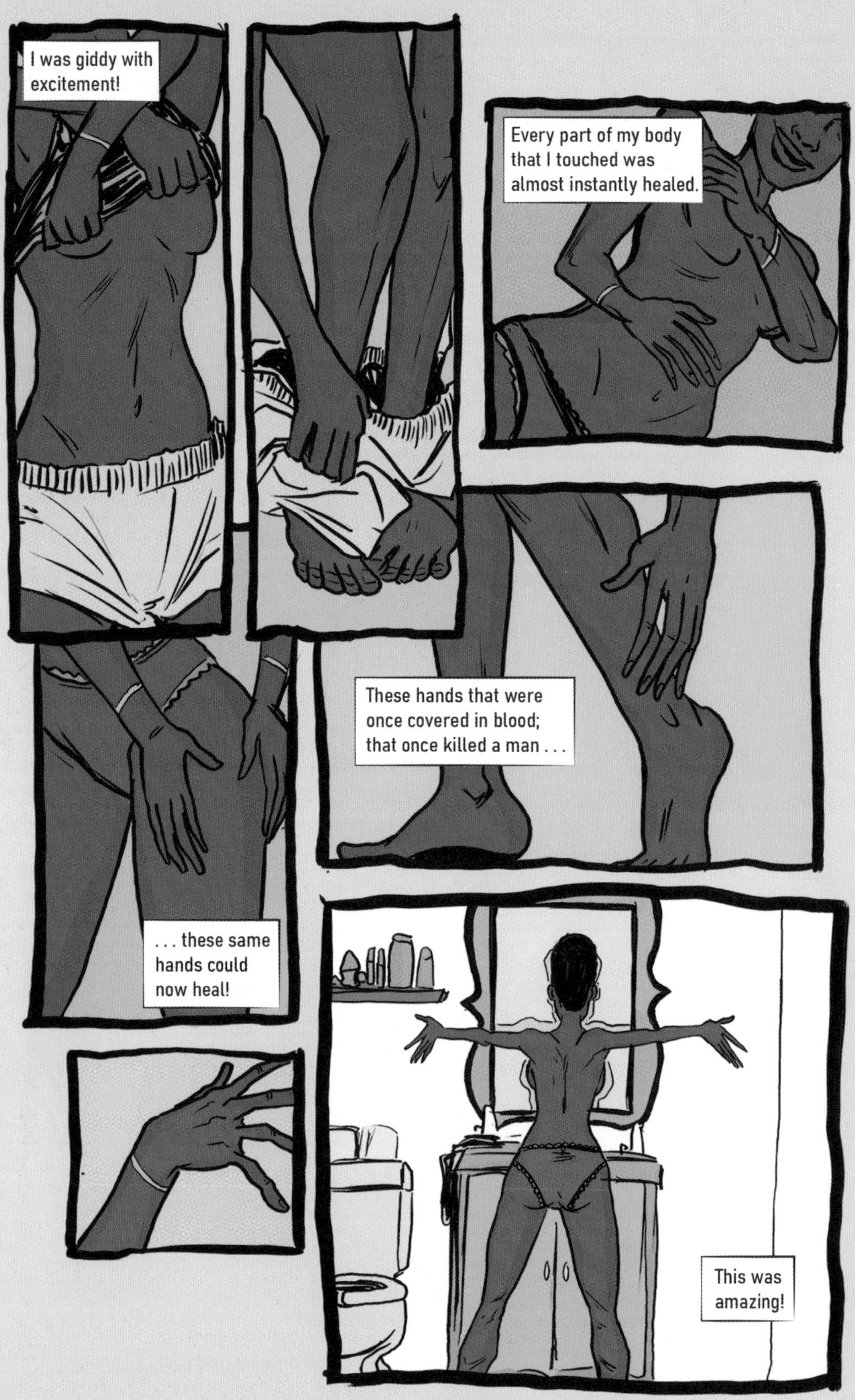
I was giddy with excitement!
Every part of my body that I touched was almost instantly healed.
These hands that were once covered in blood; that once killed a man . . .
. . . these same hands could now heal!
This was amazing!

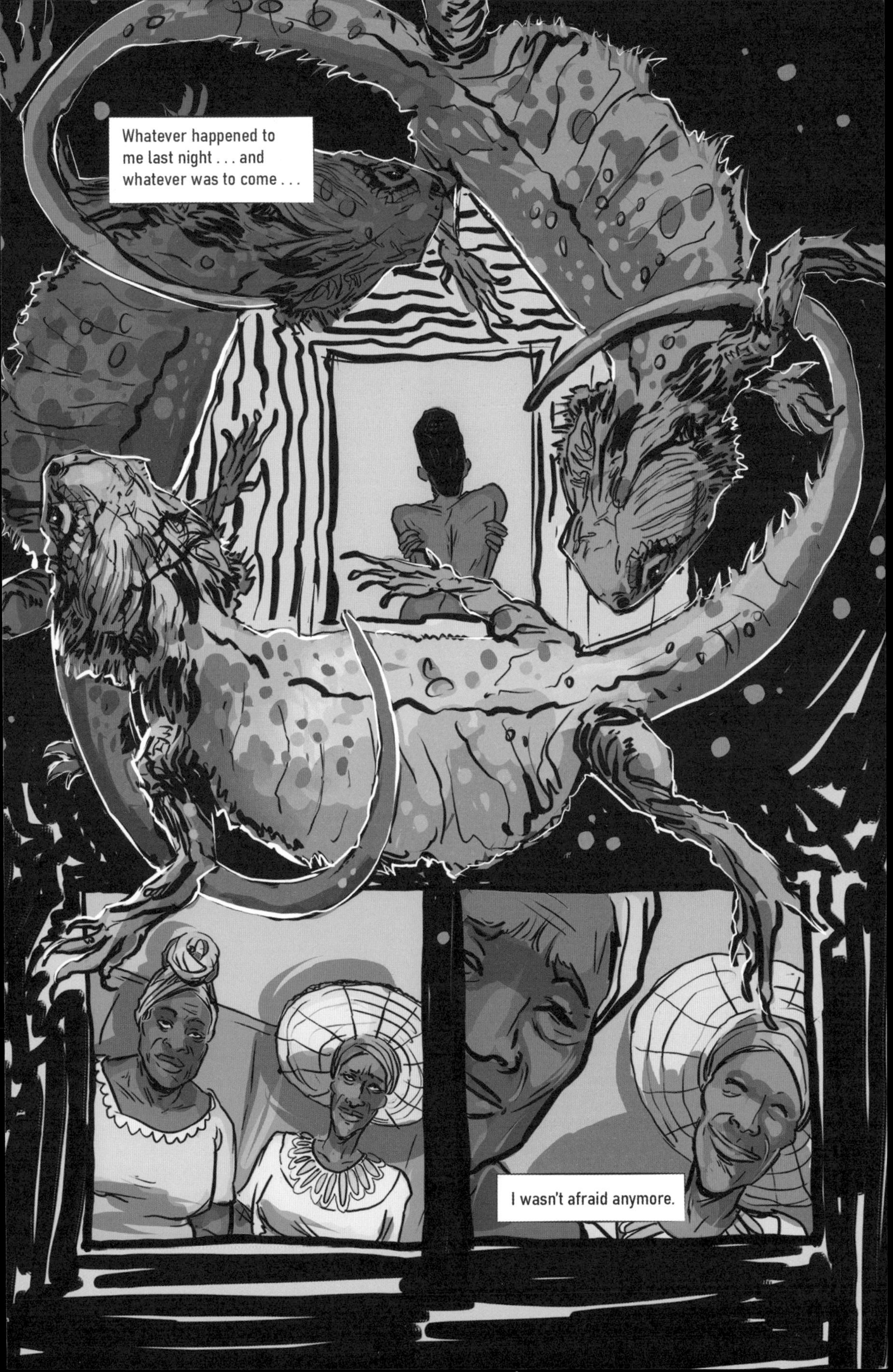
Whatever happened to me last night . . . and whatever was to come . . .
I wasn't afraid anymore.

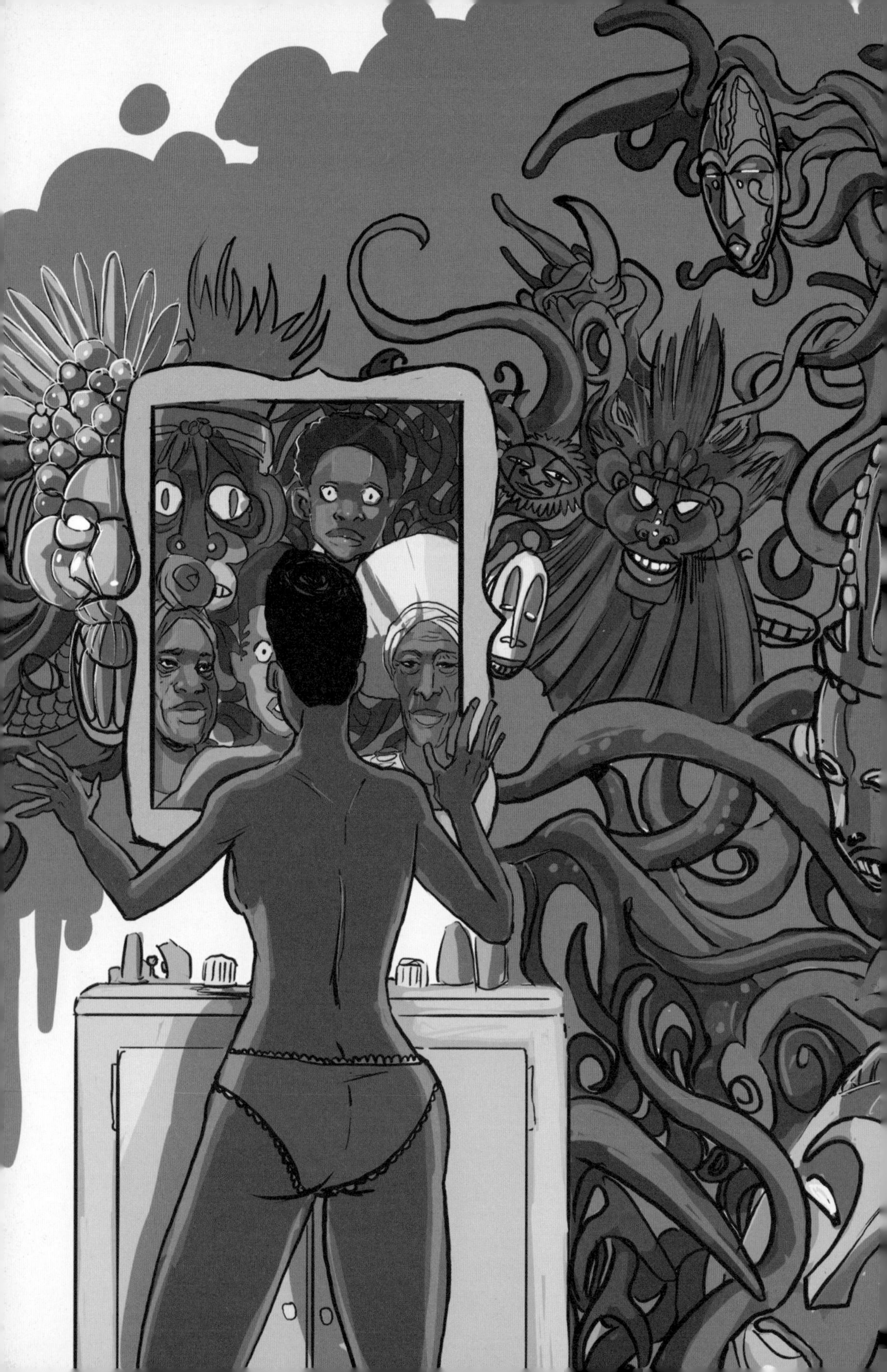

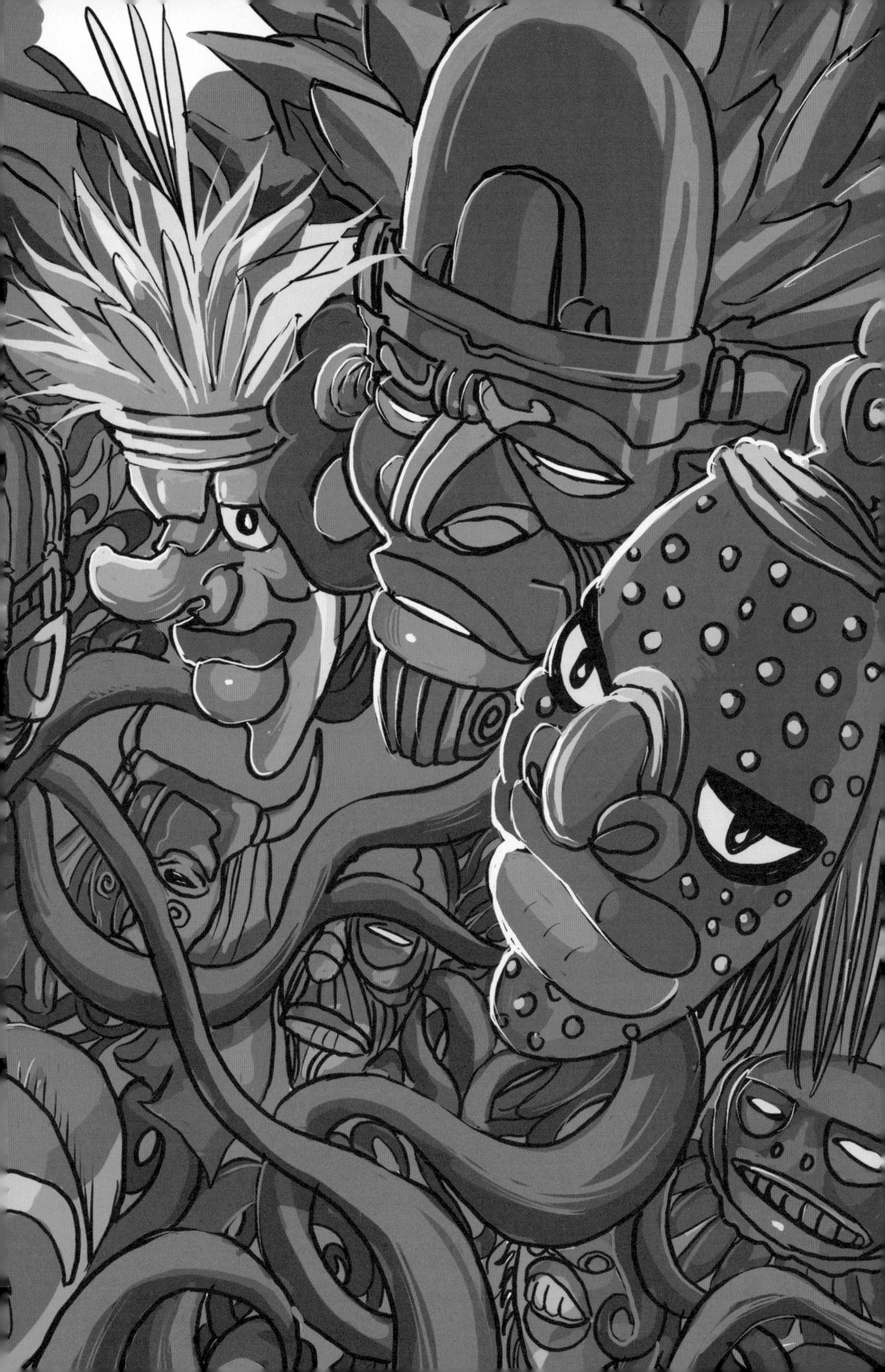

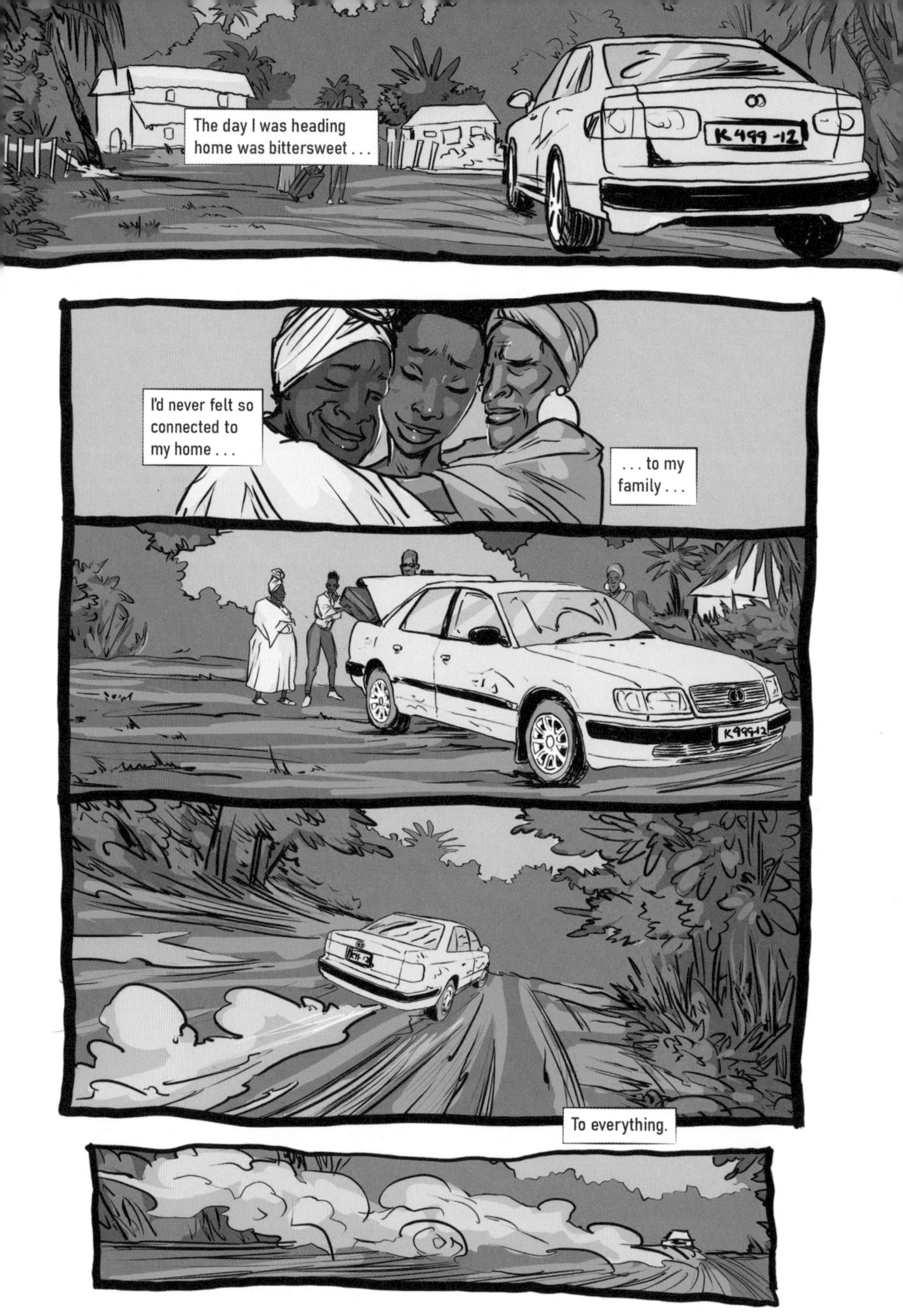
The day I was heading home was bittersweet . . .
K 499 -12
I'd never felt so connected to my home . . .
. . . to my family . . .
To everything.

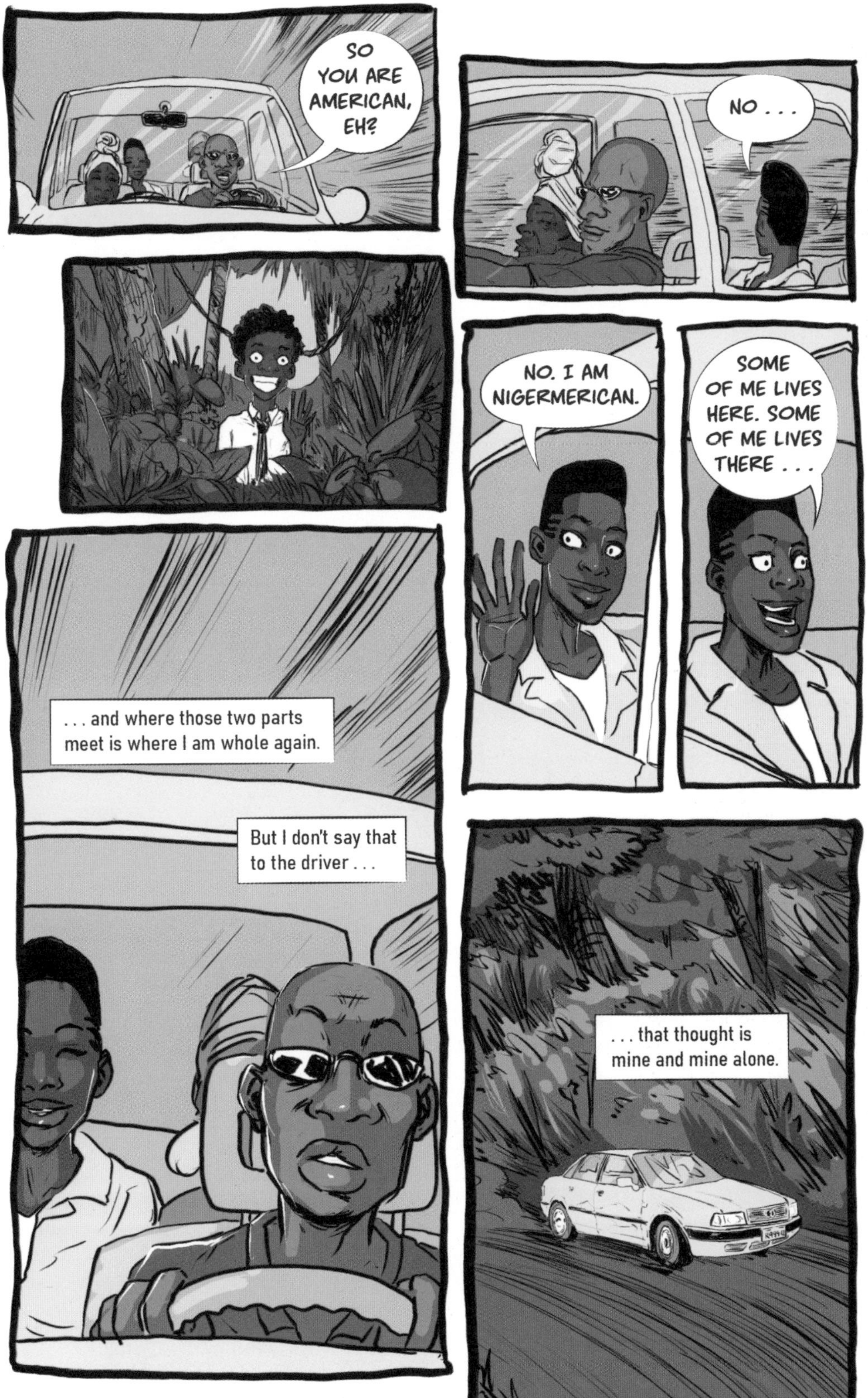
SO YOU ARE AMERICAN, EH?
NO . . .
NO. I AM NIGERMERICAN.
SOME OF ME LIVES HERE. SOME OF ME LIVES THERE . . .
. . . and where those two parts meet is where I am whole again.
But I don't say that to the driver . . .
. . . that thought is mine and mine alone.

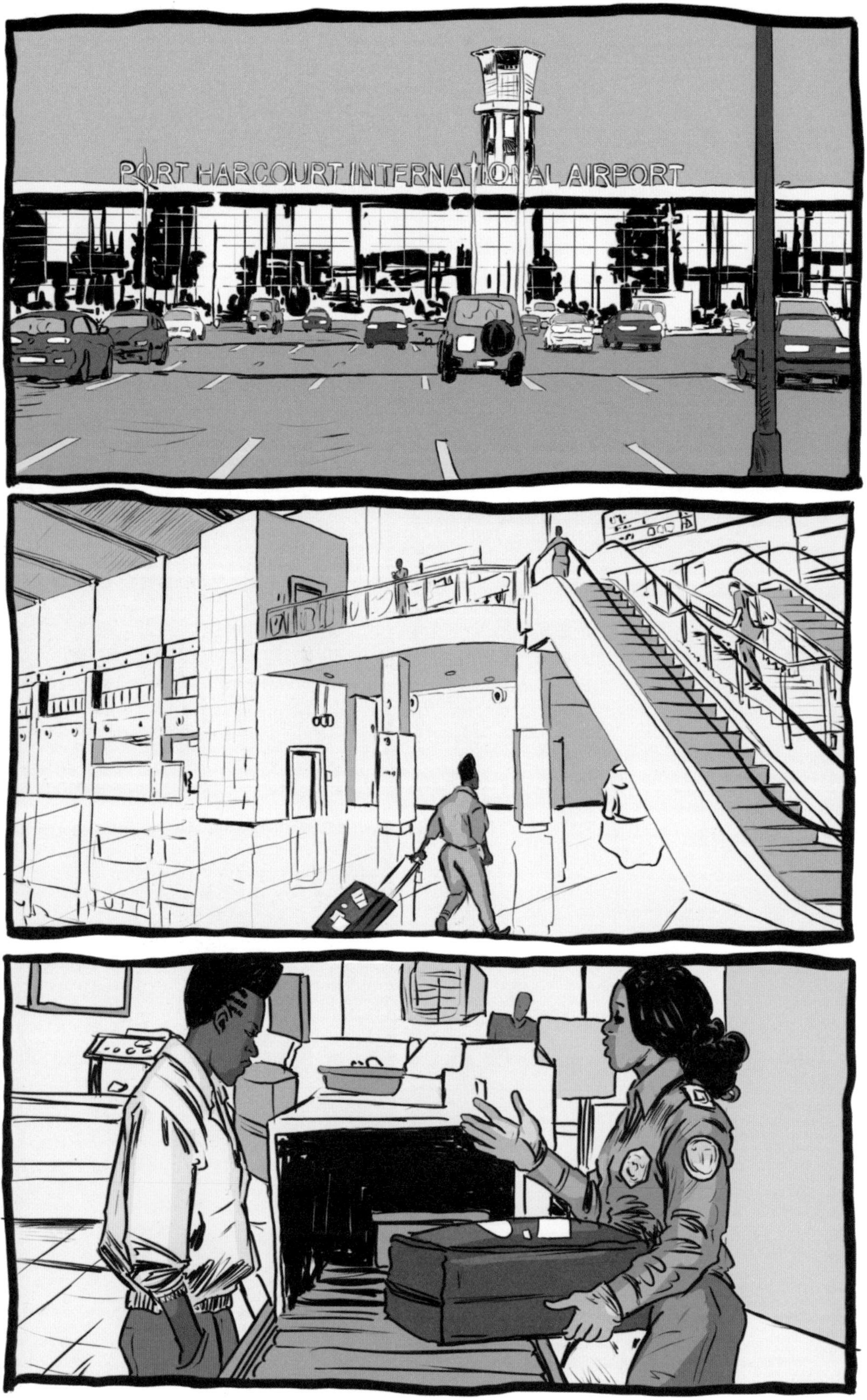

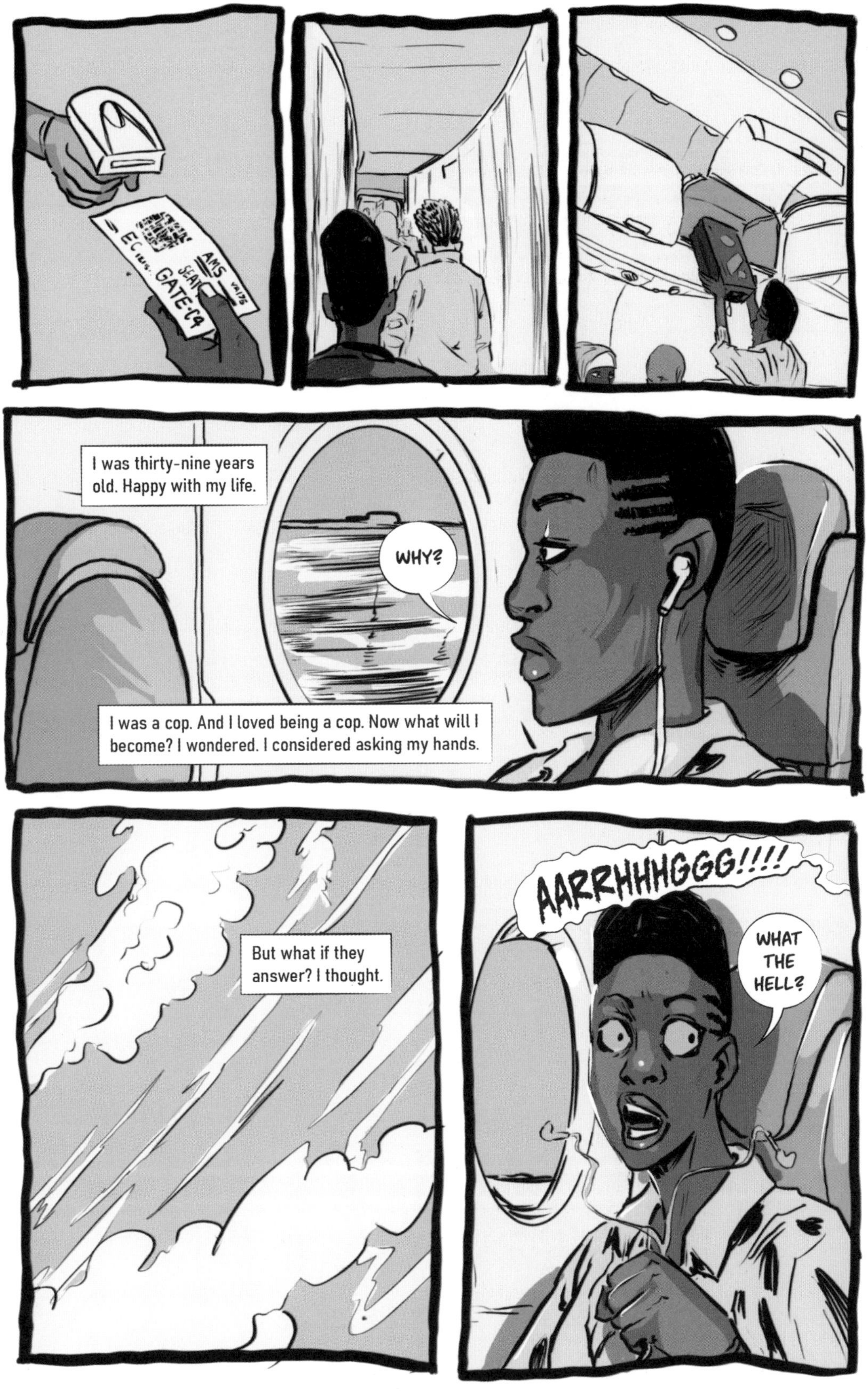
AMS
SEAT
GATE C4
EC
I was thirty-nine years old. Happy with my life.
WHY?
I was a cop. And I loved being a cop. Now what will I become? I wondered. I considered asking my hands.
But what if they answer? I thought.
AARRHHHGGG!!!!
WHAT THE HELL?

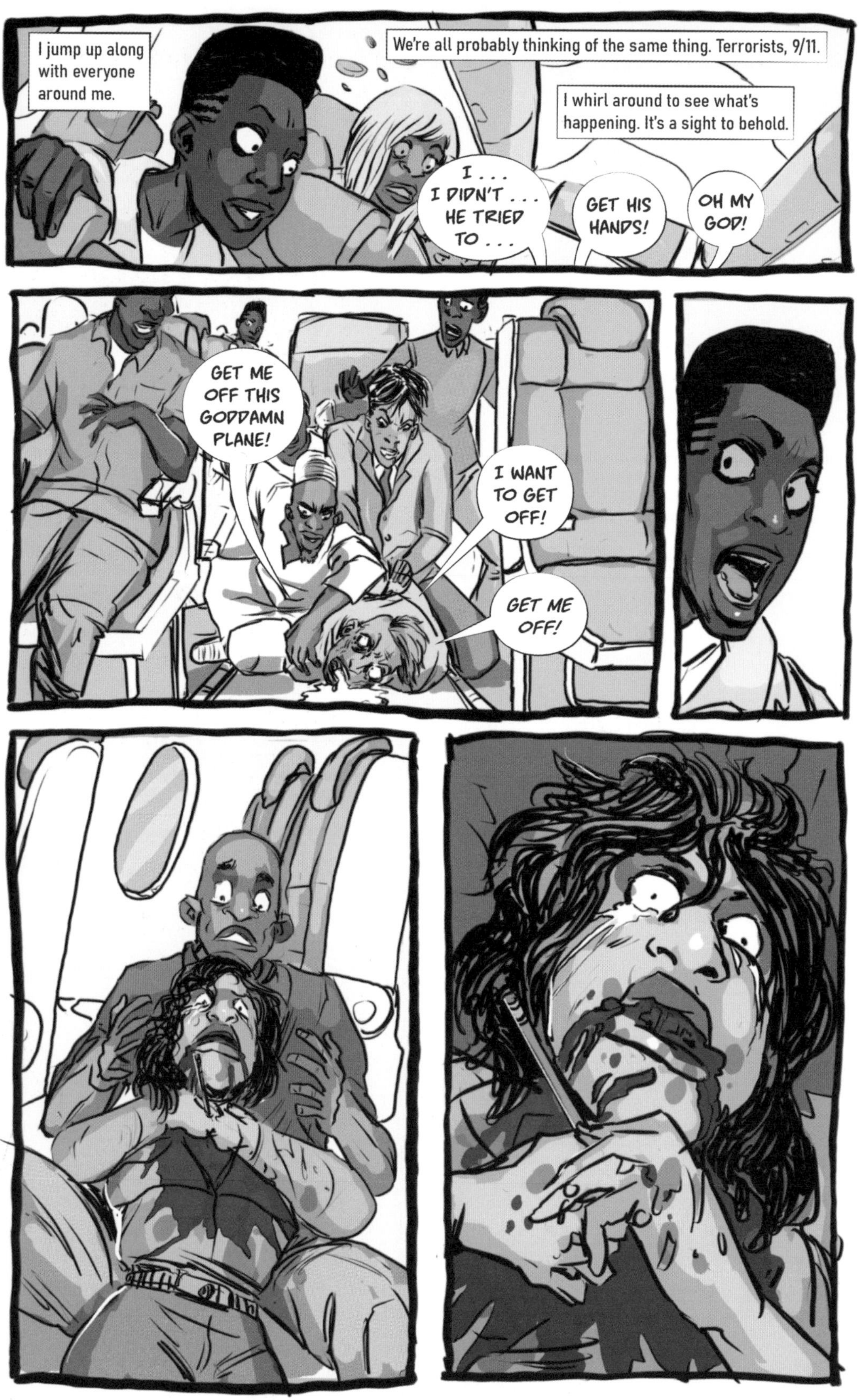
I jump up along with everyone around me.
We're all probably thinking of the same thing. Terrorists, 9/11.
I whirl around to see what's happening. It's a sight to behold.
I . . . I DIDN'T . . . HE TRIED TO . . .
GET HIS HANDS!
OH MY GOD!
GET ME OFF THIS GODDAMN PLANE!
I WANT TO GET OFF!
GET ME OFF!

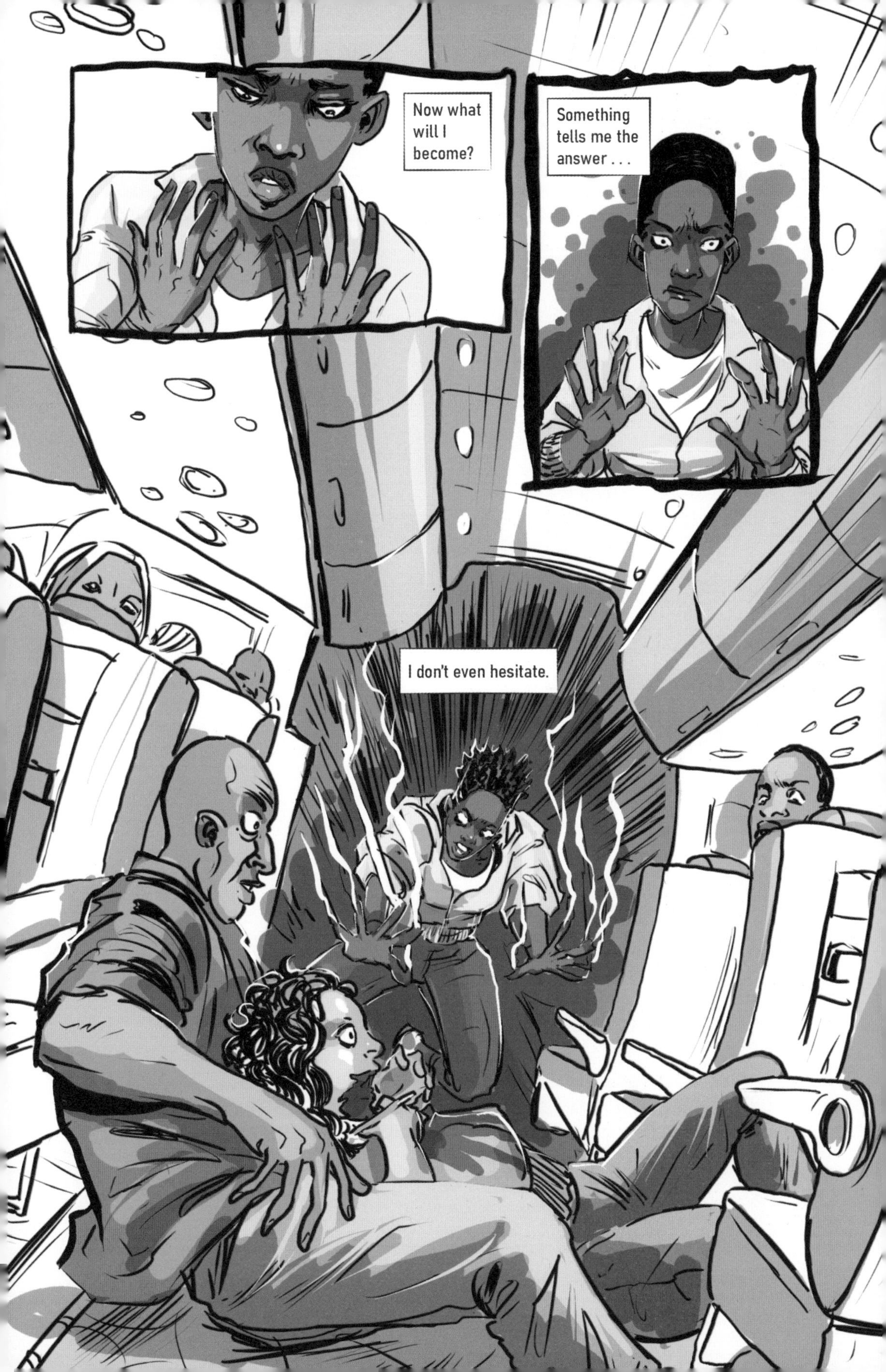
Now what will I become?
Something tells me the answer . . .
I don't even hesitate.

ACKNOWLEDGMENTS

I want to acknowledge my wife, Tawana, and my son, Jaxon, for not only helping to weather every storm but also for giving me the precious time to bring this book to life. I also want to thank my friend Nnedi Okorafor for trusting us with the translation of her words into sequential images. Thanks to the amazing David Brame for giving the adaptation such incredible lines for me to color. I also want to thank Damian Duffy for his hard work on the lovely lettering of every sound effect and voice. Thank you also to Michael, Charlie, Andrew, Charlotte, Maya, Kristen, Pamela, and the entire ABRAMS family for believing in MEGASCOPE. Finally, I want to thank our assistant editor, Jazmine Joyner, and our color production team: Cinique Lenoir, Stacey Robinson, Alex Batchelor, Anthony Moncada, and "Superior" Solomon Robinson. You make what we do so much better. **—John Jennings**

I am extremely proud of the work I have put into this book, but it couldn't have been completed without the amazing team we have been working with. They are the backbone and lifeblood of this machine. To my family, thank you for letting me disappear into the drawing dungeon for half of every day. And lastly, to my four lovely, mischievous dogs: You can't read, and get off the table! **—David Brame**

NNEDI OKORAFOR

Q: Nnedi, what was your inspiration for the short story "On the Road"?

A: The trips to my parents' villages in Imo State, Nigeria, always had a mystical element. Whenever my sisters went out exploring, from eating in relatives' homes to trekking into the forest to seeing a goat slaughtered to hearing things moving about outside at night that scared the hell out of us, we always came back with stories. We always came back affected. This went right into "On the Road."

Also, there was that day when I was a professor at Chicago State University where I met with the head of liberal arts. She knew I was a writer and she said, "Oh, Nnedi, I have a story for you!" She went on to tell me about a Ghanaian friend of hers who was in his small village . . . visiting home from the States. One day, he heard a knock at the door. When he opened it, there was a boy standing there with his head split open. He slammed the door. When he opened it again, the boy was gone. He later saw that boy perfectly fine playing soccer with other kids. That story scared me so deeply, I immediately went and wrote "On the Road." So, this isn't completely fiction . . . few things I write are.

Q: How does your experience as a Nigerian American inform this story?

A: Being Nigerian American doesn't merely inform this story, it is the foundation of this story. If I weren't Nigerian American, I would not have written this story. Everything about "On the Road,"—from the main character's internal conflicts with self as a police officer in Chicago to her being in Imo State, Nigeria, visiting her grandmother and encountering so much more because that connection remains—reflects a Nigerian American experience.

Q: Do you have a favorite scene in this story?

A: My favorite scene in the story is when *it happens*, when she's on the road that night and meets the Bone Collector, looks into every one of the spirits and ancestors, and is . . . realigned. I loved imagining the Bone Collector, and I think of those hot still nights in the village that felt so potent that I wouldn't dare go on the road because I was sure something was waiting for me. That scene captures that feeling.

Q: What first drew you to Africanfuturism and speculative fiction?

A: I didn't create Africanfuturism or Africanjujuism (*After the Rain* is Africanjujuism, not Africanfuturism), I coined the terms. I felt both needed proper names because without one, most people in our society are unable to recognize or imagine their existence and specificity. To define Africanjujuism: it is a subcategory of fantasy that respectfully acknowledges the seamless blend of true existing African spiritualities and cosmologies with the imaginative. Both Africanjujuism and Africanfuturism have existed for a long, long time.

JOHN JENNINGS

Q: What drew you to this short story, John?

A: I read "On the Road" about eight years ago and fell in love with it. I was intrigued at how the grotesque and the monstrous were deployed by Nnedi exploring aspects of the tensions she's felt as a person of American and Nigerian cultures. Nnedi references herself as "Naijamerican," and that portmanteau totally symbolizes the struggles that Chioma goes through. I could tell that Nnedi was working things out with this story, because it's one of her very early works. It lays a lot of the ground-work for the Africanfuturism and Africanjujuism genres that she currently writes in. This is actually her first Africanjujuist story, as it borrows heavily from West African spirituality for the speculative aspects of the narrative. "Juju" is another word for magic, and this story takes that magic and twists it around on its head. Also, you get the first mention of the Road Monster, which pops up again in Nnedi's first-contact novel *Lagoon*. I think that there's a rawness and fearlessness in this story and that also attracted me to it. It pretends to be a horror story but ends up being a story about self-discovery and rebirth. I still love it as much as the first time I read it.

Q: And what was the most challenging part of adapting "On the Road"?

A: It's not impossible, but it's difficult to scare someone with a comic book. "On the Road" has so many amazing visuals in it already, so it put pressure on me to make sure they were as effective as possible. We had to use pacing, color, and panel forms to get across uneasiness and fear effectively. We hope that we created a graphic narrative that gets across the feeling and meaning of the original story and also gives people a great horror story that will haunt them in the best ways possible.

Q: How did you go about transforming Nnedi Okorafor's short story into graphic novel format?

A: I actually printed out the short story and began to make notes in the margins, figuring out how many pages certain scenes should be. I was also thinking about how to translate the mystical elements in the story in a way that is particular to the comics medium. Each medium has its particular affordances, and you have to take advantage of those attributes to get the story and effects across. I think that creating the symbolic devices in the story were the most fun. I did a lot of sketches and layouts, which I shared with David Brame. Once David finished his amazing line work, we sent it over to our color flatters, who lay plain single colors into the line art. When they finished their flats, I took those images and did the final rendering. Then Damian Duffy worked his magic with the lettering to wrap everything up. It was a relatively seamless process.

Q: How was working on this adaption different in comparison to working on other graphic novel adaptations, such as *Kindred* and *Parable of the Sower*?

A: For the Octavia E. Butler projects, I am the artist and Damian Duffy is the main adaptor. Having the task of writing the script for *After the Rain* was very different for me and I truly enjoyed it. We use different parts of our brain when writing instead of drawing. It's all creative work, but the way that creativity manifests itself is so different. Another big difference is, of course, Nnedi Okorafor is alive, so she was able to help us guide the ship, so to speak. We ran everything we wanted to change past her. We didn't have that opportunity with Octavia E. Butler's books. With *After the Rain*, we got advice directly from the source!

Q: What is the cultural symbolism of the pattern on the shawl on the cover and endpapers?

A: That cloth is called ukara. It's a symbolic and ritualistic cloth used by the Ekpe society. The Ekpe is a secret male-driven organization that uses symbolic rituals to connect the community to spiritual forces that can affect all social systems. Ekpe is a powerful spirit that lives in the jungle and presides over these ceremonies. The members of the Ekpe society are indexes or connections to the ancestors of the village. The rituals maintain a connection to these ancestral beings to maintain prosperity and strength of the community. I found it interesting and significant that Nnedi's story created a maternal organization that reconnects Chioma to her heritage that her great-aunt and grandmother are members of. The centering of African womanhood is really apparent, and it makes for a robust and sometimes violently unsettling narrative.

Q: Do you have a favorite scene in the graphic novel?

A: I am in love with the scene where Chioma is outside on the porch and then she looks up and, slowly but surely, so many lizards come and watch her; like they are waiting on something to happen. It's uncanny. These Agama lizards are everywhere in Nigeria, but for them to be so focused on one point is just so unnerving. They are also such brightly colored reptiles. Using them as an index for dark mysterious spirits was brilliant.

Q: How was it collaborating and working together with David?

A: We love collaborating together. We are now a two-man studio called BLKKATZ, and we work on a lot of projects. We can't wait to share what we have in story next!

DAVID BRAME

Q: David, was there any challenge in visualizing the rich and horrifying world Nnedi Okorafor created?

A: Not having grown up in a Nigerian home or in Nigeria, I found it most challenging to create authentically terrifying and lush backgrounds and settings. I wanted the imagery to feel familiar to Chioma but unsettling to the audience. We had to find that fuzzy imaginative space where the characters in the story, the audience, and Nnedi's original voice can all fall deeply into this very mystical place.

Q: And was it difficult weaving the Nigerian culture and elements in Nnedi's original story into a visual, illustrative format?

A: I did a lot of primary research, borrowed from my own travels in Africa, and relied heavily on John and Nnedi's advice and keen eyes. It was difficult, but I didn't lament the process, it was challenging and fun—a true visual puzzle and collaborative effort to pull from all these varied sources of inspiration and coalesce them.

Q: Do you have a favorite scene in the graphic novel?

A: My favorite scene in the book is the sequence where Chioma's hands are being reattached by vines, and that this action is mirrored by a dancing child with feet that seem to have been reattached in much the same way as Chioma's hands. I find the multilayer storytelling here really inspired.

CHARACTER DEVELOPMENT

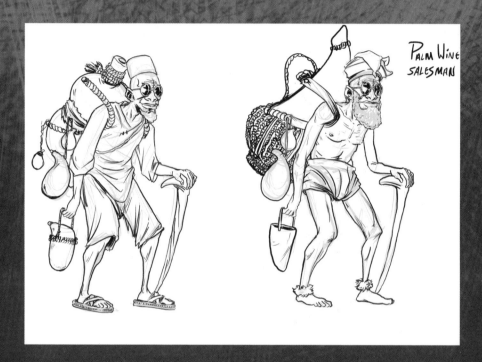

Initial character designs by David Brame for the Palm Wine Salesman (2012)

ABOVE Injured boy concept by John Jennings and David Brame, colored by John Jennings (2012)
BELOW AND RIGHT Studies of Chioma by John Jennings and David Brame (2012)

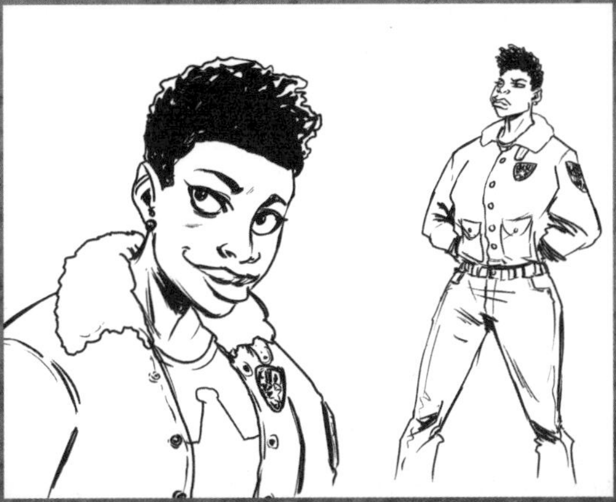

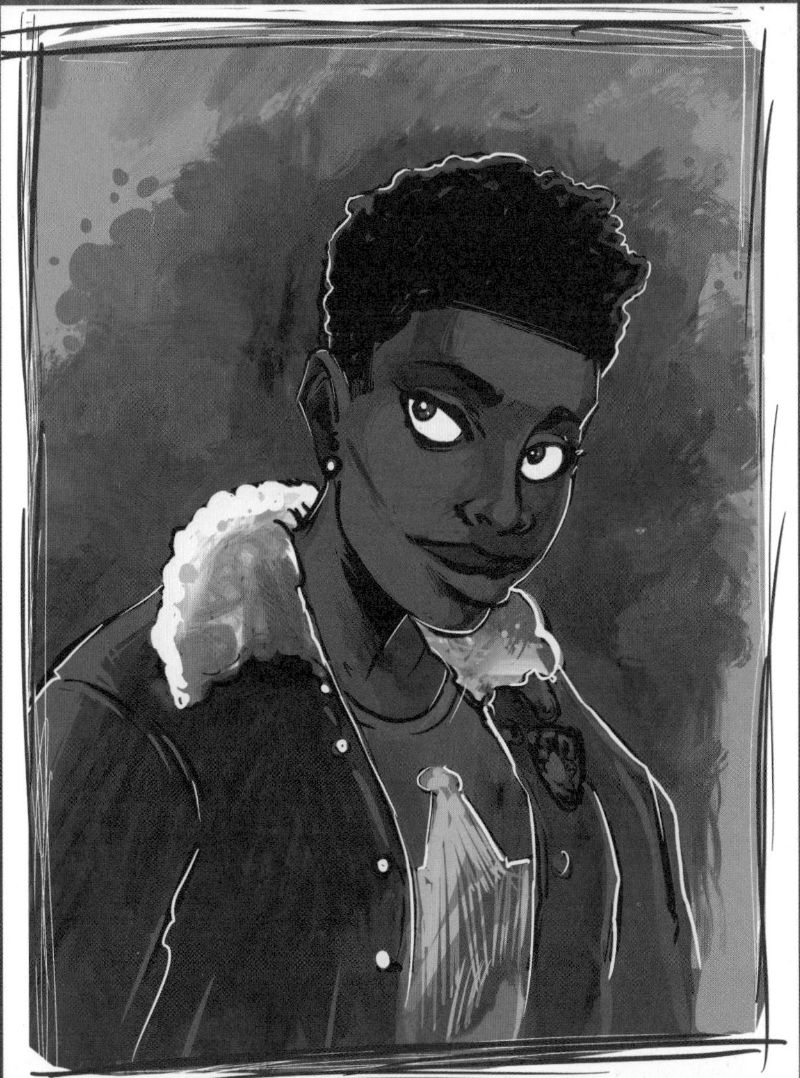

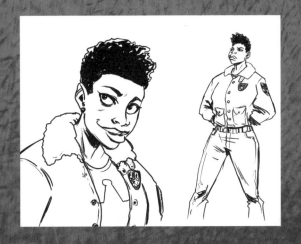

COVER DEVELOPMENT

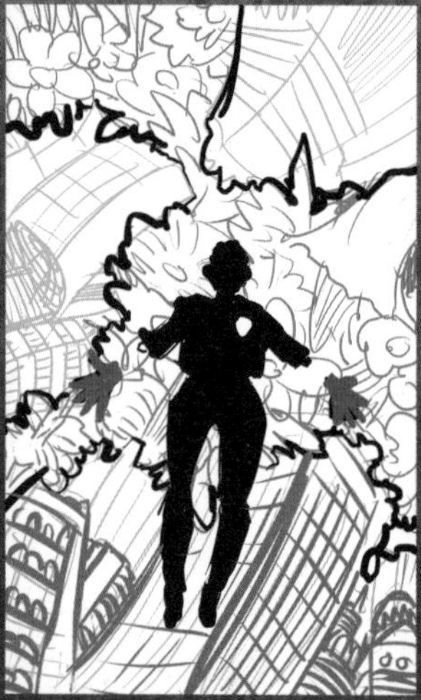

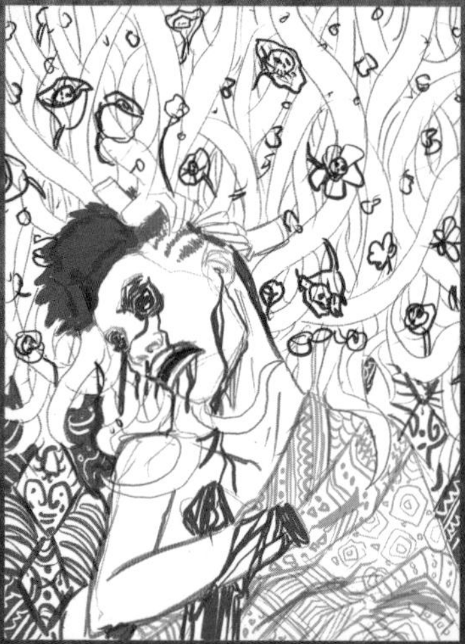

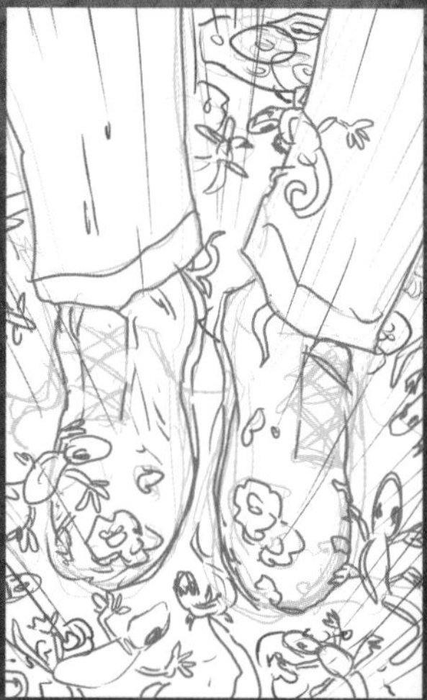

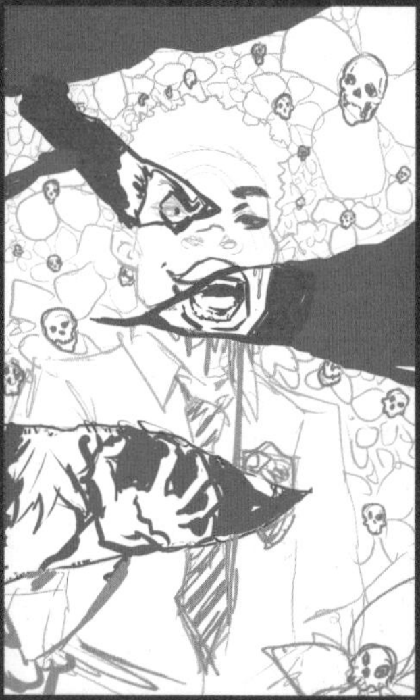

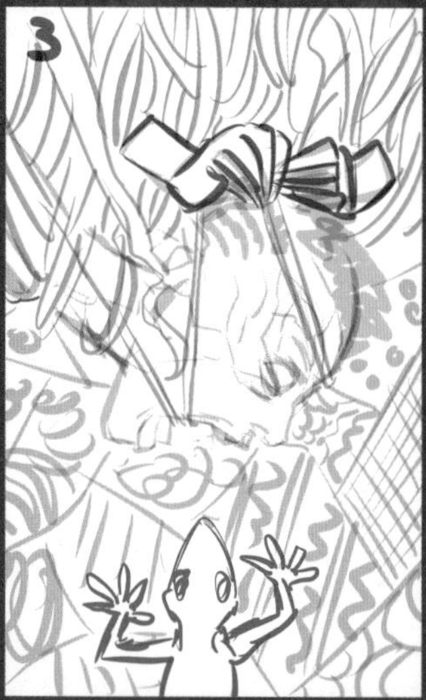

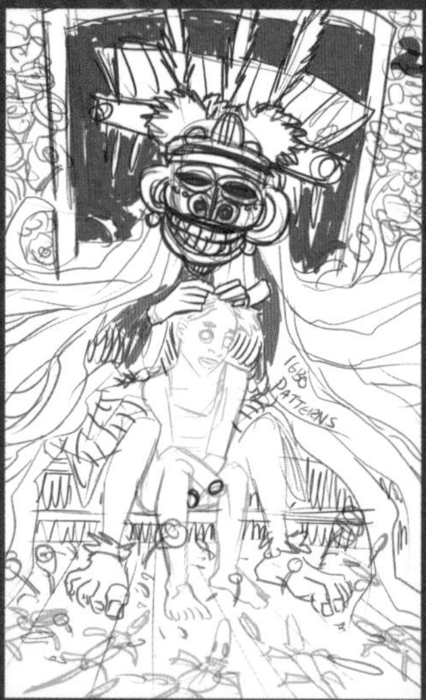

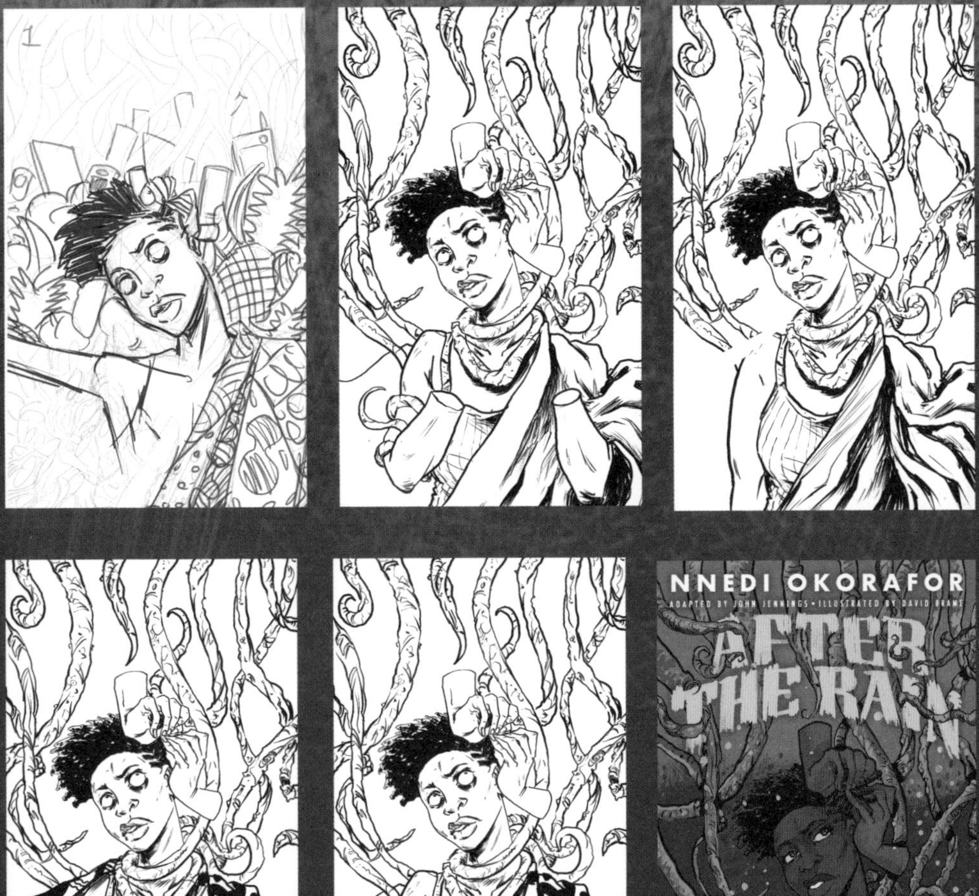
NNEDI OKORAFOR
ADAPTED BY JOHN JENNINGS • ILLUSTRATED BY DAVID BRAME
AFTER THE RAIN

Cover process from original concepts to final composition, inks, and colors.
Art by David Brame and colors by John Jennings (2019).

NOTES ON PROCESS

PAGE 89- 6 panels

1. **The women in the jungle look very happy.**

   a. Granny: I told you. She will be fine.

2. **Chioma's hands are being reattached**

   a. CAPTION: The vines were doing something to my severed hands and wrists.

   b. Chioma: Ghnnnhh!!

3. **Chioma's hands are being reattached CU.**

   a. CAPTION: I could hear a soft, wet smacking sound. When I finally chanced a look, I saw that the vines were knitting.

   b. Chioma: Heff!! Huff . . . huff.

4. **The women throw up hands in praise to the ancestors**

   a. CAPTION: They were knitting my veins and arteries.

5. **Close up of the women's hands.**

6. **The creature looks on..it seems...pleased**

   a. CAPTION: Lying on my back, I turned my head to the side and vomited.

   b. CAPTION: That road monster was hovering over me like an overattentive doctor.

   c. CAPTION: Hot pebbles and stones rained on me. The sky was brightening as the day broke.

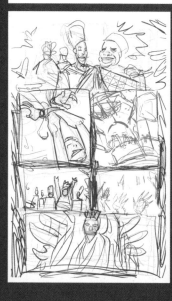

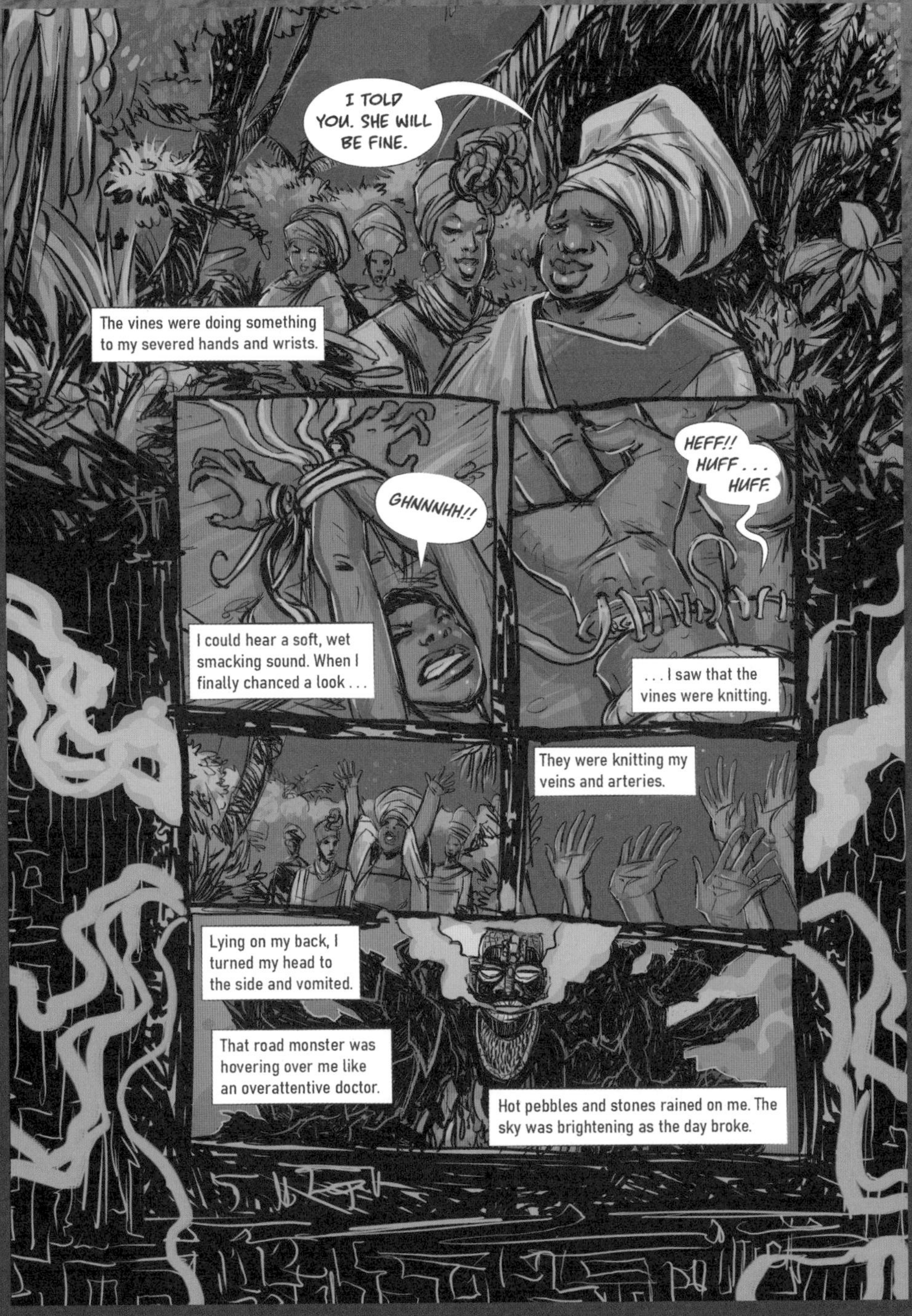
I TOLD YOU. SHE WILL BE FINE.
The vines were doing something to my severed hands and wrists.
GHNNNHH!!
I could hear a soft, wet smacking sound. When I finally chanced a look . . .
HEFF!! HUFF . . . HUFF.
. . . I saw that the vines were knitting.
They were knitting my veins and arteries.
Lying on my back, I turned my head to the side and vomited.
That road monster was hovering over me like an overattentive doctor.
Hot pebbles and stones rained on me. The sky was brightening as the day broke.

LEFT John Jennings script and David Brame's layout and inks show the stages in the creation of page 89 of *After the Rain*. ABOVE Final art

VISUAL DEVELOPMENT

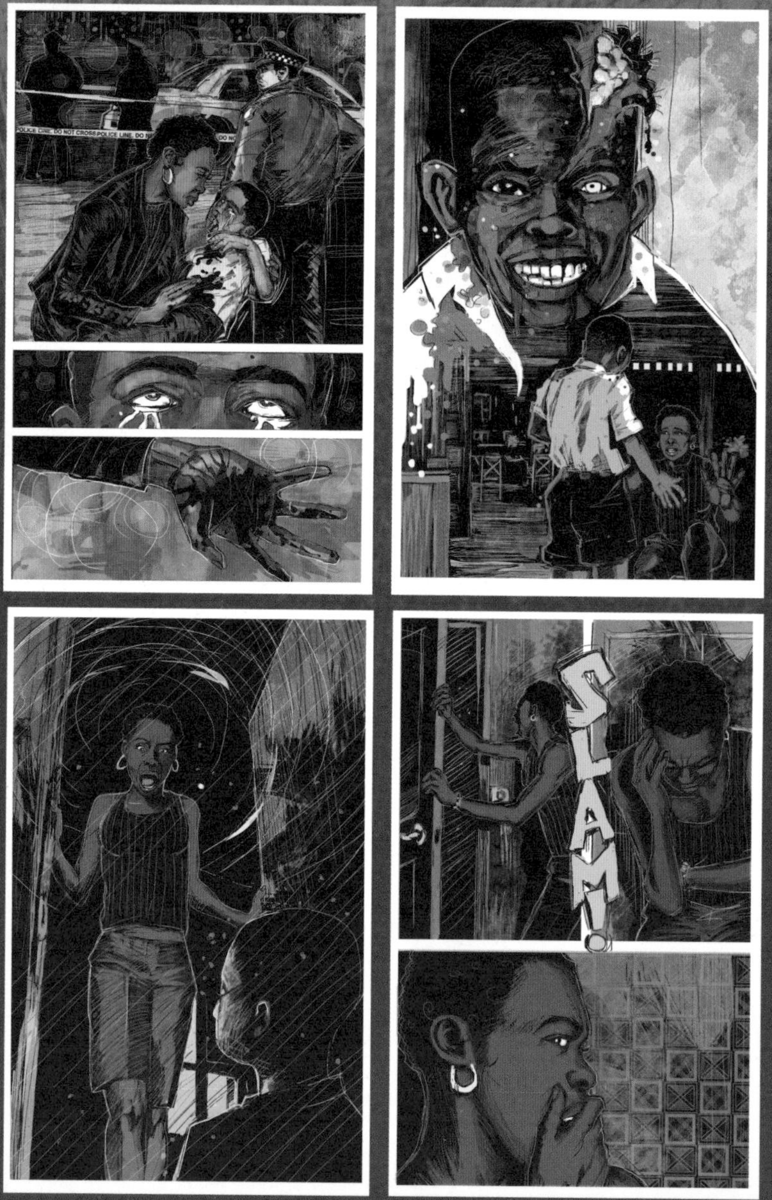
SLAM!

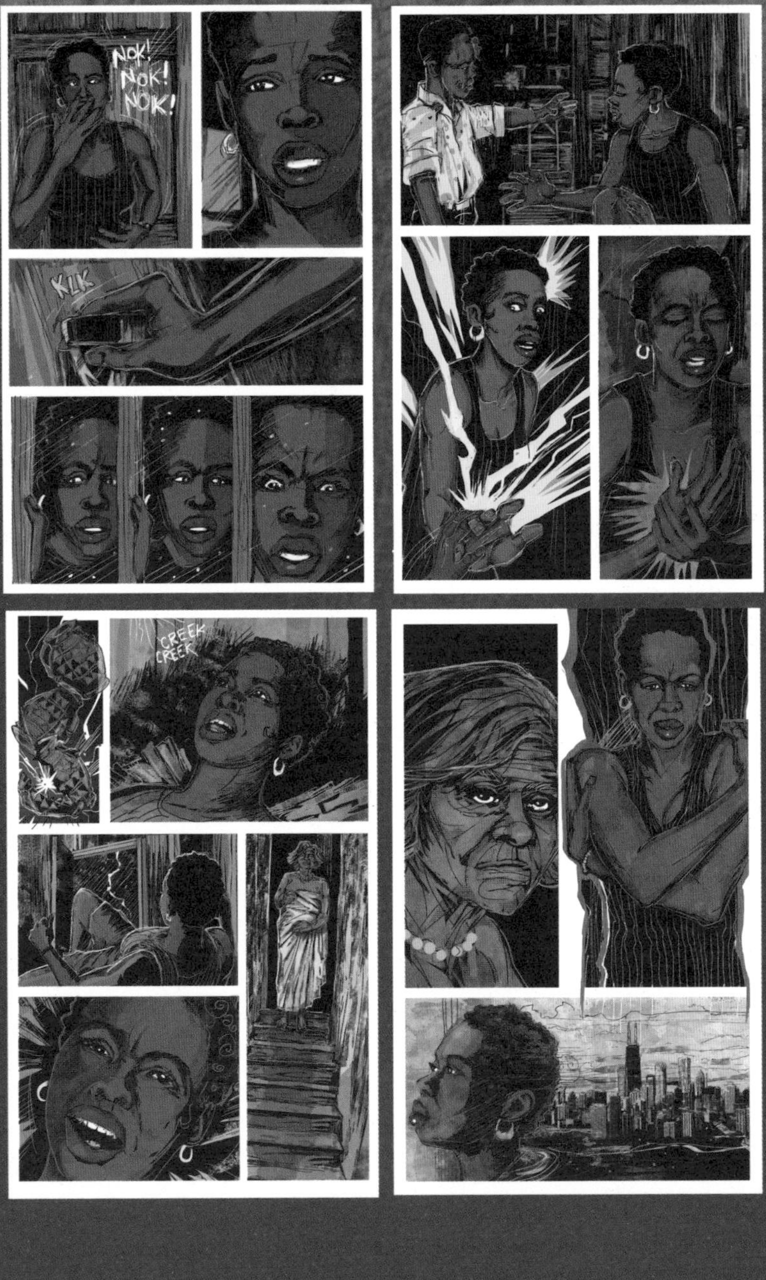
NOK! NOK! NOK!
KLIK
CREEK CREEK

LEFT AND ABOVE Original story concepts by John Jennings (2012)

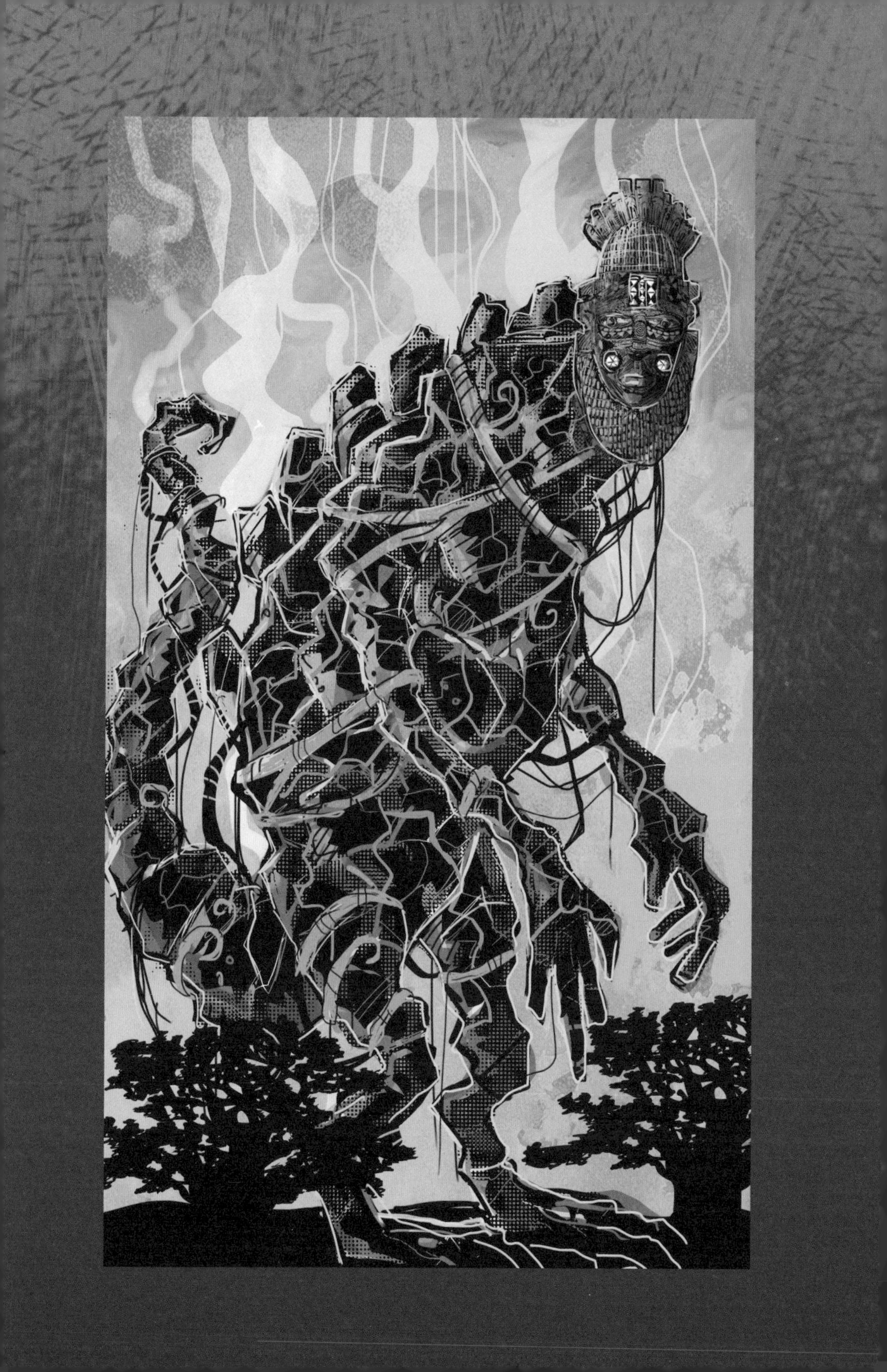

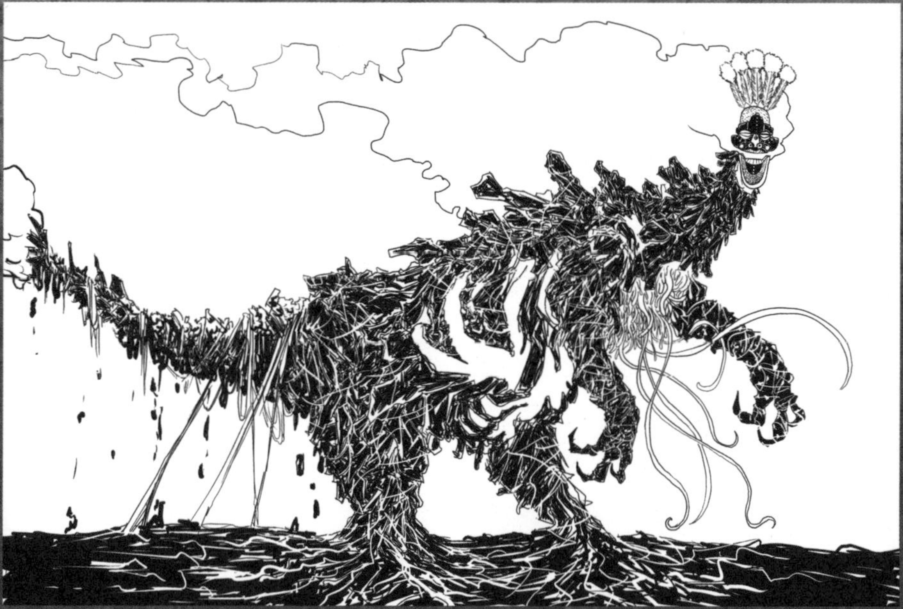

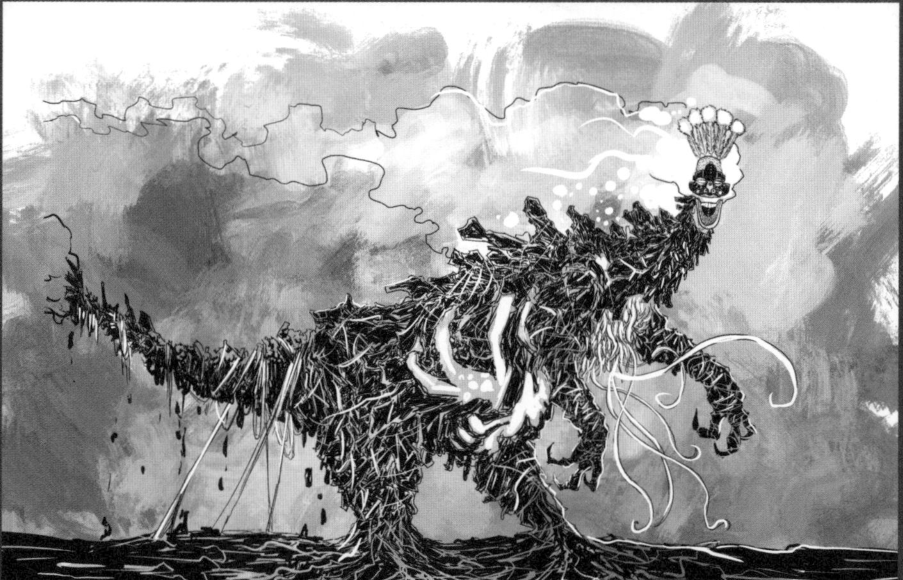

LEFT Initial Road Monster design by John Jennings (2012)
ABOVE Updated Road Monster sketch by David Brame, gray wash by John Jennings (2012)